yoga and psychotherapy

YOGA AND PSYCHOTHERAPY

the evolution of consciousness

SWAMI RAMA
RUDOLPH BALLENTINE, M.D.
SWAMI AJAYA, PhD.

PUBLISHED BY
THE HIMALAYAN INTERNATIONAL INSTITUTE
OF YOGA SCIENCE AND PHILOSOPHY
HONESDALE, PENNSYLVANIA

Library of Congress Catalog Card Number 76-356228
ISBN 0-89389-000-6
ISBN 0-89389-036-7 pb

Copyright 1976

Himalayan International Institute
of Yoga Science and Philosophy
Honesdale, Pennsylvania 18431

First Printing 1976
Second Printing 1978
Third Printing 1979
Fourth Printing 1981

Printed in U.S.A.

ACKNOWLEDGMENTS

We are indebted to Janet Boldt who devoted many evening and weekend hours in skillfully and patiently typesetting the manuscript. Caren Caraway contributed her considerable talent in preparing the illustrations and diagrams. We would also like to thank the many colleagues, friends and students who have aided in various aspects of this book's preparation over the past two and a half years. Several psychologists and psychiatrists have contributed their comments and pointed out sections where we were initially unclear in our presentation. We cannot express enough appreciation to each of the many kind and generous beings who have facilitated this publication.

TABLE OF CONTENTS

How we came
to write this book...

Two and a half years ago we were driving in a blue jeep station wagon, winding up and down the mountain roads along the edge of the Himalayas. We had just come from a week's retreat at a small, little-known, but "sacred" spot, hidden in the pine trees of the mountain forest. It was accessible only by foot along a five mile mountain road. We had parked the jeep and climbed with backpacks to this idyll of serenity, living in an earthen house, spending our days in quiet contemplation.

Now we had descended to the waiting jeep and were winding our way back to civilization. The carburetor on our wagon was having trouble breathing in the high mountain air. After choking intermittently for a few miles, it gave out completely. As we sat in a ditch by the road waiting for the car to be repaired, we began to talk about our common work as therapists.

Rudy had just met Swami Rama and myself a few weeks earlier. A year before he had given up a professorship at a leading medical school to travel to India and learn the ancient science of yoga. He came without knowing anyone and spent his first few months in his adopted homeland learning Hindi and hatha yoga and becoming emaciated. Soon after we met he began travelling with us. I had just been initiated into the Order of Swamis a few weeks earlier.

Until now we had been so absorbed in our new adventure

that we hadn't thought much about the worlds we had temporarily
left behind. We were now, however, beginning our descent to
Rishikesh. In a week we would drive to New Delhi, take a plane
to New York and a short time later find ourselves home again.
Our thoughts began to return to the work we had left. It seemed
natural enough for us, during this lull in our journey, to begin
comparing the Western approaches to psychotherapy to what
we were learning of yoga.

I began to talk about the way a yoga student relates to his
teacher. Many young adults who find a genuinely advanced
teacher think of him or her as a new parent and become less
preoccupied with hangups relating to their real parents. These
old conflicts seem to become less important and fade into the
background. I suggested to Rudy that thinking of the more
ideal guru as one's father might shortcut the whole process of
therapy. Instead of spending long hours reliving one's childhood
experiences he could just replace the expectations created there
by orienting himself toward the more constructive and supportive
expectations of the teacher. I suggested that one might thus shed
all his preoccupations and distortions related to his parents,
severing the knot of his neurosis in one swoop.

It was, as it's been throughout our writing, characteristic of me
to make broad generalizations without thinking through their
more subtle implications. Rudy, being thorough in examining
the proposition, responded after some thought. "It wouldn't
really help at all. You'd just develop a distorted concept of the
teacher. You would project your expectations onto him. In
spite of his acceptance, you would tend to see him otherwise—as
very authoritarian, for example." This led us to a discussion of
the similarity between transferring distortions onto the guru and
the process of transference that occurs in the patient's relationship
to his therapist. We began to become aware of similarities as well
as differences between the way the Eastern teacher and the therapist help the patient or student to become aware of his distortions
and to give them up. This dialogue led to an examination of a

whole host of concepts that seemed to overlap in yoga and modern psychology.

It was not long after this that Swami Rama began encouraging us to write a book together. He had begun teaching us yoga psychology more intensively during our remaining stay in India and continued to work with us when we arrived back in the United States.

He had been trained in yoga from early childhood and was selected at the age of twenty-four to serve as the successor to Dr. Kurtkoti as the prestigious Shankaracharya on the Gaddi of Karvirpitham in South India, one of the heads of the learned monastic tradition in India. In order to compete with other scholars for this position he had thoroughly learned the ancient texts and their many commentaries and interpretations. As he grew up he was sent to study with many of the great masters of India and even spent a number of years studying and teaching in the Buddhist monasteries of Tibet. Swamiji was also thoroughly acquainted with the many practical schools of yoga.

His understanding of the long history of yoga psychology and experiences with the practical application of yoga therapy is unparalleled. Furthermore, he had studied modern psychology, philosophy and medicine extensively in Europe and had earned an advanced degree in psychology as well as graduating from medical school. Swami Rama had lectured and served as consultant at several institutes and universities in Europe as well as the Menninger Foundation in the United States. With this background he was able to guide us in our comparisons of Eastern and Western psychologies.

We had not realized that we would be a means of helping Swamiji bring the rich tradition of yoga psychology to the West, to help pull together his teachings and put them up against the current Western psychology and psychotherapy that we had learned earlier.

In the two summers that followed, including several nights where we worked into the dawn, there were many consultations with Swamiji. Occasionally we'd talk until three or four o'clock in the morning as Swamiji helped clarify a confusion in our thinking. When we ran into dead ends or misinterpreted basic psychological terms from the Eastern tradition, Swamiji would give us the correct explanation, refer us to the proper texts, and we'd again revise our thoughts and writing.

But our understanding of yoga psychology does not come so much from our reading and study as from our own experiences of growth through the use of yoga methods and the direct personal guidance of our teacher. Our retrospective observation of Swamiji working with us and other students provided the deepest insights into the methods of yoga therapy.

The main thrust of this book is not to present a critique of either yoga psychology or modern psychology, but to put forth those theories and practices that we have found in our experience of them to be of value in helping one grow and evolve. We have tried to develop a comprehensive theory of personal evolution which incorporates the best of both systems.

When we began writing we grandiosely envisioned a comprehensive examination of psychology and yoga including a comparison of experimental, cognitive and social psychologies with yoga. While we speculated on some interesting similarities in these areas, we finally decided to focus on those aspects of psychology we know best. We hope to encourage others who are better versed in the other areas of psychology and Western science to broaden this endeavor.

Our experience was as therapists and the book gradually moved from the more general field of psychology to an emphasis on psychotherapy. Our backgrounds led us to focus especially on psychoanalytic psychology and to approach our subject matter from a developmental viewpoint.

Rudy's psychiatric training was psychoanalytically oriented and included several years of personal analysis. He had worked quite intensively with psychotic patients under the guidance of the teachers who later established River Oaks Hospital in

New Orleans. My own training was more eclectic, emphasizing both psychotherapy and developmental psychology. It extended from classes at the New School for Social Research to graduate work at Berkeley, postdoctoral training at the University of Wisconsin, Department of Psychiatry, in Madison, and an on-going practice of psychotherapy and mental health consultation from where the principles of yoga psychology could be applied and tested.

Our backgrounds and thinking styles seemed to complement one another, each adding a broader scope to the viewpoint of the other. Underlying these differences we shared a common disenchantment with modern psychiatry and psychology in providing adequate answers to the most basic questions regarding the nature and purpose of human life. This had led each of us to turn first toward work with psychedelic drugs and involvement with alternate life styles. While the answers there were partial, these experiences in turn brought us in contact with Eastern thought. Here the harvest has proved more satisfying.

During the two years that the book was in preparation, our work together was broken by periods of study and training in India. My original training in Rishikesh on the Ganges was supplemented by study at other mountain ashrams, while Rudy returned for a postgraduate fellowship in Ayurveda, the ancient Indian system of medicine which is so integrally related to yoga. As a result, our understanding of yoga psychology and philosophy has grown and deepened. The book reflects this process— having gone through countless revisions, growing and evolving with us.

Swami Ajaya
September 8, 1975

INTRODUCTION

Psychology has made its appearance on the stage of Western science only in the last century. After developing elaborate sciences of the external world and conquering nature, Western man has at last started to turn his curiosity back toward himself. So has begun the exciting exploration of the inner being, his behavior, his motivation, and that elusive something called his "mind." In short we have begun to look at ourselves and wonder "what makes us tick."

This exploration has met with varying success. The ingenuity and the technology which made possible the conquest of the new world and travel to outer space, often seem awkward and inappropriate as Western man steps tentatively and gingerly into the charting of inner space. We have run through our repertoire of conceptual and technological tools, sometimes with success, at other times with failure. We have gone from the speculative metaphysical pondering of the mind and the meaning of behavior to the minute reporting of sensory impressions and ultimately to the technologically sophisticated measurement of physiological processes and observable behavior. We have emerged with only patches of understanding and insight. Our field of behavioral science and psychology is a crazyquilt of theories, systems and methodologies—rich in its variety but disappointing in its lack of coherence. No matter which way we turn, we seem to stumble over the same old obstacles: where does psychology stop and philosophy start? How can we distinguish between the normal and the "abnormal?" How can we deal scientifically with a subject's report of his private experience? What is the relationship between the body and the mind? What, for that matter, is a "mind?"

There is an old Chinese proverb: "Learn from the ancient ones, and learn from those of foreign lands." Western science has at times followed this dictum, beginning with the rediscovery of Plato and extending to the search of the modern pharmacologist who stomps his way through the steamy jungles of Brazil in pursuit of some witch doctor's herb that might combat cancer.

A bit of this spirit can be sensed also in the field of psychology. Some of the more intrepid adventurers have set out to investigate the effects of ancient ritual drugs like mescaline and psilocybin. Others show a reawakened interest in the aboriginal inhabitants of America, not merely as objects of anthropological study, but as men with an insight into human nature that might offer us some fertile ideas. Social psychologists are looking with some curiosity towards the Chinese communes while in laboratories from New Delhi to Topeka, psychophysiologists are hooking polygraphs to accomplished yogis in an attempt to gain some understanding of those bodily processes which go awry in psychosomatic disease.

Yoga has attracted particular attention in part because it appears to be one of the oldest continuous disciplines studying voluntary physical and mental control and the induction of altered states of consciousness. Interest has also been due in part to the persistent rumors of outstanding physical and mental feats attributed to the practitioners of yoga. Such rumors have also served, of course, to attract those whose interest in sensationalism is stronger than their interest in science. Only now, with the advent of electroencephalographic and psychophysiological instruments, are we becoming able to test to the satisfaction of the scientific community the validity of some of those claims made by the proponents of yoga. As a result of this serious reexamination of the Indian yoga tradition, an intriguing picture begins to emerge.

Available historical data is a confusing mixture of legend and recorded facts. Because of the antiquity of the subject, many of the traditions and formulations were handed down orally for millenia. The systematized discipline of yoga has apparently been practiced in essentially the same form as today over some thousands of years. Estimates run from one thousand to four thousand years and up. From the data available, it seems clear that an unbroken chain of highly trained teachers and students have devoted themselves intensively to the rigorous practice of self-observation. Through such a systematic study of mental states and their accompanying physical sensations, a methodical and accurate means of studying one's internal organs and physiological processes gradually developed. In the usual sequence of scientific events, observation led to the ability to predict, and this ultimately to the ability to control. With the advent of this mastery it did indeed become possible to perform physiological feats which seemed "miraculous," as well as to intervene in the chain of physiological events that lead to psychosomatic illnesses. In this fashion the yogis became renowned for their health and resistance to disease.

The evolution of the discipline did not stop there, however. To those with a bent for exploring their mental processes more deeply, it became apparent that this control over physical processes enabled one to eliminate many of the physiological and sensory distractions that interfere with introspection. One could, as it were, create his own "sensory deprivation" situation. Furthermore, the control over physiological process enabled one to control his metabolism and induce changes that would serve to further alter the state of consciousness. At this point was begun the intensive and systematic study of the altered states of consciousness, a study which has continued over many centuries and attained a high degree of refinement. The under-

standing of mental and physical processes gained from the
vantage point of such heightened states of awareness became
the foundations of what is called "yoga science."

Such is the sort of history of yoga that one can piece together
from the available information. Controlled experiments done
both in the West and in India have begun to confirm this general
picture of the accomplishments and potential of yoga science.
Systematic treatment of patients suffering from physical or
psychosomatic ailments with yoga asanas and science of breathing
and meditational techniques has produced objective evidence
of definite improvement. Research in America has yielded clear-
cut data demonstrating the effectiveness of certain meditational
states in the easing of anxiety. Psychophysiological monitoring
during self-induced altered states of consciousness has demonstrated that remarkable feats of autonomic control are indeed
possible and in certain cases such techniques have been mastered
by patients with psychosomatic illness with a remarkable degree
of improvement.

In the laboratory it has been shown that an accomplished yoga
practitioner can remain alert to external stimuli even while in the
electroencephalographic deepest stage of sleep. This is in
complete contrast to our former ideas of the function of sleep and
its relation to consciousness. Such data points to the intriguing
possibility that yoga science holds the key to the understanding
of those phenomena we have come to call "altered states of
consciousness."

Such findings would seem to justify a deeper look into the
science of yoga. Unfortunately, at first blush such investigation
seems discouraging. The symbols used to express the concepts of
yoga science are even further from Western scientific jargon than
the six thousand miles separating India from America. There is a
wide gulf that separates our culture and symbol system from that
of the East. It is perhaps for this reason that the terms employed
in the ancient yogic texts often appear to us as more artistic than
scientific. It is, however, becoming clear that these terms have

been employed by the well-trained in very precise and rigorous fashion. Even so, they have remained all but inaccessible to us. The dilemma has been somewhat like trying to figure out how to attach a polygraph machine to a four-armed god.

But as one takes up and studies the theories and methods of yoga, the at first foreign system begins to take on an order. Many psychological concepts seem quite parallel to those found in the West, others to go beyond what the Western psychologist has conceived. And even the strange artistic symbols are seen to be shorthand expressions of a highly sophisticated profound understanding. At this point in the history of modern psychology we feel there is a vital need for a translation of these foreign terms into language and concepts understandable to the Westerner and for a comparison and integration of this system of psychology with those that are more familiar to us. This is the task we have undertaken in this book.

OVERVIEW

Yoga psychology is based on the concept that there are various levels of functioning. We are all aware of a "body" and "mind," but these are, from the perspective of Eastern thought, only part of the whole picture. These are only two of a number of different levels, each with its own organization and realm of function. Each, at the moment we are aware of it and think in its terms, gives a certain quality to our consciousness.

Even to the untrained mind this is not a completely foreign concept. We commonly talk of "body-consciousness," for example, or of being "lost in thought." We even acknowledge a level of functioning above that of the mind which can look down and see it when we observe, "I'm not thinking straight today," or "I can't get this notion out of my head." We may often think of our bodies as something we use. But we seldom face the logical conclusion that our minds are also "used" by us. That part of ourselves which observes our thoughts can learn to regulate them, control them and use them as we see fit.

In yoga psychology this idea of different levels of being, each able to observe and control the one below, is central. There are a number of these levels beyond the plateau of everyday thinking activity. The systematic exploration, development and experimentation with these higher levels is the work (and play) of meditation and yoga.

There are five principal levels described. They are called "sheaths" in the ancient writings since the more evolved level is conceptualized as existing within. Each sheath covers and obscures the more subtle awareness that is interior to it. These five levels or "sheaths" span the whole spectrum of human nature. The continuum they form makes up a sort of step-wise ladder that is the basis of all growth and evolution. Within this framework fit developmental theory, the therapeutic process and all the aspects of philosophy, religion and art that focus on the unfolding of man's higher potentials. Growth is a unitary process: biological evolution from protozoan to man, psychological evolution from the child to adult, therapeutic evolution from mental illness to health and the development of universal consciousness in the mystic are all included in this process of growth. Each deals with one leg of a long journey. Each describes one segment of the whole.

From this perspective a grasp of the notion of levels of functioning or sheaths seems very useful and important. It provides perhaps the only framework within which one can compare and contrast such diverse subjects as yoga, biofeedback, sleep research, medicine and psychotherapy. This multi-leveled conceptualization comfortably accommodates all of these. For this reason the chapters have been arranged to bring this hierarchy into focus. Each of the first five chapters deals with one of the sheaths. They are described in sequence. Each chapter provides a basis for the next.

Chapter I deals with the physical body and how working with it through yoga postures, bio-energetics or "Rolfing," for example, affects the psychological makeup. We look at biofeedback as a means of teaching people to tune in to and to control that internal part of the body which is ordinarily considered involuntary, a process mastered long ago by advanced yogis. The importance of this discipline is not its sensational value but its role in cultivating awareness of internal states.

The world that opens to one who becomes more aware of this inner experience is described in the second chapter, which deals with breath and energy, that level which provides the intimate connection between mind and body. This aspect of yoga psychology is concerned with breathing patterns and their effect on internal processes and the mind. In yoga science it is assumed that the concentration, the build-up and the controlled release of latent energy provide the key to integration and the achievement of higher states of consciousness. This energy is so subtle that we do not readily perceive it. The way in which a knowledge of breath control can be used to conserve and focus energy both physically and mentally is discussed.

The third chapter deals with the third sheath, the mind. It contrasts the Western method of observing the mind by observing behavior with the yogic method of studying it through the direct experience of introspection using meditational techniques. Where the primary thrust of Western psychology is to strengthen the ego, yoga psychology emphasizes that the ego is only a stepping stone to further evolution. What is often called "higher states of consciousness" and "mystical" is simply a completion of human development. It is "mysterious" for the ordinary adult in the same way that an adult's understanding is "mysterious" to a child. This simple but profound and enduring psychology that originated over four thousand years ago in the Vedas is outlined and compared with parallel concepts in modern psychology. Such notions as "conscience," "will," and "habit" take on a new meaning when viewed in terms of this psychology which was evolved to guide one to the attainment of a higher consciousness.

Chapter IV goes beyond the mind to take a look at those systems of Western psychology that have approached the study of altered states of consciousness. The psychologies of Jung and Freud are each seen to provide some guidance for the exploration of the "unconscious," or unknown parts of the mind. The ways in which this unknown mind serves as a barrier between usual waking consciousness and the levels beyond it is discussed. The next level or sheath comes into being with the refining of a non-verbal discriminative faculty whose use is often experienced in terms of imagery.

In the next chapter, the fifth, it is seen how a further evolution of this power of discrimination and "passive volition" is related to the development of what is called in yoga "a state of bliss." There are good reasons for concluding that this blissful state is the natural propensity of human consciousness and that we all have an inherent need to experience it. In fact, current research on sleep is compatible with the ancient notion that higher conscious-ness is experienced in a split-off, disassociated way during deep sleep. Changes in consciousness from waking to dream sleep to deep or dreamless sleep are examined in terms of the alpha, theta and delta waves as they have been studied in biofeedback. The possibility of a fourth state of consciousness which results from the integration of these three and which corresponds to highest human development is discussed and its description from the ancient Indian writings is recounted.

Within the five sheaths lies a pure consciousness. The sixth chapter compares this consciousness with the state of psychosis with which it is sometimes confused, since both depart radically from ordinary awareness. When, however, put in the perspective of growth and evolution, it becomes clear that they are at opposite ends of the spectrum. The long process of the evolution of consciousness that lies between these two extremes is outlined and the step-wise cycle of growth which comprises the process of evolution is analyzed. We see how facilitating this process is what psychotherapy is all about and how its failure to take place is what constitutes psychological illness.

The last chapter, Chapter Seven, concentrates on the *chakras,* the seven centers of consciousness which come into prominence during the process of meditation. They seem to constitute the structure of inner reality and their framework provides a sort of workshop within which one operates to explore himself and evolve a higher consciousness. The chakras are defined and there is a discussion of the behavior manifested when energy is focused at each. Psychological aspects of each chakra and the results of successfully or unsuccessfully integrating the dualities of each are presented. Here we look at the reasons for meditating on different chakras and how it is that an indifference to the higher chakras has accounted for a lack of a unified, comprehensive psychology in the West.

CHAPTER ONE
THE BODY

"The infinite is Brahman. From it, from this Self, space came to be, from space the wind, from the wind fire, from fire water, from water earth, from earth the plants, from plants food, and from food the body of man. This body of man composed of the essence of food is the physical sheath of the Self."

Taittiriya Upanishad, II. 1

chapter 1
THE BODY AND HATHA YOGA

In the minds of many people in the West, yoga is associated primarily with strange contortions of the body, but the major focus of yoga is actually on the alteration of one's self awareness and his relationship to the world. It is a complete system of therapy which includes work on developing awareness and control of the physical body, emotions, mind and interpersonal relations.

There are many forms of yoga including physical yoga (hatha), devotional (bhakti), service or action (karma) and philosophical yoga (jnana). The most comprehensive and scientific yogic system for developing awareness is raja yoga, the "royal path." This system was codified by the sage, Patanjali, who wrote the Yoga Sutras, over a thousand years ago. This is also called ashtanga yoga or "eight-rung ladder" since it is a systematic eight-phase approach to mastery over all aspects of our functioning. Mastery of each step leads to work on a more subtle aspect of our being, beginning with habits and behavior then proceeding to work on the body, breath and then mental functioning.

The physical positions or postures are important, though as one of the early phases in yoga training. By learning to discipline his body, the student becomes physically supple, healthy and relaxed so that he can comfortably pursue the main aspects of yoga which involve mental work and introspection. But this is more than mere physical preparation, for the discipline involved in training the body serves as a model for later work on other levels of functioning.

Although the body is worked with intensively, actually the goal is to become less bound up in the body and to gain some distance from it and perspective on its functioning. Working properly with the body in this way cultivates an objectivity and detachment which permits the neutral observation of the body as it assumes each position and gradually leads to increased control.

In this chapter we will look at the relationship between physical and mental states and how working with the body can affect the mind. We will then turn our attention to how body awareness can be extended and how this can lead to the ability to control bodily functions usually thought of as involuntary.

THE INTERACTION BETWEEN
PHYSICAL AND MENTAL TENSION

The posture a person takes is a reflection of his state of mind. In this sense, the physical state is an "embodiment" of a mental state. That is, the mental state takes physical form. Posture is a stance from which we face the world both physically and mentally. For example, those who mentally shrink back from the world will be likely to have a posture that expresses the same attitude.

Mental tension is revealed by the body in many ways. Under strain, for example, the brows are knit and the muscles of the forehead become tensed, the stomach is pulled in and is rigid. When the body is tense in this way, movements lose their natural fluidity and become stiff. Each person has characteristic ways of responding to mental tension by tensing particular parts of the body. Not only does a posture reflect the way that we're feeling inside but the posture and feeling become so fused that one readily leads to the other. For this reason, holding the body in a certain way can provoke or accentuate the feelings or the thoughts that are associated with it. Therefore, a body posture which has become habitual, beginning as a reaction to a certain mental state, may actually come to sustain and perpetuate that state. For example, the person who has developed the habit of raising his shoulders when he feels defensive and overwhelmed by the stresses around him may eventually adopt this as a part of his customary posture. On a day when he would have the opportunity to feel relatively relaxed, the constant tension in his shoulders will increasingly create in him a feeling of fear and defensiveness. In this way posture and body habits come, not only to reflect character, but to actually sustain it and so may hinder growth and evolution. Therefore, working with the body and posture as a way of promoting personal growth is a natural and inevitable development in psychotherapy.

The Body in Modern Psychotherapy

Wilhelm Reich, who worked extensively with character disorders, came to call habitual positions and tensions "character armour." He felt that the tense muscles associated with different psychological problems had to be dealt with and resolved before the person could gain access to the problems themselves. One of Reich's students, Alexander Lowen, describes the characteristic postures that go with different types of personalities.[1] For example, the passive-dependent "oral" character is typically swaybacked. He pulls his shoulders backward, thrusting his head, buttocks and pelvis forward.

Lowen has also described a pattern of chronic tensions or muscle barricades. [2] The use of muscle tensions as a shield is seen in those who have never developed secure identifications and hence feel vulnerable. An inability to distinguish between the "I" and the "not I" results in a more primitive way of separating oneself: It is done physically by keeping the muscles in a tense, partly contracted condition which serves as an artificial boundary between oneself and others. This lends a sense of security and compactness and protects one from imagined "invasion."

In contrast to this, Lowen describes the individual with "strong ego boundaries" who is able to maintain his unity and identity. Such a person is more secure about his self-definition and can allow his muscles to be relaxed.

Based on these notions, a form of therapy called Bioenergetics has evolved. It focuses the patient's awareness on his tense muscles. Through placing the patient in a stressful posture, the effects of his chronic tension are brought to light. There may be trembling, pain and loss of balance which should not normally result. The patient can see how tense and uncoordinated his body really is. Through the use of this and similar maneuvers, Lowen feels he is able to increase contact with the body and produce a release of tension through the tremor and involuntary movement which ensues.

Dr. Ida Rolf has developed another approach to working with postural disorders which she calls "structural integration." She and her students use methods of physical manipulation ("deep massage") to release tightened muscles and connective tissue and correct postural distortions. Although she doesn't call her methods "psychotherapeutic," those who have been "rolfed" report that the resulting new posture affects their mental and emotional states in sometimes dramatic ways.

One well known writer has vividly described his experiences while being rolfed. He recalls his first session:

> The ten hours of processing...would involve manipula-
> tion of the connective tissue of all the major muscle
> groups in my body... after the trauma of the first
> hour, slight but unmistakable changes in my posture
> and stance in life began to be obvious. My feet made
> more substantial contact with the ground; my leg
> muscles seemed to be freshly lubricated; there were
> ball-bearings in my joints.

He becomes aware of the intimate link between his emotional
state and his bodily tensions.

> As the rolfing continued, it became clear that I was the
> cause of most of my pain. Anxious anticipation, sus-
> picion and resistance made my muscles tensely rigid. I
> learned to relax and most of the pain ceased.

It is common for patients undergoing bioenergetic analysis or
rolfing to find that repressed memories are released as the
characteristic muscular tension is relieved.

> In the seventh hour of processing, pressure on a
> muscle in my shoulder released a memory of child-
> hood conflict with a person I loved deeply — a
> memory that had become encysted in my chest. I
> wept. The release of the memory and the grief it
> occasioned eased the panic and tension...[3]

Of course, unless there is concurrent work being done on the
underlying mental and emotional problems, their persistence
will constantly tend toward a return of the previous poor
postural habits. In the case of bioenergetics, Lowen's techniques
are coupled with more traditional psychotherapeutic techniques.
Normally, yoga combines a regular practice of postures and the
introspective study of meditation to produce a well-integrated
improvement in bodily functions and mental attitude.

The Body in Yoga Therapy

Yoga has traditionally involved the notion that bodily position and physical posture are intimately and basically linked to personality and emotion. Hatha yoga is that branch of yoga which includes a series of postures to stretch and strengthen each of the muscles and tendons that may have become shortened and contracted due to mental tensions and faulty posture. Simultaneously, muscle groups which have become weak from disuse are also gradually strengthened.

During the development of bad postural habits, like curvature of the spine, normal balance and equilibrium are lost. Certain muscles must become increasingly tense to hold the body in the out-of-balance or off-center position. Other muscles which would normally operate in opposition, to keep the body balanced, are used less and shrink or become weak. Eventually, the person is unable to correct his posture even when distortions are pointed out. The muscles necessary for maintaining the proper position are too weak. Attempts to straighten up can be sustained for only a few seconds before the body begins to tremble and feel uncomfortable, lapsing back into the previous poor position.

Therefore, merely being aware of one's postural errors may be of little value. A gradual strengthening of those muscles which are necessary to restore the body to its proper position may be the only remedy. This is especially effective if it is accompanied by systematic stretching and loosening of the contracted and tightened tendons and muscles which maintain the abnormal position. The resulting increase in freedom of movement allows one to become aware that a more comfortable posture is possible. Moreover, there is now the muscle strength and flexibility to maintain it. What is at first a "discovery" becomes a habit and the new posture becomes customary.

In addition to the sustained, chronic posture that characterizes a person there are more temporary body positions and gestures that reflect more transient mental states. Waving the arms when excited is an obvious case, but the position one assumes as he faces a friend for a casual chat is a less obvious item of vocabulary in the "body language." Open arms reflect a willingness for interchange while crossed legs with arms folded over the chest can indicate a refusal of input from the other persons.

The many such correlates of gesture and posture were consciously utilized in yogic training for millennia. The teacher who sits with one leg folded over the other asserts his position of authority. In the orthodox tradition, the student who sits down in this fashion before his teacher is recognized immediately as impudent and insolent. It is obvious that he is less receptive. This posture is called the "heroic pose" and is one of many that have been identified and named according to the attitudes they involve. Other postures emphasize relaxation, for example, the "corpse pose." By assuming certain positions *(asanas)* and gestures *(mudras)* the student learns how to create the mental state he wishes.

Techniques of Relaxation in Yoga and Modern Therapy

Cultivating a relaxed and tension-free posture facilitates introspection, an approach which is not unknown in the West. In many varieties of behavior therapy, the therapeutic sessions are begun with a process of "progressive relaxation," a procedure similar to that employed in yoga. Beginning at the tip of the toes, the muscles are brought one by one into focus, and relaxed. The student lies on his back comfortably cushioning the head so that no effort is expended. By concentrating on each muscle group in sequence, the whole body is brought to a calm and quiet state, systematically creating a state of total relaxation.*

Autogenic training which is used widely in Europe for a great variety of psychosomatic illnesses incorporates a number of relaxation techniques.[5] Another obvious example of the encouragement of relaxation is the psychoanalytic couch. As Freud abandoned the use of hypnosis, he discovered that having the patient assume a reclining position promoted relaxation, allowing the train of associations to flow more freely.

In behavior therapy, a variety of relaxation techniques have been used. Some are strikingly similar to those traditionally used in yoga. Postures are also thought to gradually help those muscles

---

* See the recent review and comparison of relaxation techniques used in both modern psychology and in some aspects of yoga.[4]

which are tense to relax, which withdraws the energy bound up in rigid musculature making it available for other uses. Moreover, when the voluntary muscles become quiet, one becomes more clearly aware of internal states. Random static from postural tension no longer drowns out subtler signals from within. As we shall see in subsequent chapters, elimination of the noise of the "grosser" contents of consciousness in order to bring into awareness the subtler ones is a major aspect of the philosophy and practice of yoga.

The Body as a Model for the Mind

Yoga postures, in addition to these more direct functions, serve another more subtle purpose in preparing the student for the practice of meditation. Learning their correct and precise execution, the student becomes aware that there is more involved than simply positioning the body. In order to accomplish the stretch of one muscle group and the required tension of its antagonist, attention must be focused. The mind cannot be allowed to wander. It is held firmly but gently on the area of the body involved (see illustration). Absent-mindedly attempting a posture can lead to injury. A lack of attention to the muscles and supporting structures can result in carrying the stretch beyond that precise point where it is beneficial, which may result in a tear, dislocation, or milder, less obvious damage that leaves those muscles stiff or sensitive. For such reasons, one is counseled to:

> Bring your awareness to the area of tension. Carry the posture far enough to feel a good stretch, but not pain. If your mind wanders, allow it to wander but immediately and gently return it to the task at hand. Now turn your attention to the breath. Observe your breath and gradually eliminate jerks and irregularities. Allow it to become smooth and even. Next return to the area of stretch.

Search it out and pin-point its location in the body.
Use your mind to create an image of this area and
mentally outline the tension. Now, tell that part to
relax. If the tension fades, extend the posture a bit
further, increasing the stretch a bit more. Now once
again return to the breath. Bring it back to an even
flow. Let its rhythm be regular. Now go to the area
of stretch...

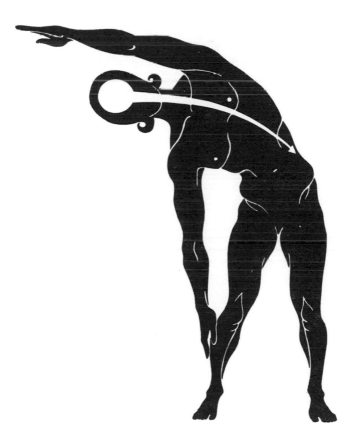

The process is repeated until the tension will no longer respond to attempts to relax it. Then, returning to the relaxation posture, the body is stretched out and rested.

If carried out correctly, this sort of exercise is not only an effective physical discipline, it is preliminary training in mental discipline. At a later point, a similar methodical approach will be suggested for working with the mind during meditation. By first learning concrete, easily understood physical tasks, the student is able to begin that mastery of attention and concentration which will later be necessary in the introspective work of meditation. A systematic approach will have been acquired which can then be applied to the study and regulation of the mind.

For in meditation it will also be found that the attention wanders. The method of dealing with this will be similar to that used before. The student will be instructed not to struggle against the wandering but to gently guide the attention back to the "platform" where thoughts are observed just as it was earlier returned to the part of the body being studied. Having learned this technique of detached observation in the practice of yoga postures, it can now be applied with less difficulty to the mental realm. Otherwise, such an approach might seem confusingly abstract.

Exploration of the Inside of the Body

Through the careful study of physical sensations experienced during the practice of yoga postures, the subtle feelings that are produced by each position can be identified. They gradually become apparent through the repeated experience of each posture and its immediate effects. Instruction at the termination of each posture to pause, close the eyes and go inside encourages such awareness. Through this process of introspection, it becomes obvious that each position affects bodily sensation and also the state of mind. For instance, after the headstand, an increased sense of alertness may be noticeable.

This "tuning-in" to the internal situation of the body is one of the most important facets of hatha yoga. For many it is the first contact with a whole realm of experience which had been outside awareness. Generally, there is a tendency to ignore information from the inside of the body until it becomes painful or uncomfortable and one is "ill." The surface of the body instead receives most of our attention.

In many cultures, the surface of the body is regarded as most important. Our own culture, for example, is preoccupied with surface appearances. If the skin color is poor, we use cosmetics. If body odor is unpleasant, deodorants are used. Self-esteem often depends on superficial looks. A person's whole self-image may revolve around his or her outward characteristics and the use of surgery to change facial features or enlarge female breasts has become a growing medical sub-specialty.

There is often less concern with possible internal derangements which might be manifesting themselves at the body's surface. Not only is there frequently a denial of the importance of the inside of the body, there may even be a revulsion experienced toward it. Such negative attitudes toward internal processes are seen when yoga instructors attempt to teach the various cleansing exercises or "washes." These involve passing water through the nasal passages or swallowing and throwing water out of the stomach. In order to practice internal cleansing techniques, students must often overcome strong feelings of revulsion.

MODELS OF DISEASE:
INTERNAL ECOLOGY VERSUS THE INVASION BY GERMS

The Body as an Ecological System

In yoga it is traditionally assumed that the inside of the body can be "polluted" by metabolic wastes, chemicals or other toxins. These pollutants are viewed as a major obstacle to health and mental clarity.

Normally the body excretes those wastes which result from the digestion and breakdown of food through the urine and feces. There are, however, alternate routes for this excretion. For example, many wastes other than carbon dioxide are thrown off by exhaled air. The skin is also known to excrete a certain amount of wastes through perspiration and, in yoga, mucus is thought to serve an excretory function.

We can see from these examples that the body is constantly undergoing a self-cleansing process. There is a natural internal ecology within which all of the organs are working to maintain a waste-free environment.

In yoga there are several important cleansing techniques or washes to promote or accelerate these natural functions. Washes such as those described earlier concentrate on removing accumulated mucus in the sinuses, nasal passages, throat, stomach, intestines, colon and lungs. Fasting is sometimes used in conjunction with cleansing exercises in order to allow the body's metabolism to focus on waste removal.

In addition to these washes, there are certain breathing exercises which have as one of their functions the facilitation of elimination through the skin and breath. *Kapalabhati,* an exercise consisting of rapid inhalation and exhalation, "washes out the lungs," removing so much waste material that an unpleasant odor can sometimes be noticed. Other breathing exercises are designed to promote perspiration and facilitate waste removal by this route. Through learning deep breathing, the yoga student increases the effectiveness of respiratory excretion of carbon dioxide and other toxins.[6]

The Germ Theory

In modern medicine, less importance has been placed on the internal ecology, cleansing and in developing a sensitivity to internal experiences. Instead, more attention is given to external appearance. For example, if a patient has acne or a skin rash, the emphasis is on *suppressing* the external manifestation rather than focusing on the underlying disturbance in the organism. Physicians are now beginning to feel, however, that such suppressed symptoms may reappear in other forms. For example, in some cases where eczema is suppressed it seems to reappear as asthma.

Our ignorance of the inside of our bodies is related to our attitude toward disease. It seems to have played a major role in the rise of a theory of disease peculiar to our culture. The conviction grew that most diseases were "caused" by invaders from the outside: micro-organisms or "germs." The ways in which poor management of one's internal environment could contribute to the illness was largely ignored.

The emphasis on germs was only one of a number of perspectives in modern medicine until it gained great impetus during the 1930's and 40's as a result of the discovery of antibiotics. "Miracle drugs" seized the public's imagination. It was quickly assumed that every disorder of the body would eventually be discovered to have its cause in the malicious attack of some invasive micro-organism. There was a great sense of relief, for it seemed that medical science would also eventually discover an effective drug to annihilate each of these invaders. Though a micro-organismic culprit did not materialize for every known disease, the concept of "miracle drugs" prevailed. This search for new drugs to reverse illness continues today.

Thinking of ourselves in terms of the surface of the body and not developing an awareness of the interior leads to looking about in the world to find the cause of discomfort whenever we feel vaguely that things are not right. From this perspective it is natural to assume that the remedy will also be something external — a "pill" or drug which can be put inside ourselves to make everything all right again.

This approach is also seen in the current attitude towards drugs which influence the mind and emotions. Feelings of unhappiness are glibly blamed on "pressures," "difficulties at work," or other external influences. An "upper" is taken for a lift, a "downer" to relax, or whatever is handy to feel different. The term "disease," of course, means *dis-ease,* a "lack of ease." But attention has turned away from a focus on this internal experience to the external world where the causal agent and remedy are both thought to be found. We have now come around to the point where "disease" means something that comes from the outside.

The Psychosomatic Model

But the search for ever more powerful drugs has not succeeded in abolishing all physical disorders. Where even the tiniest viruses have been identified and the most potent drugs employed, people continue to get sick. For this reason, perhaps, attention has increasingly been turned toward the relationship between physical disease and those disorders which are mental and emotional. This has given rise in recent decades to a new medical specialty called "psychosomatics."

Currently, it is fashionable to say that sixty to eighty percent of all illness is "psychosomatic." But the relationship between the emotional and the physical is not well understood, and there has been little success in finding effective treatment for illness which involves both. Therefore, most physicians

continue to fall back on their disease model and on potent
medications when faced with psychosomatic problems.

Control of Internal States

Motivated by the present need to cope with such disorders,
some psychiatrists and physicians have become more interested
in how physiological functions are normally regulated and how
their regulation becomes upset. How does an ulcer patient come
to secrete too much gastric acid? How do the bronchi of an
asthmatic come to constrict in such an inappropriate way? How
do we "learn" to regulate and to use our internal organs? More
to the point, how does one "learn" to misuse them so that
diseases like asthma, ulcers or high blood pressure result? Is the
mind involved or does this happen on some more primitive level
of regulation? Psychoanalytic investigators avoided this difficulty
by explaining that the mind *is* involved but that such mental
functions are carried on in the "unconscious mind" outside one's
awareness. For this reason, most of us are unaware of such
regulation.

Two Types of Learning

Behavior therapists have a different explanation for how
such "mislearning" occurs. Their theory is based on the distinction between two types of learning or "conditioning," classical
and instrumental. Classical conditioning is typified by Pavlov's
dog, who learned to salivate at the sound of a bell. It has been
thought to be involved in the learning of responses by the internal
organs. But this is a sort of "reflex." It was therefore thought to
be easily distinguished from the second kind of learning which is
considered to be more purposive. The best known example of
this second kind is Skinner's rat, who discovered pressing a lever

led to receiving a pellet of food. This "instrumental" conditioning seemed to involve forms of behavior operating in the outside world and involving conscious choice.

From this point of view, it seemed logical that "classical" or reflex conditioning was involved in the more *primitive* aspects of the organism and instrumental conditioning was reserved for "higher levels" of functioning. Thus, scientific psychology developed a theory which was acceptable to the cultural preconceptions from which it grew: that which involved the outside of the body was reasonable, rational and purposive (volitional). That which involved the inside of the body was automatic, reflexive and primitive.

Ulcers, for example, are thought to be influenced by emotional factors but in a reflexive way — beyond the patient's control. Treatment, then, is also externally oriented through the use of antacids, medicines and so forth. Volition and personal responsibility are not thought to be involved. In this way, a rationale was developed for having banished the interior of the body from awareness. Not only was it repulsive and irrational but it also was incapable of being voluntarily controlled.

When the external environment is populated by potentially disease-producing invaders and the internal body is thought of as "bad" and incomprehensible, we are left only the surface of the body with which we can identify. Trapped between an unknown interior and a threatening external world, we opt for that which is, at least, somewhat familiar, our outer surface.

Learning to Control the Inside of the Body

Within this cultural context it is understandable that psychology and psychosomatic medicine have tended to think of one's interior as vegetative, containing organs that act automatically, governed by the "autonomic" or "vegetative" nervous system. For this reason recent research by Neal Miller demonstrating that internal organs can be volitionally and purposefully controlled has aroused great resistance and controversy.[7] His experiments clearly show that in animals, control of the internal organs can be achieved in "instrumental learning situations" where awareness of, and intentional control of, internal organs are possible. This would suggest that a person suffering from ulcers, for example, could learn to control gastric secretion if he were to become more sensitive to his internal organs.

It is the denial of the interior of the body and its isolation from our awareness that makes dealing with psychosomatic illnesses so difficult. The control of internal processes cannot be learned as long as the response to efforts made remains outside awareness. For instance, if one attempts to control his heart rate and has no way of knowing whether it is increasing or decreasing, then bringing it under conscious control is not possible. In order to monitor the activity of the internal organs, electronic equipment has recently been developed to detect and give information to people about their own internal workings. The success of results obtained when one has access to this "feedback" information has been remarkable. There is now a whole new field of psychological and medical investigation and treatment called "biofeedback."

BIOFEEDBACK AND SELF-CONTROL

When a child is learning to walk, he must learn to balance himself. If he leans too far, he falls. This fall can be called "feed-back." It gives the child information on how successful his effort was. By means of this information or feedback he can gradually learn to adjust his body in such a way that he stands upright easily. Though the use of such feedback is hardly new, the term itself is of relatively recent origin. Its use dates back several decades to the beginnings of work with electronic equipment. It has been technically defined as "a method of controlling a system by reinserting into it the results of its past performance."[8]

Our ability to operate effectively in the world depends on our gradually refining our actions through a constant process of learning by using feedback. Steering a new car is, at first, difficult. We quickly become adept at it as we see the results of turning the steering wheel a few degrees. We gauge the effects of a lecture we are giving by the responses seen in the faces of the audience and we attempt to make adjustments accordingly.

But, for most, the inside of the body is cut off from this feedback process because we have not learned to pay attention to our own internal feedback information. There is little or no awareness of the heartbeat so we do not know how it responds to something eaten, to a movement made or to a mental image. Having no information on the effects these actions may have on the heart rate, "control" of it is never "learned." It remains outside the realm of the "voluntary" system and seems rather automatic and unrelated to volition.

Yet, in Miller's experiments, voluntary muscles were completely paralyzed so that they could play no role in the control of the heart. He found that despite this, the animals were able to learn to control their heart rate when feedback was provided in the form of rewards adjusted according to electronic measurements of the slightest increase or decrease in the number of heart beats per minute.[9] In this case, the heart, previously thought of as an "involuntary" muscle, was apparently controlled volitionally. A series of such studies showed that kidney function, gastric changes, responses of the blood vessels and the blood pressure could similarly be controlled. It is becoming clear that we *can* learn to control internal organs if we are provided with appropriate feedback from them. The ability of animals and humans to alter their physiological functioning is now being studied and developed beyond that which was previously imagined.

When information about the responses of his internal organs is relayed to an individual, the feedback is called "biofeedback."

In the last few years, instruments have been developed for biofeedback training. Subtle aspects of internal functioning that belonged before to an unknown territory can now be brought into awareness and controlled through biofeedback training.

This mushrooming of biofeedback has numerous clinical applications. For example, it was discovered that by monitoring the activity of the forehead muscle (frontalis) and displaying a signal (through an auditory tone) to a patient suffering from headaches, relaxation of the muscles around the head could be learned and the common "tension headache" relieved.[10]

Other headaches of the "migraine" type have also been studied from this perspective. Migraine headaches are not related to muscle tension but seem to be due, instead, to contraction and subsequent excessive dilation of the blood vessels in the head. It was gradually discovered that learning to control the blood flow in the hands through biofeedback information could somehow influence the blood vessels in the head. Patients learned to "warm their hands" in this fashion (by increasing blood flow to the fingers). This seemed to simultaneously shift blood flow away from the congested arteries of the head, often relieving their migraine headaches.[11]

Other aspects of the circulatory system have been studied in this fashion. Psychophysiologists at Harvard have demonstrated that blood pressure can be controlled through biofeedback learning.[12] They indicated that elevated blood pressure can be lowered, (at least temporarily), in some hypertensive patients.[13] A study by C. H. Patel in England reported lasting effects of biofeedback training in lowering blood pressure when the biofeedback was combined with yogic relaxation. Improvement was still sustained twelve months after training had been completed.[14,15]

In another study patients with irregular heart beats were trained to alter their heart beats. When they were shown a green light, increasing the rate would bring a "reward" signal.

When they were shown a red light, a decrease was necessary to bring a reward. A couple of hours a day of such training over a three-week period was sufficient for most of the patients to learn moderate control of the heart rate. This was found to be quite effective in reducing irregularities of the heart's rhythm.[16]

Other work using biofeedback demonstrated that subjects could learn to change their stomach acidity, suggesting a "volitional" treatment for ulcers.[17] It has even been shown by one group of research workers that men could voluntarily produce scrotal heating through temperature biofeedback, reducing their sperm count below fertility level.[18]

BIOFEEDBACK AND YOGIC FEATS

Even without bio-feedback technology, isolated individuals have periodically appeared who have shown the ability to control their internal organs and physiological states. For example, in the laboratories of the Menninger Foundation, Jack Schwartz, who calls himself a "Western Sufi," demonstrated his ability to pass a metal spike through his biceps and remove it, suffering no bleeding from his arm and apparently no pain. Follow-up examinations showed that the openings left were largely healed and, in many cases, had completely disappeared within a few days.[19] In view of what has been learned about the ability to control internal states through biofeedback, it would not be surprising that the ability to constrict blood vessels and prevent bleeding could be developed. All that would be required is learning to "tune-in" to the level of awareness where internal states are reflected. One then has his own internal "biofeedback" and is in a position to exert control over his blood vessels. In other words, "involuntary systems" can become "voluntary" when access is gained to internal cues.

Seen from this perspective, the aura of "magic" surrounding

reports of remarkable bodily control by yogis falls away and such feats seem much less "miraculous." If it is true that through the discipline of yoga, one learns to tune out external distractions, focus attention inward, and become aware of internal states, then, in view of what we now know, it would not be surprising if yogis also showed a remarkable ability to control their breath, heart rate, or metabolism. From the perspective gained through biofeedback research, it seems that a fresh look at yogic "feats" is in order.

"Stopping the heart" is one of the feats of yogic self-control that has attracted much attention. It has been studied for several decades beginning in the year 1935 when Therese Brosse, a French cardiologist, took a portable electrocardiograph machine to India and recorded the ECG's of several yogis as they attempted to control their hearts. One of her published reports was intriguing and aroused a great deal of interest. She made a recording which apparently indicated that the yogi in question had succeeded in completely stopping his heart.

In the early fifties there was a report from an Indian medical college on observations of a 34-year old practitioner of yoga who called himself Ramananda Yogi. When studied under fluoroscopy, his heart showed a "cessation of pulsation" when he attempted to "stop" it. The authors admitted, however, that a closer examination revealed a "very slight flicker extending along the border at the left apex of the heart."

In 1961, three researchers at the All-India Institute of Medical Sciences in New Delhi studied four "yogis" who claimed they could stop, or slow, their hearts. One, a 37-year old man, who had been studying yoga for about five years, had accidentally discovered a way of reducing his heart rate. By assuming a special posture, which he invented, he was able to briefly slow the heart to a rate between forty and fifty beats per minute. At times, the interval between two beats extended to three seconds. Another experimental subject showed some weakening of the pulse and reduction of heart sounds heard through the stethoscope but the electrocardiogram indicated little or no change in his heart rate.

The third subject in this study was a Shri T. Krishnamacharia, the same gentleman who had "stopped his heart" for Dr. Brosse in 1935. At that time, the electrocardiogram had been made with only one "lead" or electrode attached to the body. This time more modern equipment with multiple leads was used. The now elderly gentleman repeated his maneuver. It was evident that his heart "tilted" in his chest cavity as a result of muscular contractions and that the change of its position eliminated the recording from lead 1, the lead which had been used by Dr. Brosse. But the other electrodes continued to register the heart beat as before. It was concluded that, had Dr. Brosse had the benefit of more modern equipment, she would not have reported that the heart had been stopped.

The fourth subject in this experiment was Ramananda Yogi, whose heart had been previously observed under fluoroscopy. On this occasion, an electrocardiogram was done and only a slight and insignificant slowing was recorded.[20]

It is such results which have led researchers in this area to conclude that "this field, which at one time appeared so promising to throw light on psychosomatic problems, is not likely to do so to any extent at all."[21] Closer scrutiny of the feats of control often show them to be more apparent than real.

Those scientists investigating yoga have repeatedly commented, however, that one of their major difficulties is in locating "qualified yogis." The research team in New Delhi mentioned that they could locate only four practitioners of yoga who claimed to be able to stop the heart and, of these, none turned out to be able to, in fact, do so.[22]

Other researchers distinguish between those who are authentic yogis, having pursued the different facets of yoga training to higher states of awareness, and those who work with only certain aspects of yoga such as the physical postures. A person of this latter type "is simply practicing a few yogic exercises; he is not practicing yoga in the strict sense."[23] In India there are also those who have never seriously practiced *any* part of yoga but, nevertheless, label themselves "yogis." There are the "bogus yogis;" they are the free-lance performers of India's street scene, who, through their sleight of hand and clever stunts, capitalize on the legends and traditions which have grown-up around those more truly accomplished.

It is rare to find a yogi who can demonstrate some evidence of having attained a highly developed sensitivity and ability to control internal states, who is willing to submit to laboratory testing of his physiological control. One of the authors of this book, Swami Rama, was recently studied at the research laboratories of the Menninger Foundation. In a series of experiments, he demonstrated an ability to alter his EEG pattern. Moreover, he was able to create a temperature differential of ten degrees Fahrenheit between the two sides of his palm.

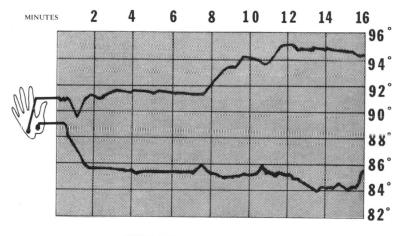

EXPERIMENT WITH SWAMI RAMA: CHANGE IN
HAND TEMPERATURE OVER SIXTEEN MINUTE PERIOD.

DEGREES F°

In another experiment, he produced a state of atrial flutter during which the heart ceased to pump blood for seventeen seconds.   This length of time was shorter than that which had been planned as the researchers became so alarmed at this often fatal condition that they abruptly interrupted the experiment asking the Swami to return his heart to normal.[24]

The experimenters were surprised that, instead of stopping his heart, the Swami actually increased its speed to such an extent (300 beats per minute) that it was not pumping any blood (since the ventricles had stopped and the atria merely fluttered).   The effect on the circulatory system was thus the same as if the heart had completely ceased to beat.

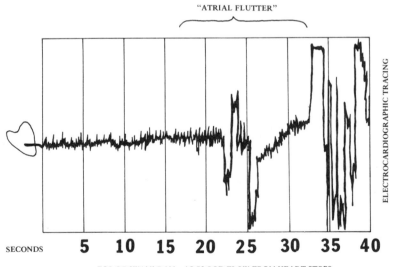

ECG OF SWAMI RAMA AS BLOOD FLOW FROM HEART STOPS.

A recent report describes the use of the same technique to control the action of the heart by another Indian. In this experiment, yogi Satyamurti was confined in an isolation chamber at a medical institute in India. Heart activity was monitored with a modern twelve-lead electrocardiograph. At first, a rapid rate of 250 beats per minute was observed, similar to that seen in Swami Rama's recording. In this case, however, the experiment was not interrupted and eventually, to the surprise of the research team, "a straight line appeared on the ECG recording." This was maintained for an extended period but, at the designated time, "electrical activity returned." The researchers were "left rather perplexed and confused." They were expecting some tachycardia (slowing) and possible signs of decreased oxygen supply to the heart wall.

> "...but, contrary to this, there was severe tachycardia followed by a complete disappearance of all complexes. Any instrumental failure was ruled out by thoroughly checking the machine and also by spontaneous reappearance of the ECG....A disconnection of the leads by the yogi, quite a likely explanation, ought to have given rise to considerable electrical disturbance, but there was hardly any. Later on, we tried all sorts of manipulations with the leads to simulate what the yogi could have done...(notwithstanding the total darkness and his ignorance of ECG technique), but in every case there was a marked disturbance. Therefore, although it is obviously difficult to believe that the yogi could have completely stopped his heart or decreased its electrical activity below a recordable level, we still had no satisfactory explanation for the ECG tracings before us."[25]

Those who can demonstrate control over such internal processes are neither the bogus yogis nor those who practice only the physical postures and exercises—though it is these who most often make themselves available for laboratory investigation. In order to attain the level of consciousness that will permit such control, various aspects of the person must be painstakingly trained and gradually integrated: body, mind and that consciousness which goes beyond the usual mental states must be brought into harmonious coordination.

It is not a matter of simply learning to control an organ. In fact, biofeedback training, in which an isolated physiological function is altered, may have serious drawbacks. For example, to change one aspect of the system without an awareness of how it interacts with other body systems or with the mind may be, in the words of Erik Peper, a current biofeedback researcher, "useless and possibly harmful." He typifies a recent, more sober assessment of the value of biofeedback when he suggests that its clinical use must be "integrated with a variety of methods such as: psychoanalytic techniques, relaxation training, gestalt, family counseling, hypnosis, behavior shaping, job counseling, etc..." He adds that: "To be successful, a patient may have to change his habits or life style to gain health... In order for a patient to get well, he must be free to grow in all dimensions." [26]

Such a comprehensive approach is a traditional characteristic of yoga training. Although similar to biofeedback in its potential for developing physiological control, it stresses a more holistic approach to the human being. In the philosophy of yoga, the physical body is seen as only one level of existence. There are others, ranging upward from the gross physical, past the mental, and into the higher states of consciousness. Concern is not only with the regulation of the physical body but with that of the mind and intervening levels of function.

Besides working to control the body in a direct manner, one can approach it from the next highest level of organization, that which involves the study and regulation of what, in yoga, is called energy or *prana*.

CHAPTER TWO
PRANA

"Quite other than this physical sheath which consists of food and interior to it is the energy sheath that consists of breath. This is encased in the physical sheath and has the same form. The one is filled with the other. The first has the likeness of a man, and because it has the likeness of a man, the second follows it and itself takes on the likeness of a man. Through this vital sheath the senses perform their office. From this men and beasts derive their life. For breath is the life of beings and so is called 'the life of all.' "

Taittiriya Upanishad, II. 2

chapter 2
BREATH AND ENERGY

In the first chapter we explained that the preliminary steps in yoga which involve the body serve as a preparation. The physical postures should leave the body supple and calm, free from nervous movement or muscular tension. However, even when the body is totally relaxed, one is not completely still because the movement of the breath breaks the silence. Therefore, as the body is brought under control, attention inevitably turns toward the breath. The breath and its intermittant ebb and flow is the next subject of study. This is the link that stands midway between the grosser material body and the more subtle realm of the mind.

But breathing is more than simply an obstacle to be conquered before reaching the mind. Its proper use is a key to mastering the mind and passing beyond it into other realms of consciousness. Breathing techniques have always been an integral part of meditational training in the East. One of the Sufis has said, "The subject of breath is the deepest of all the subjects with which mysticism or philosophy is concerned, because breath is the

most important thing in life."[1]   Gurdjieff is said to have spent
years in the Middle East learning breathing from a Sufi master.
Swedenborg, who lived in Europe in the 1700's before there was
any awareness of Eastern tradition, found it expedient to
"invent" a technique of breathing that would facilitate his entry
into altered states of consciousness.[2]   In the previous century
Robert Fludd, the English philosopher and physician had maintained that a "supercelestial and invisible force" in some way
"enters the body through the breath."[3]

Jung tells of observing a group of primitive people who began
their day by breathing into their hands and offering the breath
to the rising Sun.   When Jung questioned them, carefully
observing what he could only regard as a superstition, the
tribesmen laughed at his inability to see the obvious "rightness"
of surrendering the first breath to the source of energy which
sustained their world.

The fundamental relationship between breath and "spirit" is
reflected in most languages, viz: our "expiration" and "inspiration," the latter meaning not only to *inhale,* but to become filled
with creative energy or spirit (inspired). The word "expiration"
denotes death, or loss of life-energy as well as "exhalation."

The breath begins at a strategic point in development. The first
great adaptation to the outside world made by the newborn is his
initial gasp for air. The beginning of respiration transforms the
dynamics of the circulatory system and gears the infant's
physiology to its new environment. Nothing so arouses primitive
survival instincts as does the feeling of suffocation. For this
reason, the flow of breath and its alternations and rhythms is
intimately tied in with the earliest, most fundamental layers of
mental life.

Breathing is the only physiological function which is both
voluntary and involuntary. We can control it consciously or we
can ignore it and allow it to run more or less automatically as do
other internal processes. It can be regulated by the mind or left
to the body. In this sense, then, breathing is a strategic inter-

mediary between mind and body. It is not controlled by either of them exclusively, but is subject to influence from both of them. And it can, in turn, affect them both. Breathing is the key to the interaction of body and mind.

Breath: The Tide of Life

The rhythm of the breath is one of the most obvious physical indications of a person's emotional and mental state. When relaxed, the breathing reflects an emotional calm and indicates a state where the attention can be focused. Disruptions of breath generally are associated with emotional or mental disturbances. The breath becomes "agitated in anger, stopped momentarily in fear, gasping with amazement, choking with sadness, sighing with relief, etc."[4] Where the mind is randomly influenced by fleeting emotions and thoughts, it is not calm and this is reflected in the breathing.

Though emotional and mental states are difficult to control, they are intimately connected to irregularities in breathing, and the breath *can* be controlled. This suggests that learning to consciously and deliberately regulate the breath is a key to mastery of both emotions and the mind. Beginning students of yoga are often amazed at how quickly they gain control over their emotions by working with the breath. Anyone can verify for himself the notion, long held in yoga, that pauses and jerks in the breath disrupt the continuity of thought. By learning to breathe gently, smoothly and without irregularities, students of meditation are able to reduce distracting thoughts and achieve heightened concentration.

The breath not only serves as a link between a person's body and mind, but is also the most direct channel of interchange between the person and the surrounding medium. Through breathing we take in oxygen, tying ourselves into the larger ecological system which connects plants and animals in an overall cycle of energy exchange. The act of breathing unites us with this larger energy pool and integrates us into the greater context of nature. The breath "is the result of a current which runs not only through the body, but also through all the planes of man's existence...the current of the whole of nature...is the real breath... It is one breath and yet it is many breaths."[5]

But when the breath is not free-flowing, interchange with surrounding sources of energy is limited. The above descriptions of breathing habits such as "choking with sadness" portray constrictions in this interchange. Thus emerges a "breath language" which is in many ways analogous to "body language." It reveals the characteristic ways in which one relates to his surroundings: holding the breath, sighing, and wheezing are other items of vocabulary in this language of breath.*

Breath and Relaxation

Training in various patterns of breathing is one of the most crucial parts of yoga discipline. According to traditional yoga psychology, the breath not only influences the body and the mind but can serve as a powerful instrument for inducing states of higher consciousness.

Beginning students in yoga are taught exercises in which they learn to completely empty their lungs and then fill them to capacity. One such exercise, called "the complete yogic breath," requires the student to slowly exhale as he focuses on different parts of his lungs. The lower lungs are emptied by using the muscles of the abdomen, then the middle part of the lungs through pulling the ribs slightly in, and finally the chest and

* For a review of the research on breath and emotions, see "A Psychological Study on the Relationship Between Respiratory Function and Emotion," by Hiromoto Matsumoto, Chapter VII in *Psychological Studies on Zen,* edited by Yoshiharu Akishige. There is also a discussion of the relationship between chronic breathing disorders and character structure in Chapter VII of the present work (Section IV, "The Heart Chakra," pp. 243-248).

shoulder area. This is followed by a slow, even, regular inhalation, again concentrating on each part of the lungs as the breath comes in. The exercise helps to correct shallow and incorrect breathing, familiarizes the student with the structures that are involved in respiration, and allows full use of the lungs.

The movements of the rib cage, the diaphragm and the abdominal muscles come to be identified through experiencing this process. Most people are unaware of the intricate series of movements involved in breathing, especially the part played by the diaphragm. The full use of the diaphragm, achieved by slow, even and deep breathing, leads to relaxation of the chest and other muscles, and hence a calm and relaxed state of mind. The reason for this is simple: the diaphragm is perfectly located to expand and contract the lungs most efficiently. By using it, a maximum of air exchange can be produced with a minimum of work. When the movement of the diaphragm is replaced by the use of the rib cage and other chest muscles, much more movement is involved and much more effort is necessary. Moreover, the use of the chest muscles in respiration seems to be involved in some biological way with "emergency reactions." *

Breathing exercises strikingly similar to those traditionally used in yoga are also used in behavior therapy, and as a preparation for most bio-feedback training. In the latter case, such techniques help patients to relax in the face of stimuli which previously aroused anxiety.

Proskauer, a well known breathing therapist, has reported that simply teaching breath awareness (a procedure traditionally used in meditation) leads her patients to correct irregular breathing patterns. The emotionality which goes along with their irregular breathing is consequently replaced by a state that is more calm—physically, emotionally and mentally. [6]

In a study referred to earlier, [7] such breath awareness was used successfully in the treatment of hypertension. In this case

* See Chapter VII, pp. 246-248.

watching the breath was combined with other yogic relaxation techniques and bio-feedback to lower the blood pressure of the patients studied. Another study compared effectiveness of deep breathing exercises derived from yoga with systematic muscular relaxation in reducing anxiety. While each treatment led to a significant reduction of anxiety as measured by psychological tests, the greatest improvement was in those who had undergone a combined treatment where both breathing and muscle relaxation were used.[8]

RIGHT AND LEFT: A UNIVERSAL POLARITY

Besides the depth and rhythm, there are other properties of the breath which show variation. One of these, intriguingly enough, seems to be an alternation in the flow of breath between the two nostrils. At times the breath flows predominantly through the right side, at other times the left. Though this has been considered a trivial thing by modern physiologists until recently, it has always been an important matter in yoga. In western psychology, however, there has been a growing awareness of how significantly the right or left predominate in other ways.

In treating patients who have suffered damage to the brain, physicians over the last century have gradually come to feel that the symptoms vary according to which side of the brain is affected. Patients who have had a stroke that destroys tissue in the left hemisphere, for example, will most often have difficulty with speech. They may be unable to pronounce certain words or make clear sentences, although they may, after some recovery, report that their ability to *understand* had not been impaired. By contrast, patients who suffer damage to the right side of the brain will more often experience difficulty in orienting themselves in space. They may easily lose their way, even in familiar places such as their own homes. They have great difficulty in

identifying objects by touch.   While a key might be quite
recognizable to them when seen on a table, locating it by
feeling in a purse or pocket seems impossible.

It is felt that the left hemisphere, which controls the right
side of the body, is predominantly involved with logical thinking,
analysis, and verbal and mathematical functions. Robert Ornstein,[9]
who collected a great deal of data on this dichotomy, feels that
the mode of the left side of the brain is "primarily linear." It
processes information sequentially. In other words, it is concerned
with cause and effect and the temporal sequence of events.
The right hemisphere, which is connected to and controls the
left side of the body, tends, by contrast, towards "holistic
mentation." It is not so much involved with language ability as
with orientation in space, ability to be artistic and the capacity for
recognizing familiar people and places.   Rather than being
concerned with *analysis* and the sequence of events, this side of
the brain is able to *integrate* many inputs at once, permitting a
response to the situation as a whole.

When a large number of subjects were asked to characterize
their right or left sides they tended to identify the right side of
their bodies (left brain) as more "masculine," bright and strong
and associated it with "day." They saw the left side as more
"feminine," dark, mysterious and related to the night.[10] Though
the mode which is most valued may vary between cultures, the
recognition of this basic polarity is almost universal. For instance,
the Hopi Indians in the American Southwest see the function of
the right hand as that of writing, while the left is for making
music.[11]   The Mojave Indians traditionally view the left hand as
the passive, maternal side of the person and the right as the active
father.   The left is often the territory of the taboo, the unconscious.   It is the world of mysteries, rituals and dreams.   In
mythology the feminine side is usually on the left, whereas the
masculine is on the right.[12] Ancient Hindu sculptures depicting
masculine and feminine gods in the same figure invariably show
the male on the right and female on   the   left   (figure   2a,

p. 40). Medieval drawings by the alchemists show a similar right/left polarity (figure 2b, p. 41).

Right and Left Breaths in Yoga

The study of these two aspects of the personality is fundamental in yoga. They are thought to represent not only two sides of mental life but also two distinct modes of physiological functioning. The tempo of metabolism shifts to correspond to the shift in the mode of consciousness. For example, the system involving the right side of the body is thought of as more active in terms of internal metabolism as well as in external behavior. It includes such metabolic processes as digestion, defecation and physical exercise.

Students of yoga have long understood that these two systems or modalities alternate. First one is predominant, then the other. It was also discovered that this alternation is correlated with a cycle involving the nostrils. Gay Luce, a prominent writer on bio-rhythms, has noted:

> Anyone with a bad cold...knows that we do not breathe evenly through both our nostrils at once. We alternate. Yogic masters, who learn deliberately to alternate breathing through one nostril and then the other... know about this normal breathing rhythm. Ordinarily, a man will breathe through one nostril for about three hours while the tissues of the other are slightly engorged. Then in a three-hour exchange, he will breathe predominantly through the other nostril. Three-hour rhythms may be among the basic sub-units of our physiology.[13]

This has been recently documented at the Kaivalyadhama research institute in India. Ninety-nine subjects recorded which nostril was open at three hour intervals for a month. Analysis

figure 2a

Siva Ardhanarisvara: showing right-left **polarity,**
and its correspondence to the male-female **principles.**

of results when plotted on graphs showed a rhythmic pattern of
nostril alternation which varied from person to person and day
to day.[14]

A normal person will breathe mainly through one nostril for
two to three hours while the tissues of the other are engorged,
closing it off. By the end of this time, the situation will have
gradually shifted. He will have begun to breathe through the
opposite nostril. Midway through this cycle he passes through
a period when both are momentarily open. The pattern continues:
first one nostril is clear, then the other.

When the right nostril is clear, the right side of the body (and left hemisphere of the brain) are predominant. During that time one finds he is "in the mood" for more aggressive tasks and assertive interactions. Those yogis who have studied this matter in depth have discovered that operating in the world effectively and being assertive is easier during these periods. On the other hand, more passive functions are to be performed when the left nostril is open and the opposite system is predominant. At this time the physiology and mind are inclined toward rest and receptivity. There is a great deal of information on this subject in the yogic literature called *Swar Swarodayam*. These ancient writings advise:

> ...in learning from some spiritual teacher...in singing, in playing upon instruments...in disease, sorrow, dejection, fever and swoon...in establishing relations with one's masters,

the left nostril should be open. By contrast,

figure 2b

Medieval representation of the "Alchemistical Marriage" again reflecting the polarity between right and left and its correspondence to the active and passive.

In all harsh acts, in the reading and teaching of difficult sciences...in hunting...in climbing a high place or mountain, in gambling...in the breaking in of...a horse...in athletic sports...in practicing with swords, in battle, in eating...in harsh and hot deeds,

the right nostril should flow. [15]

It is explained to the student that: "It may happen that when something is to be done, the breath is not rightly flowing..." In such a case, the proper nostril "is to be set in motion."[16] There are maneuvers which are employed for activating one or the other of the nostrils. For example, lying on the right side or keeping a pillow pressed tightly under the right arm will, after several minutes, open the left nostril. However, those who have advanced further in their training, effect control through mental concentration alone.

Ida and Pingala

If, through patient practice, one sharpens his sensitivity to the movement of the breath, he becomes aware of a complex pattern of subtle sensations resulting from its flow. When the body is in good health, relaxed and calm, each inhalation and exhalation can be sensed as it moves in the chest and sends a spreading network of currents through the body. These sensations follow the course of the air and radiate out from it like the ripples around a stone which has been dropped into quiet water. The most vividly experienced pathways are called *nadis*. They are thought of as the major channels through which the body is energized. When air enters the right nostril and the system involving the right hand side of the body is activated, there is a subtle feeling of energy coursing down the major channel on this side, which is called *pingala*. This channel or *nadi*, is associated with the activation of the right nostril and the right hand side of the body whereas its mirror image, called *ida,* the major pathway on the left, comes into play when the left nostril is open and the left hand side of the body is predominant.

The more active right channel is associated with warmth or heat and stimulates metabolic processes. In traditional yogic symbology it is associated with the sun. *Ida,* on the other hand, is associated with coolness. When one is hot and tired, lying on the opposite side to open the left nostril is said to have a cooling and soothing effect. *Ida* is symbolized by the moon.

Swar swarodayam, the ancient yogic study of breath is a vast and intricate science which details the relationship between breathing rhythms and states of consciousness. The flow to different parts of the body affects the consciousness in very specific ways.[17] There is also an appreciation of the fact that the rhythmic cycle is a necessary part of one's natural balance. If one nostril remains open for more than several hours, signifying an extended predominance of one aspect of the person, this is taken as an indication that something is amiss. It has been observed that when one nostril remains active for as much as twenty-four hours, a serious illness will usually ensue.

There are a number of different yogic breathing exercises which involve using the hand to close first one nostril and then the other, creating patterns of flow that alternate between them. These help to establish the natural rhythm. The more advanced student also learns to become more aware of and constantly regulate (without using the hands) the flow of breath through the side appropriate to time and activity.

Union of the Sun and Moon: Synthesis in the Microcosm

Although a rhythmic alternation between the two sides is usually appropriate, a third possibility exists. The breath may flow equally through both nostrils. This facilitates an integration

of the two modes of functioning represented by the right and
left.   A synthesis of these two aspects of the personality leads
to functioning on more creative and satisfying levels.

Hatha is derived from two roots, *ha* meaning sun, and *tha*,
moon.*   *Pingala*, or the major right channel, is symbolized by
the sun and *ida*, on the opposite side, the moon. *Hatha yoga* is
the discipline which leads to an integration of these two.

figure 2c
Nadi shodhanam

* Actually, these roots can have other meanings related to male/female polarities,
but in this context "sun/moon" is the traditional interpretation.

Upon first beginning hatha yoga, which involves breathing as well as postures,* the student is likely to notice that he is not equally flexible on both sides. He may find, for instance, that his right side is drawn and tight whereas the left side is looser. Measurements taken at the beginning and again later in hatha yoga training indicate that these imbalances are gradually corrected.

When these two aspects of one's self are integrated, a fullness of the whole personality is experienced. The energy flow in the body is sensed as less off-balance and more "central." During that time a synthesis replaces the usual rhythmic alternation and a sense of tranquility, joy and clarity may be noted. This is a state especially conducive to the practice of meditation. At this point the internal energy is experienced as moving more centrally, closer to the axis of the body. One is said to have "opened" the third or central channel *(nadi)* called *sushumna.* At such a time one is counseled to involve himself neither actively nor passively with the world: "Do neither harsh nor mild acts at that time, both will be fruitless." [18]   This is, instead, a time for turning inwards.

SWAR SWARODAYAM: THE STUDY OF ENERGY

The notion of a pervasive energy phenomenon that underlies the tangible, material world, seems to span many cultures and ages: "The Chinese called the energy *Chi;* the Hindus, *Prana...;* the Polynesians, *Mana;* and Amerindians, *Orenda.* In modern times it has been called Orgone (Wilhelm Reich)....and bioplasma" [19] (Russian researchers). Paracelsus, often considered the father of Western medicine, describing this energy, stated, "The vital

* Although hatha yoga today is associated mainly with the physical postures or asanas, in its original form as described in the classical texts, the emphasis was on breath. See *Hatha Yogapradipika of Svatmarama* (translated by T. Tatya) Adyar Library & Research Center, Adyar, Madras, 1972.

force...in man...radiates within and around him like a luminous
sphere...."[20] More recent investigations of a contemporary neuro-
psychiatrist have found "a 'vital energy body or field' which sub-
stands the dense physical body, interpenetrating it like a sparkling
web of light beams."[21]

Other prominent medical doctors have also described such
"energy fields." Galvani, a professor of anatomy and one of the
first discoverers of electricity, described an energy underlying
biological functioning, a "life force" which was different from
ordinary electricity, but which still ran "like a circuit from one
part of the animal to the other."[22] Later, Mesmer, one of the
most famous teachers of hypnotism in Europe, postulated a
magnetic force ("animal magnetism") in the human body, which
ran through all of nature. More recently in research at Yale
University School of Medicine, electrodynamic field shifts have
been documented during hypnotic states, "inadvertently resurrect-
ing...Mesmer's animal magnetism, now more suitably based on
the laws of modern physics."[23] Freud, who learned hypnosis
from Mesmer's student, Charcot, formulated his notion of this
energy mainly in sexual terms, applying to it the term *libido*.

None of these concepts of biological energy has ever met with
wide acceptance by Western science. Their subtlety has made
them difficult to verify through observation and measurement.
Moreover, each has been a partial theory, explaining only a
limited aspect of the total spectrum of energy phenomena. Such
diverse concepts as libido, psychic energy, mental energy, sexual
energy, bio-energy and even orgone are currently used. Each
emphasizes a model which looks at psychological and biological
functioning from a particular limited perspective. We stand in
need of a unifying and comprehensive understanding of energy
in the biological and psychological realms. Our current understanding of energy is similar to our understanding of chemistry
before the periodic table was discovered. There has been no
overall integrating system.

By contrast, the study of energy in yoga is more comprehensive.

Here a unitary concept is employed which has sufficient breadth
to encompass manifestations of energy both within the person—
biological and psychological—and in the external world. There is
no parallel discipline in modern science. Western theories tend to
reduce the human to a variety of systems such as the circulatory
system, the nervous system, or the mind. These are studied
individually, each in terms of its own dynamics and energy
properties. Yoga tends instead to study the subjective effects of
the totality of these systems working in concert. This notion of
energy, however, may be obscure and difficult for the Westerner.
Not only is it framed in symbols unfamiliar to him, but it's based
on a study which is experiential and introspective. In yoga, energy
is studied as it is sensed during the inward focusing of the attention, a practice not usually cultivated or developed in the West.
The result is a sort of constantly evolving "internal map" of
experiential "energy patterns" as they are discovered during one's
personal exploration of inner space.

Field Theory and Energy Patterns

   The concept of electro-dynamic fields has become increasingly
important in current atomic physics. The old notion of electrons,
protons and other such particles being assembled like so many
tinker toys to make up an atom of matter seems to be giving way
to an emphasis on fields.
   As Dr. H. S. Burr has pointed out, the organization of sub-
atomic particles "is, to a considerable degree a function of such
fields." The characteristics of matter from this point of view,
are "determined by the interplay of electro-dynamic fields" and
the particles contained therein. But electrical phenomena underlie
biological processes too. Therefore, electro-dynamic fields are also
present in living systems. It is then, reasonable to extend the field
concept into the biological realm. Potential fields and polar
differences exist in living systems. The fields they create relate

"the entities of the biological system in a characteristic pattern." [24]

Carrying this perspective into our approach to experiential
energy, we can begin to understand how a pattern of "pranic"
or energy flow becomes apparent to the student of yoga. Each
organ system, like the circulatory system, the digestive system,
etc., though it may have its own organization, involves a certain
amount of energy. When the potential fields and polar differences from the various systems are experienced as they summate,
then an appraisal of the total situation results. Any attempt to
sum and calculate the total effect of the various physiological
energies working in even one small area of the body would be
nearly impossible.

Although it's not feasible to calculate mathematically such a
combined effect, it is obvious that the various forces cancel each
other and combine in various ways to create some total effect.
But this overall summation is not static; it is constantly changing.
At one moment the most intense energy will be experienced in
one area, at the next moment it has shifted slightly to another
area. As it varies through time, a pattern of energy "flow" comes
into awareness.

If we look, for instance, at the nervous system, and focus on a
large nerve as it courses through the upper arm, we will find that
as a result of electrical impulses moving through this nerve there
are changes in electric potential. If we examine another organ
system in the body, the circulatory system, which operates in
close parallel to the nervous system, we find that it also has its
own energy properties. The movement of blood through the
vessels involves energy and pressure operates to create the flow.
Meanwhile, tiny nerves supply the walls of the vessels, and to make
matters even more confusing, tiny vessels supply the nerves! It is
this totality of the energy state as it changes through time which
is studied during the internal experience of prana.

To make this summation principle clearer, we might use an
analogy from basic physics: The course of a boat on a windy

river is the combined effect of a number of forces such as wind, motor propulsion and water currents. But it is only the resultant of these which is experienced as the boat moves. The interrelation of the various energy shifts taking place in the different organ systems of the body is a similar resultant pattern of energy. But it is much more complex.

Dr. Burr and his co-workers at Yale have been able to measure electro dynamic fields, or "L-fields," in and around the body which seem to reflect the summation of some of these forces. But their measurements are limited by the range of phenomena the instruments can pick up. The overall pattern of energy flow sensed by the inward explorer, the yoga student, is probably broader and includes more elusive and subtle forms of "energy."

Prana: A Unified Theory of Energy

The yogic notion of energy is unitary and includes not only those energies involved in the physical processes. It also includes what is called "mental energy." Both are included in the yogic term for energy, *prana*. In this context, *pra* means "first unit" and *na,* "energy." *Prana* is the energy which underlies all activity, physical and mental.

In psychoanalysis mental energy or *libido* is said to be invested in objects or persons toward which one turns his attention or affections. Originally Freud coined the term to designate sexual energy, which he saw as "dammed up" in neurotics. The inability to direct and regulate such energy led, he felt, to the symptoms of emotional illness. This "hydraulic" notion of sexual energy, as something almost material that could be "blocked," was widely criticized. Eventually orthodox psychoanalysis came to use the term in a much more *mental* sense, to designate the tendency to relate oneself to persons or objects.

Meanwhile Reich, one of Freud's most brilliant but controversial students, held onto the original sexual meaning of Freud's

energy concept, and in his hands it became even more physiological and nearly tangible. Its flow could be blocked by muscular
tension, its escape from the body prevented by such devices as the
orgone box, and it could be measured with mechanical devices.
He came to feel that attention to the energy was more important
than to the mental content, and eventually shifted from talking
therapy to more physical maneuvers, such as breathing exercises
and the manipulation of body parts in an effort to reduce what
he saw as "muscular blocks" to the flow of energy. In the words
of one critic, he "pushed psychoanalysis to the utmost biological
extreme, reducing all of psychic life to a manifestation of bodily
streamings and spasms." [25] This energy he came to call *orgone*.

The bio-energetic therapists have followed Reich's lead, while
orthodox analysts have made of *libido* a primarily mental
phenomenon. Yet Freud's earlier notion of libido is broader in its
scope and closer to the Eastern notion of *prana*. He saw it as an
energy that was readily expended through relatedness, especially
of a sexual nature, but which can also, at least potentially, be
shifted and transformed (sublimated) so that it becomes the
force behind less gross, more mental and creative (sublime)
activity. All attempts by Western science or psychology to
integrate this sort of concept with the prevailing notions of
physical energy have been unsuccessful. The more "scientific"
psychologists have therefore found it necessary to reject notions
of mental energy and libido. In yoga, however, this is more
easily placed in perspective. The entire spectrum of energies is
included. The internal energy pattern which is experienced
results from the merging of mental energy with the physical
energies which we discussed. The two find a common meeting
ground in the phenomenon of *prana*.

The fusion of the mental and physical energies creates that
level of existence known in yoga as the *"pranic* sheath" or the
"energy body." Where mental and physical energy come
together, the total energy state is reflected. From the perspective
of yoga, most Western concepts of biological energy have proved

unsatisfactory because they have encompassed only one fraction of this totality. For example, Reich's orgone energy was more physical, in contrast to Freud's *libido,* which became more mental in nature. In a similar way, the concepts of Mesmer, Galvani, or current researchers on Kirlian photography, appear to be fragmentary. Each seems to be related to the area of experience to which the writers have had access.

Where the total energy state is reflected might be called the level of pure energy. The level of pure energy is this *pranic* level or "sheath." This energy manifests in both the mental and physical spheres, though their basic nature is different. The basic nature of the physical level is matter and of the mental level, thoughts.* However, the *pranic* or energy level which connects or relates consists purely of energy.

There is a hierarchy of such levels in yogic theory. They form a sort of continuum. At each there is a higher degree of consciousness than in the previous. On the lowest level exists the physical body, on the next level is the energy make-up of the person and on the level above that is the mental plane.

Because of this interrelationship between the three, the total energy situation may be changed, either through inputs from the mental sphere or inputs from the physical level. Thus, one may do a certain posture or breathing exercise which physically increases or shifts the focus of energy, altering the total energy picture. He may, on the other hand, employ certain mental exercises by concentrating attention on a certain point in the body, thereby shifting mental energy and altering the total balance. Many of the meditational practices used in yoga might be viewed from this perspective.†

The energies involving the movement of the limbs and the grosser physical processes are found in the practice of yoga to be

* See Chapter VI, section on "Purusha and Prakriti," for an explanation of how consciousness relates to matter in the yogic system.

† See Chapter VII.

"noisier": that is, the sensations produced by these movements are more easily noticed and can "drown out" the sensations of subtler energy shifts that may be taking place. For this reason, one who wishes to study *prana* and its movements within himself must first assume a quiet, relaxed and steady position. This is another way of looking at what is accomplished by the yoga postures that were discussed in the first chapter: when the body and muscles are relaxed, the "grosser" *pranas* are quieted. When the situation is calm in this way, the subtle sensations inside that normally may not be noticed come into awareness.

But in unusual circumstances they may also be noticed anyway when, accidentally, they are accentuated enough. An example is the feeling of intensity in the chest that comes with "opening one's heart" to another with compassion. Another is the experiencing of "butterflies in the stomach" with stage fright.

The experience that ensues when one aspect of the subtle energy comes into awareness suddenly is graphically described by Gopi Krishna, a student who stumbled onto this level of consciousness through his own reading and practice without the aid of a teacher.

> I found...a...tongue of flame licking my stomach, as if a part of the streaming energy...was being diverted to the gastric region to expedite the process of digestion. I lay awake, dumb with wonder, watching this living radiance moving from place to place through the whole digestive tract, caressing the intestines and the liver, while another stream poured into the kidneys and the heart. I pinched myself to make sure whether I was dreaming or asleep, absolutely dumbfounded by what I was witnessing in my own body, entirely powerless to regulate or to guide the current...all that I could feel was a gentle and soothing warmth moving through my body as the current travelled from point to point.[26]

Shifts in this total energy pattern can be sensed and the

courses which such energy shifts follow have been mapped out in great detail by those who have immersed themselves in this study (see figure 2d). These paths or courses which such energy movements follow are the *nadis* which we have called "channels." Their configuration and distribution is extremely complex. It is said that seventy-two thousand of these channels or pathways have been described by those who have developed an extreme sensitivity to them.

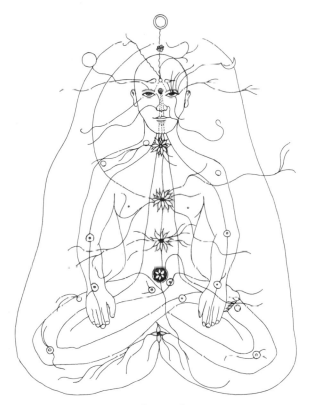

figure 2d

A certain range of the more physical *pranas* has been mapped in acupuncture, an ancient system of medicine which is practiced primarily in China. On this level of energy, twelve main channels are described coursing through the body. These are energy circuits which have been likened to electrical wiring.[27] From the perspective of yoga, they are a part of a grosser level of energy fields that can be physically manipulated through the insertion of needles, etc. Though these seem again to represent only a fragment of the spectrum of energy forms, they are of some practical interest because they are easily accessible to input from the outside. The yogic *nadis,* which are experientially derived from "inside," seem, however, to encompass all the various polarities and "energy fields," including those described by acupuncture.

These energy pathways described in the yogic tradition intersect and converge at certain centers which are located along the axis of the body. This roughly corresponds to the spinal cord and the energy centers located along this line are termed in Sanskrit, *chakras.* These centers have been rediscovered and described in many different cultures. Identical locations are noted in such cultures as far away and unrelated to India as that of the Hopi Indians in America[28] and more currently in the description documented by Dr. Karagulla.[29]

PRANAYAMA: DISCIPLINE OF ENERGY CONTROL

The study of energy shifts and movements within the field of awareness is a preliminary step. It is only after one studies these energy patterns within himself and, in some personal terms, maps them out, that he is able to begin to learn to control them. Even before that, however, preparation is necessary to reach the degree of sensitivity which will allow the perception of such internal states.

The Role of Breathing Exercises

There are certain breathing exercises which are used to sharpen this acuity. One aspect of this is accomplished through an exercise called *kapalabhati*. It is a bellows-like pumping of the stomach muscles which flushes the lungs with air. The result is removal from the blood of carbon dioxide and other wastes which, if allowed to remain, would dull sensitivity. Another technique is rhythmic breathing, alternating between the left and right nostrils. This practice is done seated, pressing one nostril closed while breathing slowly through the other. It is called *nadi shodhanam* which literally translated means "clearing the pathways *(nadis)* through which energy flows" (see figure 2c, page 44).

This alternately traces a path of energy movement along the left side of the body and then the right. The repetition of this pattern gradually establishes a smooth and consistent course which becomes increasingly well-defined. This retracing of the same path then "illumines" or "lights up" the *nadis* just as repeatedly tracing a letter in the palm of the hand makes it more vivid. In this way the *nadis* are more easily sensed and mapped out in the internal consciousness. One's usual breathing, by contrast, is jerky and variable from breath to breath so that no consistent flow is discernible and the picture is murky. This is analogous to the difference between discharges of static electricity and its flow through a wire. The erratic flashing of lightning in one part of the sky and then another involves movement of electrical energy, but its course is haphazard. By contrast, in a wire the electrons move in concert, flowing in a directional path, and an electrical current is detectable.

The Conservation of Energy

Breathing exercises have even been recommended as a means of helping the psychotic to deal with the chaotic energy situation with which he is struggling. Without a return to stabilization and balance, energy is constantly depleted and this can result in the "burned out" picture which is often seen in schizophrenics who have been hospitalized for many years.

Such breathing exercises may also be helpful in "reducing the static" of a system which has been disorganized through the use of powerful psychoactive drugs. Here again, through the injudicious use of psychedelics or amphetamines, not only is the smooth flow of energy disrupted, but considerable energy may be dissipated. Such a drug experience is like a "blast." There is a spectacular and explosive release of energy without the ability to modulate. This results not only in depletion but in a sort of deafening or blinding of the sensitivity to more subtle energies within. After such an experience, the delicate work of internal exploration becomes difficult. After an explosion, one cannot hear because of the ringing in his ears. Similarly, the state of dulled sensitivity which follows a drug experience may last for months. Breathing exercises will often promote the return to a balanced energy state, whereas the use of medications may only compound the chaos or produce an exaggerated slowing and lethargy.

In yoga this is often described in terms of the opposite characteristics of *"rajasic"* and *"tamasic."* When the energy state is agitated, restless and disturbed, the term *rajasic* is employed. When there is a dullness, a lethargy or inertia, this is called *tamasic.* A state of equilibrium and balance is referred to as *sattvic.* It is the establishing of a *sattvic* or balanced state in the energy sphere that provides conditions optimal for meditation and personal growth.

There are special breathing exercises designed to increase and restore the supplies of energy which are held in reserve. One of these *(agni sara)* uses diaphragmatic movements to stimulate the solar plexus area and increase the body's energy store. There are also other practices besides breathing exercises which aim towards the elimination of energy waste and dissipation.

Learning to distinguish between important *needs* and more whimsical "wants" enables one to eliminate the wasteful expenditure of time and energy that may go into the pursuit of encumbering and unnecessary luxuries. This can often reduce a hectic schedule to one more manageable and conserve much physical energy. Moreover, such an approach may serve as a model for the more psychological methods of energy conservation. Once more what is easily applied in the physical world can become a useful model for managing the less tangible problems of the mental world. Just as one can learn to avoid the automatic pursuit of products thrust at him through commercial advertising, he can similarly learn to avoid slipping into the pursuit of pointless and uncomfortable fantasies or obsessions. As a result, less mental energy is wasted.

There is special emphasis on the notion that energy is likely to be lost through speech, thus voluntary silence *(mauna)* for periods of time may be practiced. This provides an opportunity for learning to control the tendency toward trivial chatter and the dissipation of energy which it brings. Random and impulsive sexual activity is also avoided since this brings about the discharge of energy before it reaches a level where it can be usefully employed.

This way of viewing energy loss finds a parallel in the Western psychotherapeutic notion of "acting out." Certain persons seem to tolerate poorly a build-up of energy and the resulting "tension." Such people, finding this state of heightened energy unpleasant, will frantically search for the closest available outlet for discharge. Emotional outbursts and random sexual activity are frequent methods of releasing this energy and reducing tension to a level that can be tolerated. This may interfere with therapy to the extent that this device serves to reduce tension and make one comfortable; he may lose his motivation for finding a new psychological organization. Such an erratic discharge of energy also makes it difficult to pursue the discipline of yoga, since one does not have at his disposal adequate energy with which to work.

The Control of Prana and Higher States of Consciousness

The development and exploration of higher states of consciousness requires maintenance of higher levels of energy. The flow of energy cannot be clear and vivid if it is discharged before reaching a significant degree of intensity. Moreover, the work to be done on the mental level is demanding. Without sufficient energy one will feel too weak and distracted to carry it through. But there must be a gradual development of the capacity to handle comfortably this greater quantity of energy. (110 wiring cannot handle 220 volts!)

When the student learns to conserve and tolerate higher levels of energy, he is at last prepared to approach its control and channeling. As the patterns of energy flow become familiar and can be correlated with mental and physical events, he gradually gains the ability to alter them. But first these movements and patterns must somehow be catalogued. One must arrive at some set of symbols into which the energy can be organized. To this end, such terms as *nadi, chakra, ida* and *pingala* have evolved in the yogic tradition.

The study of such a vast field of experience necessitates a very complex system of symbols for its conceptualization. Since these symbols and terms refer to an area of experience that has not had a counterpart in Western culture or science, it is understandable that attempts to translate them would often lead to misunderstandings and distortions. Western science has had no symbols which represent experiences of internal energy. In order to interpret such symbols from other traditions in our own terms, we must resort first to mental and then to physical approximations, both of which are necessarily misleading. The use of physically oriented terms, for example, has led to confusing the energy pathways with anatomical structures. For instance, the *nadis* are often mistakenly equated with nerves. It's almost like learning a new language. There is a complete vocabulary and a set of grammar principles which govern its use. But learning the words is not helpful unless the phenomena they represent have been consciously experienced. The Eskimo's half dozen or more different terms for snow are incomprehensible to one who has always lived in the tropics. Not only must one learn the vocabulary and grammar, he must be absorbed in the environment where it has meaning.

As *prana* enters with the breath, it becomes divided into five subsidiary energies. Each of them has its own characteristic distribution and peculiar function and has been studied in detail.* When one goes a step further and develops control of these *pranas,* he gains the ability to energize directly any mental or physical aspect of himself that he chooses. Once the "language" is mastered, it becomes an effective tool.

In this context, disease is seen as a disturbance in the balance of *prana.* In a series of tests the subject studied by Dr. Karagulla was able to accurately diagnose physical disorders through her sensitivity to the energy patterns of patients. Since the energy imbalances preceded physical maladies, she could predict illnesses. "The energy web or body showed the condition clearly many months before it became apparent in the physical body."[30] When the energy becomes deficient, excessive, or poorly modulated in a body part, disease occurs.† Regulating the pranic flow is said to

---

* These are *prana vayu, apana vayu, vyana vayu, samana vayu* and *udana vayu.* Their functions are respectively: respiration, excretion, coordination and integration, digestion and providing body heat, and speech and communication. For a more detailed treatment of this subject, see Rama Prasad, *op cit.*

† Even by monitoring the more limited range of energy phenomena which register on electrical devices, gynecologists were able to identify changes in electrical potential in the pelvic area that correlated highly with cancer of the female reproductive tract. (L. Langman, M.D., "The Implications of the Electrometric Test in Cancer of the Female Genital Tract," in Burr, *op cit,* pp. 151-172.) Later, when 102 cases were identified where there was such a change, 95 of these were found in surgery to have cancer (Burr, *op cit,* p. 54).

return the system to balance and cure the disorder. The function of acupuncture stimulation, which seems to at least temporarily affect some of the grosser *pranas,* is said to be: "primarily to take energy out of one limb of the circuit and put it into another—to shift these energies around so that one obtained a balanced system."[31]

Mental Energy and the Study of Mind

We see, then, how *prana* serves as an intermediary between body and mind. The current of *prana* is the "currency" of the psychophysiological system: it is the medium of interchange between mental and physical worlds. Its role is analogous to that played by money in the conversion of ideas to physical work. One may not be able to think a house into existence but he can sell a poem or an idea and have the house built. Money is the "green energy" that serves as the link, just as the *pranic* sheath links the mental to the physical. Through money or through *prana,* the forces at one level can be converted into energy and fed into another. The degree of control possible, then, is a function of the amount of energy available, just as what can be done in the world is partly dependent on how much money one has at his disposal.

Energy is tied up on different levels through inefficient operation. We've seen, for example, how muscular tension traps significant quantities of energy. In working with the body through hatha yoga exercises this is released and made accessible. But energy is bound not only by muscle tension. It is consumed by mental tensions as well. When there is a preoccupation with fears and anxieties, vast quantities of energy may be wasted. Even when the fears and anxieties cannot be clearly identified, one may notice and complain of a drained, tired-out feeling. Habitual ways of handling such tensions may become so much a part of the fabric of one's life that they can no longer be perceived. In addition to the energy they unobtrusively consume, further energy is expended in keeping them outside the field of consciousness. This vast world of mental tensions that lies outside our awareness represents enormous quantities of energy that are potentially available. Much of the practice of yoga revolves around gaining access to, and control over, this energy.

Ultimately it becomes evident that the immediate control over the energy level of *prana* is exerted by the mind. Yet the mind itself is notoriously changing. It is given to conflict, confusion and contradiction. At this point the student of yoga realizes that he is confronted with the question of how the mental world can be regulated. This dilemma can only be solved through a careful and systematic study of the mental field, bringing into awareness and integrating its disparate parts. First the conscious mind must be studied and understood. Then gradually the areas that lie outside awareness can be approached and brought into sight. This is the next step in the science of yoga.

CHAPTER THREE
THE MIND

"But other than the sheath that consists of vital breath and interior to it is the sheath that consists of mind. The one is filled with the other. The first has the likeness of a man and because it has the likeness of a man, the second follows it and itself takes on the likeness of a man."

Taittiriya Upanishad, II. 3

chapter 3
THE MIND:
ANCIENT AND MODERN CONCEPTS

We are, according to the traditions of yoga, encased in a series of bodies. Until now we have discussed the physical body which is operative on the physical plane, measurable by physical means and studied by anatomy and physiology. We have also described the energy or pranic body which is approached in yoga through the study and control of the breath but whose study has, until recently, remained outside the orthodox scientific establishment. We now turn to the mental field or "mental body," which can be examined by focusing the attention inward toward the workings of the mind.

Just as calming the body makes possible the quietness necessary for the study of breath and energy, in the same way, regulating the breath brings the mind into focus. When the grosser levels are brought under control and tamed, then the subtle functions of the mind come to the fore of consciousness, standing out in clear relief and taking on a vividness that makes them more available for observation.

In modern psychology, the mental field has most often been studied indirectly by making inferences about mental functioning through observing outward behavior. Unfortunately, this methodology tends to lead away from the mind toward a preoccupation with the behavior being studied. By contrast, in yoga psychology, the mind is studied directly through a special kind of introspection. The various methodologies developed in the East for the study of the "mental body" are called "meditation." Through the process of meditation one develops a capacity for observing the functioning of the mind without being swayed or overwhelmed by thoughts.

The ordinary mind is not able to study itself accurately since it is too much a part of what is being studied. This is analogous to what happens in physics, where certain atomic phenomena cannot be evaluated with precision because the instruments themselves affect what is being observed. The study of mental processes is similar: an untrained mind which tries to look at itself will become involved in the thought processes it is trying to observe. This difficulty has interfered with the development of a viable introspective psychology in the West. In the East, however, through a gradual process of evolution, meditational methods have been developed which provide a means of objectively observing the mind without becoming caught up in the train of thoughts.

The mind is seen by the practitioner of yoga as not only an obstacle to that consciousness he seeks, but also as the bridge over which he may reach that consciousness. From this perspective he calls the mind a "bag of tricks." He regards it warily, yet studies it devotedly. Yoga psychology is a tool for this study provided by those who have already crossed the bridge and viewed the mind from a vantage point beyond.

Well-developed concepts of mental functioning have evolved using this approach. They are organized around the idea that within the mind itself there is a hierarchy of functional levels. Though there are many schools of Indian psychology which relate to different systems of yoga, this chapter will focus

primarily on two of the most ancient and influential, raja yoga
as outlined by Patanjali and the Vedantic tradition established by
Shankaracharya.

In modern psychology the mental levels responsible for control
in the adult are conceived of in terms of a unitary ego. In yoga
psychology there is a level beyond the Western ego, though
movement toward it may be problematic. Just as difficulties are
involved in developing control over impulses through growth to
the ego level, there are also difficulties encountered in making
the transition to levels beyond this. Whereas modern psychotherapy limits its attention mainly to the development of an
ego, yoga psychology deals with what lies beyond, outlining a
path to further evolution. We will trace this path from its
beginning.

THE MIND AND INSTINCTS

Nature is a complex of interdependent patterns: plants take
their nourishment from the earth and animals feed upon them.
They co-exist in a cycle of energy exchange involving a flow of
carbon dioxide and oxygen. Seasonal changes are based on the
movement of the earth around the sun, and the flow of the tides
and shifts in physiology are influenced by the cycles of the moon.
The whole of the natural world is made up of complementary
patterns of biological activity that move in harmony. Animals
exist in this complex matrix and instinctively move in such a way
as to flow with its overall pattern. They are at one with nature.

But they have little freedom of choice. Their behavior is
rigidly established by the demands of their environment. Their
responses to threats or sexual stimuli, for example, are laid out
in a programmed way. There is little flexibility or capacity to
anticipate and plan. Although animals move harmoniously with
nature and form an integral part of the fabric that is the beautiful

order of nature, they are subject also to the brutal side of the law of the jungle. As an animal kills and eats, so is it killed and eaten. There is no security. The animal who lives in the wild must be constantly alert to possible danger and ready to react with his limited capacities. Those actions which succeed in preserving him are passed on to future generations and become part of their basic nature. For example, certain signals set off defensive patterns that unfold automatically. If they serve him well, he survives. If not, he dies. The reaction to danger, then, becomes part and parcel of the hardware of the animal's "bio-computer."

The animal's ability to learn is limited and his awareness of alternatives is negligible. In a word, he has little consciousness and his survival depends not on knowledge and understanding but on those inherent patterns of action which serve to regulate behavior and integrate him into nature. These are "automatic survival mechanisms" over which the animal has no control.

This is especially true of lower animals. The nervous system of the frog, for example, is designed in such a way that when a dark spot approximately the size of a fly moves across its visual field, its tongue flies out. This will happen quite automatically since this way of responding is built into its "computer hardware." It's not the sort of thing that is learned or unlearned and there is no flexibility. In higher animals, the situation is somewhat different. Automatic or instinctual mechanisms only come into play when the pressure of needs reaches a certain level. A male bird, for instance, will respond to the silhouette of a female bird by beginning his mating dance when his sexual need has not been satisfied for some time. If he is isolated from the female of the species, however, the urge becomes stronger, and the stimulus needed to trigger the response is less specific. He will eventually respond to any semblance of another bird by beginning his mating dance. If he is isolated for a long enough time, researchers have even found that this behavior pattern could be set off by simply flapping their arms!

In the case of mammals, the instinctual urge becomes less important for organizing behavior and increasingly comes to serve as an emergency measure only. Behavior is largely governed by habits—learned patterns of response that are semi-automatic but can be changed. The bio-computer is larger, has more capacity and is capable of being programmed in a variety of ways. Its response can be changed. It can be reconditioned, in contrast to the set mechanical response that must appear in lower animals. Habits operate from a somewhat higher level of organization to govern behavior and replace instincts. Through these less automatic mechanisms, the animal gains increased flexibility of response.

In man there is not only the capacity for a variety of conditioning or habit programming, but there exist levels of functioning which can create or alter the program that is used. He can judge which habits most suit his purpose and create them in himself. Nevertheless, underneath all this sophisticated capacity and higher levels of consciousness, there persists the more basic of the automatic survival mechanisms such as those associated with fear or sex, which are present in animals throughout the evolutionary hierarchy.

The Instincts in Yoga

In order to reduce emotional and instinctual distractions, yogis have found it necessary to study the instinctual side of themselves in detail. As a result, four primary underlying instinctual or primitive urges are described. These are: the need for food, the need for sex, the need for sleep, and the need for self-protection. The way in which these needs are met in man are, of course, not as mechanical as in lower animals since the patterns of response are a result of a more sophisticated, flexible programming. More of man's behavior is consciously directed. However, the underlying drives persist. They push toward providing for those needs that are most essential for survival. Without them, left to his own devices, man might neglect to provide for what is essential and perish. Whenever his more recent programming and sophisticated intelligence lead him away from providing for these basic necessities, the instinctual mechanisms come to the fore, and push for more urgent action. However, with the ability to think in a larger time frame, man can provide for himself comfortably and smoothly and anticipate his needs. He can arrange to procure what is necessary without waiting for a push from the emergency instinctual urgings. He thus frees himself from the tyranny of automatic reactions: he achieves control over his behavior and gains greater freedom.

"Choice," "freedom," and "control" imply a new level of awareness, a further stage in the hierarchy of consciousness. This stratum of being we call "the mind." It has the capacity for self-awareness and the anticipation of the future.

THE MIND: THE INTERNAL INSTRUMENT

Just as the physical and energy "bodies" are seen as external "instruments" in yoga, the mind is traditionally called the "internal instrument." In jnana* yoga, the system which has the most elaborate conceptualization of psychological processes, the workings of the normal conscious mind involve three main functions. The "lower mind" is that part which is in most direct contact with the incoming data. It collects sense impressions and coordinates them with motor responses. It takes the form of perceptions which shift from moment to moment. Because of

---

* Jnana (pronounced gyana) comes from the same root as the Greek gnosis, "knowledge" (e.g., agnostic, "to have no knowledge of"). Jnana yoga is the yoga of knowledge, intellect and reason.

the many stimuli coming in, the lower mind is constantly in flux. It's like a television screen monitoring the events of the outside world. On it, sensory input is displayed. It can also register memory traces. This lower mind is called in yoga, *manas*.*

But intelligent use of the data flashing on the screen of *manas* depends on the action of two other functions. The first of these is *I-ness*. When sensory impressions come in via the lower, sensory-motor mind, this *I-ness (ahankara)* serves to transform them into a personal experience by relating them to individual identity. It provides a sense of separateness from the rest of the world, a feeling of distinctness and uniqueness. It is the agency which defines what of the sensory data and memories is "I." It is the property of subjectivity. It takes what has come in and relates it to a sense of *I-ness*. When the sensory-motor mind functions, "a rose is seen." But when *ahankara* adds its influence, "I see a rose."

Once an incoming impression has been flashed onto the screen of *manas* and related to *I-ness*, then some decision must be taken. Some judgment must be made and in some cases, a response selected. This discrimination or judgment is the third major mental function. It evaluates the situation and decides on a course of action. This power of decisiveness in yoga psychology is called *buddhi*. It is called the "crown jewel" of discrimination and understanding. *Buddhi* means, then, a special kind of intelligence or wisdom.† It is from this word that *Buddhism* takes its name since much of its practice centers around the sharpening of this faculty.

These three functions comprise the yogic conception of the mind and occupy the center of the stage in yoga psychology. Their interrelated functioning produces what we recognize as

* This comes from the same root as the English word "man." In some schools of psychology *manas* means "mind," the essence of man. In the Vedanta system, which we are here following, *manas* is used in a more restricted sense: it refers only to the "lower" mind.

† This is often translated into English as "intellect," but this can be misleading. That paralyzing and unproductive mental activity called "intellectualizing" is certainly not a creation of *buddhi*. It is carried on by the lower mental functions. It is the repetitive re-exhibiting of certain thoughts and fantasies on the screen of the lower mind without any decision resulting.

"normal waking consciousness." Together they make up the "mind" of which we are aware. But they are not to be regarded as three different independent substances or faculties, nor should they be conceptualized in an anthropomorphic way. They are not like three independent little personalities which can oppose one another. Conflict does not arise in the mind as a result of their contrary tendencies as it does in western psychoanalytic theory where the ego, superego and *id* "disagree." It is for this reason that the three functions in yoga psychology (*manas, ahankara* and *buddhi)* are collectively called the "internal instrument." They function as a whole.

There are a number of other structures which surround, support and relate to this central mental complex. One of these is the memory bank or *chitta,* which principally lies outside awareness. It is the storehouse of past impressions and experience. It is from here that memories bubble up to appear on the screen of the lower mind. Situated externally to these more internal mental components are the five senses, which feed in data to be registered by *manas.*

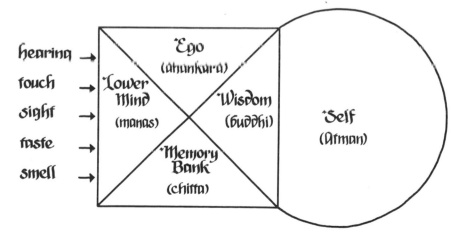

THE VEDANTIC CONCEPTION OF MIND

On the "other side" of the mental complex lies the "innermost" or "highest" field of human consciousness. This is variously called the Self, the *Purusha, Brahman, Atman,* or *Jiva* by different schools. This is the key to yoga psychology, for it is around the attainment of this level of consciousness that yogic discipline is organized. It is thought of as both the highest state of consciousness and the innermost center of the psyche. Reaching this results in a serene, encompassing awareness, and because of its contrast to the clamour and restlessness of the usual mental plane, it may be compared to the eye of a hurricane.

This concept of mind is an "operational" conceptualization, organized in such a way as to provide a scheme optimally suited to promoting growth. It is a way of understanding the mind that facilitates going beyond it and observing it.

Raja and Jnana Yoga: Two Major Schools of Yoga Psychology

What we have discussed so far is essentially the theory of mind as it is laid down in the tradition of Vedanta. This school of thought is based on the teachings contained in the *Prasthana-trayi* (i.e., the Upanishads, the *Brahma Sutras,* and the Bhagavad Gita), which is the culmination of the Vedic tradition and considered by many to be a distillation of the most profound aspects of ancient Indian philosophy. In its purest form, Vedanta psychology is a very intricate and refined theory of mental life. Perhaps more than any other school of Indian psychology it has conceptualized the functioning of the mind in a highly intellectual fashion which is relatively compatible with, and acceptable to, Western thinking.

Vedanta psychology and jnana yoga use the concepts of *manas, ahankara, buddhi* and *chitta* in order to arrive at a thorough-going understanding of mental functions.* But this

* For a detailed source book which differentiates between Vedanta and other Indian systems of psychology, see J. Sinha's *Indian Psychology.*[1]

intellectual path is admitted to have many pitfalls. One can easily become enmeshed in the intricacies of psychological analysis and become diverted from genuine self-exploration and evolution. For this reason the path of jnana yoga is often called "the razor's edge."

Jnana yoga is necessarily based to some extent on the experiences of others. It is organized around teachings and concepts framed by someone else. This stands in contrast to the yoga of Patanjali, raja yoga, which is based much more directly on personal experience. Patanjali's psychology is simple. He doesn't talk in terms of *manas, ahankara* and *buddhi*. Rather, he deals with the mind holistically and often uses the term *chitta* in an inclusive way to designate this constantly fluctuating, changing phenomenon. Patanjali's path is not restricted to those who can master the complex concepts of a refined psychology.

In Patanjali's system, the mind is likened to a lake. Like a body of water it is potentially calm and crystal clear, but the thoughts, "modifications of the mind," stir it into activity and obscure its true nature. These thoughts or modifications are called *vrittis* and are compared to waves appearing in the body of the lake. They may arise from the lake bed (memories), or from the effects of the outside world (sense perceptions). When the waves are quieted, the water is clear, and one can see through it to its innermost levels. If this process of calming and quieting is brought to perfection, the water becomes completely transparent and the inner man, the highest consciousness, comes into evidence.

Patanjali's system is set forth in his Yoga Sutras, a terse compilation of one-hundred ninety-six aphorisms.[2] The first four of these give the gist of the whole system. The rest of the work is an explanation of these and detailed instructions on how the student can realize and experience for himself, through his own practice, the knowledge contained therein.

The first aphorism (sutra) says, "Now," that the student has established himself as motivated and properly prepared, "the

system of yoga is being expounded."[3]   A certain degree of
preparation is a prerequisite. Patanjali classifies four types of
minds existing in prospective students: 1) the mind which can
easily be concentrated; 2) that which is concentrated with
difficulty; 3) that which has little ability to achieve concentration; 4) and that which is completely imbalanced and not yet
fit for yogic discipline. The theory and methods of yoga are
expounded only to those who are properly prepared. Besides,
preliminary steps must have been taken to awaken a strong sense
of purpose before the student is ready to undertake the training
itself.

The next three aphorisms explain that yoga (which is bringing
into force the highest consciousness) is basically a matter of
developing voluntary control and regulation of the thought
processes *(vrittis)*. When this is accomplished, then that consciousness which underlies the thoughts becomes apparent. It
ceases to be obscured and limited by the thoughts and mental
changes. Prior to this, consciousness identifies with the thoughts
and one automatically assumes that he *is* his thoughts.

The concept of identification is as central in Patanjali's Yoga
Sutras as it is in modern psychology. However, Patanjali's
concept of identification goes to much more subtle levels than
does that of modern psychology. Whereas the latter assumes
that the ego identifies with objects and people (with inputs
from the external world), Patanjali suggests that there is something beneath and behind even the most miniscule thought
which is identifying with it. Unaware of this, we naively
believe that we *are* the thoughts we are thinking. To propose
anything different would seem strange to those of us brought up
in the Western philosophical tradition where the notion, "I think,
therefore I am" forms the basis of the way we see ourselves.
Yet Patanjali assumes that we are in essence different from our
thoughts. Therefore, we can observe them. This provides the

foundation for a truly scientific psychology since it makes possible the objective, first-hand study of the mind.

Patanjali goes on to classify the "thought forms" or "modifications of the mind" *(vrittis)* in two ways: first, as to whether or not they serve as obstacles along the path to expanded awareness;* and second, in terms of five categories which reflect their function in mental life: 1) accurate perception or cognition; 2) inaccurate perception; 3) fantasy or imagination; 4) memory; and 5) sleep. Without realizing it we have a natural tendency to be constantly sorting our "thought forms" or *vrittis* into these five pigeon holes, viz.: without at least some tentative distinction between what is accurate and inaccurate perception, for example, we are hard put to carry out the simplest of our activities—mental or physical; among internal images and thoughts we must constantly differentiate between correct recollections and imagined ones; the routine separation of fantasy from reality is what sets us apart from the psychotic; our usual waking consciousness ebbs away as that *vritti* called "sleep" comes into prominence. Patanjali uses these five practical operational categories as a first step to bringing order to the complexity and chaos that greets the observer as he first steps back and looks at the mental field.

Through cultivation of the ability to disentangle oneself from his thoughts, consciousness gradually evolves. Patanjali outlines a systematic and detailed path for gaining such self-mastery. Briefly, this path has been called ashtanga (eight-limbed) yoga, or more recently, raja yoga† (the royal path).

---

* Whether they are *klishta* or *aklishta*, i.e., whether or not they serve as obstacles *(kleshas)*. See introduction to Chapter VI.

† Usually this eight-fold path in its entirety is referred to as raja yoga (the royal path), however, it is also common to refer to the first four steps inclusively as hatha yoga and the last four which focus more directly on the mental realm and beyond as raja yoga. For a contemporary description of this eight-fold path, see: Swami Rama's *Lectures on Yoga.*[4]

The first two steps in this eight-step path involve ten guides to living habits and life style that can minimize disturbances in the mind and body *(Yamas and Niyamas)*. Whereas Vedantic tradition concentrates on inner discipline, Patanjali is more practical and does not hesitate to include a detailed discipline of external behavior in his attempts to take advantage of all available means to promote the process of growth. His training program then goes on to work successively with each of the sheaths we have been describing. The preliminary regulation of everyday behavior has prepared the student by freeing him from tension, worries and anxieties so that he can focus his attention enough to gain some mastery of the body through hatha yoga. The next step in this progressive path toward total self-mastery focuses on work with the second, or energy sheath, involving primarily breathing practices which can lead to the control of *prana*. In the fifth of the eight phases, the student learns to regulate sensory input *(pratyahara)* so that impacts from the sensory organs are cut off and do not distract the mind from its observation of itself. Of course, one of these phases is not stopped before the next is begun. They are rather coordinated and integrated to work synergistically.

During the final three steps the student learns to make his mind one-pointed and concentrated.* The more gross aspects of our being have been brought under control; behavior, body, energy and senses have been mastered and the student is now ready to focus more directly on controlling the thoughts which come before his mind and distract it. This work is achieved in three steps: concentration *(dharana)*, contemplation *(dhyana)*, and finally *samadhi*, that highest state of consciousness. Each of these latter three stages is simply an expansion of the former. When concentration is developed and occurs for a longer

---

* Patanjali's description of right knowledge as being based on direct perception, inference or authoritative testimony as distinguished from wrong knowledge, forms the basis of a scientific attitude and approach to understanding which precedes the development of science in Western civilization by over 1,000 years.

period of time, it becomes contemplation, and when this is deepened, it leads to that state known as *samadhi*.

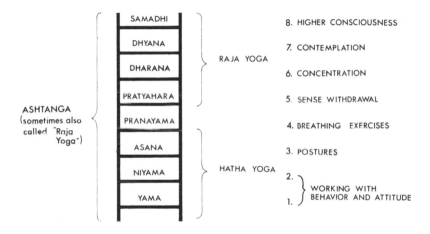

Patanjali's yoga and the psychology of Vedanta differ primarily in their emphasis. In their essence they are not contradictory. Vedanta focuses more on the theoretical and abstract, while Patanjali's is primarily an applied and experimental psychology. Our detailed formulation of mental functioning will, of course, draw most heavily from the teachings of the Vedanta school, but in general our approach is a synthesis of these two major and complementary points of view.

THE SENSORY-MOTOR MIND (MANAS)

Since the lower or sensory-motor mind has no ability to evaluate the information it takes in, it continues to collect more and more. In a sense, then, it acts as a collecting device, taking in as much sensory data as possible. It has no ability to make decisions or to evaluate. It accumulates information and responds to it by habit or through the intervention of the *instincts*. But neither habits nor instincts involve evaluation, so judgment and discrimination are beyond the capacity of *manas*. It is *buddhi*, the power of discrimination which arrives at decisions. *Manas* carries out its orders, coordinating a response with the sensory impression it has received. "*Buddhi* is like a sword. Its function is only to cut whatever comes before it."[5] Strictly speaking, it has no other quality and performs no other function. Such things as planning, desiring, memory, affection, gratitude, sexual impulses, shame, fear, love, attachment, hate, jealousy, anger and so forth are all phenomena which are properties of the lower mind. One is prompted to a particular act when a certain mental impulse springs onto the screen of *manas*. But it is *buddhi* which decides whether or not to give in to the impulse.

For instance, one may plan an evening out for himself. The fantasies and images of what will occur come on to the screen of *manas*. Past memories of previous evenings of diversion, of movies or plays, of various entertainment rise from *chitta* and mingle along with the fantasies about the future, creating a flow of thoughts in the lower mind. When one of them is selected and offered to *buddhi*, it says "yes" or "no," making a decision. This sets into motion a course of action which once again will be coordinated by *manas*. Once *buddhi* makes its clear-cut decision, accepting the proposal to attend a play, for example, then *manas* sets about coordinating phone calls to find out curtain time, the price of tickets, and plans for dinner and transportation. We may say, then, that planning is primarily a function of *manas*, though the core of the plan, the essential decision, is made by *buddhi*.

Manas itself has no ability to make a decision. For this reason it is said in yoga that the basic nature of *manas* is to doubt. Being unable to size up or evaluate things and getting no help in this respect from the instincts, it simply doubts the validity of everything.

The main job of the lower mind is to see that information is received and that action is coordinated smoothly. But without orders from above, it will respond by habit or botch up everything. It might be thought of as a rather dull and unimaginative drone who does his job without understanding why. When the boss is away and the lower mind is left to fend for itself, its responses will not be "decisions" in the true sense of the word. At best they will be covered over with rationalizations, but underneath they will be essentially reactions to whatever is happening, based on habit or impulse. In the absence of influence from more evolved parts of the mind, the sensory-motor mind is extremely susceptible to the push and pull of the instincts and emotions.

Perhaps this is seen most clearly in the case of a young child:

> Mary, a four-year-old, is playing outside with her friends when the "Good Humor Truck" comes by, ringing its bell. She impulsively leaves her tricycle and runs inside to ask her mother for change to buy some ice cream. She's told that she's going to be eating supper in a few minutes, and that this is not the time for snacks. But Mary is so swayed by her immediate impulses that she cannot tolerate such frustration. First she tries to convince her mother that if she's allowed to have the ice cream she'll still eat her supper. When this fails, she becomes sullen and demanding. She gets more and more angry, crying: "I don't like you!" and becoming so upset that she begins to sob. Unable to control her anger, Mary lies on the floor, kicking her legs about. She becomes so distraught that it takes some hours

to calm her down. Finally, she has not only missed her ice cream cone but her dinner as well—and even her favorite television program!

The sensory stimulation of seeing an ice cream truck and the instinct of hunger have interacted on the screen of Mary's lower mind to produce an automatic and unmodulated effort to get an ice cream cone. No thought of the future or the cost of becoming angry occurs to her.

But unregulated action of *manas* is not limited to children. In the midst of doing a yoga posture, for example, the mind may begin to wander to thoughts of dinner, to dessert, or to what to order for lunch. The thoughts straying from the job at hand represent a lapse of the higher mental functions. As a result, the lower mind comes under the influence of the basic urge for food. The body is deserted by the mind and the energy is split: the physical energy involved in movement, the mental energy in a fantasy of food. There is no higher level of functioning to integrate these two. The situation is chaotic: it can't be productive. The posture is poorly executed and could even result in an injury. The mental activity is pointless and distracting— draining and wasting energy. A higher integrating function is missing. There is nothing to coordinate the various systems into a meaningful whole. It's like a switchboard whose operator has gone on a coffee break. The signals are jammed and the connections are made without any meaningful coordination. The lower mind, *manas,* when functioning alone can only react mechanically to circumstances or impulses.

To the extent that *buddhi* is weak and unevolved, one is swept along by reaction to circumstances and impulses. When it is ignored, decisions are not really made. Responses are colored by emotional influences. Action is determined by impulses and the effects of past conditioning. However, as we shall see later, as the *pure buddhi* is progressively uncovered, it brings the capacity to step outside the vicious cycle of impulse-driven behavior.

As it becomes more refined it becomes able to make decisions
that are more independent and creative.

THE MEMORY BANK (CHITTA)

When the lower mind is not receiving a constant stream of sensory input, it is open to input from within. Underlying *manas* is a
pool of memories containing the traces of past experiences. This
storehouse of impressions *(chitta)* is the foundation or mental
stream in which the rest of the mind operates. It is, in a sense,
the river bed over which the other parts of the mind flow. The
sensory mind or stream of consciousness is simply a series of
ripples on its surface. It is from this memory bank that thought
waves arise which surface in the sensory-motor mind.

Chitta is then the basic stuff out of which mental functioning
arises.* It is the "unconscious" of modern psychology, lying
outside awareness. In part it acts as a passive reservoir, receiving
and storing impressions from all the impacts the world offers.
Even before the more advanced, conscious aspects of the mind
come into being, *chitta* is accumulating, like an immense lake
bed, a huge pool of sensory impressions and data. All of the
mind, *buddhi,* the capacity for decisions, *ahankara,* the sense of
I-ness or identity and even *manas,* the sensory-motor mind, arise
out of this basic consciousness called *chitta.*

But *chitta* has two functions. Besides its passive and receptive
role, it has a more active one. When it is struck by influences
from the outside, it throws up certain instinctual reactions or
primitive urges. Out of those the emotions arise. This concept
of *chitta* is in some respects similar to the psychoanalytic

---

* In Patanjali's system, as set forth in the Yoga Sutras, the term *chitta* is used in
a more inclusive sense. It comprises the sum total of mental functioning. This is in
keeping with Patanjali's emphasis on simplicity and the avoidance of complex
psychological theory.

notion of the *id,* which is the underlying pool of instinctual energy or *libido* which sends up waves that energize mental functioning.

It is when the senses are quiet and the sensory-motor mind is receiving no information from the outside world that memories and impressions from the past begin to bubble up. When the grosser noise of the outside world is quieted, then what appears in *manas* are memories and fantasies—an associational stream of past impressions and experiences. In this sense, *manas* serves as a stage or a screen. It is like a platform on which the thoughts parade. Or, it is like a television monitor: whatever is fed into it flashes onto the screen. If the senses are occupied in providing input, then sense impressions appear. When nothing current or "live" is being broadcast, then "replays" and old movies are seen. *Chitta* is plugged in and memory traces and impressions from the past begin to flash onto the screen. Daydreams and experiences from long ago come to occupy the mind.

The suspension of sensory input has been explored recently in numerous experiments by laboratory psychologists. Subjects have been isolated in a chamber where they are allowed no sound, no visual input, and even wear special gloves to minimize the sense of touch. After remaining in this situation for some time, they often become aware of very vivid imagery, voices, and sounds. The experience as it is described sounds similar to what follows the ingestion of psychedelic drugs like LSD. These experiments in "sensory deprivation" cut off the sensory input to the lower mind. In the quiet that ensues, traces and impressions from the memory bank begin to appear. When sensory experience is suspended, the mind is cleared so that material arising from the unconscious can be more clearly observed.

Filtering Sensory Input

However, reduction of sensory input can be accomplished without going into a laboratory. The higher aspect of the mind has the ability to voluntarily and selectively limit what sensory data is admitted to the lower mind. In yoga practice one will usually begin working with the sensory stimuli which bombard the mental field by simply finding a quiet place. This in itself will limit sensory input. Gradually, however, one learns to "tune out" the senses. In the yoga system of Patanjali, this "voluntary sensory deprivation" is called *pratyahara*. Voluntary control of the senses gives one greater access to the unknown parts of the mind.

When sensory input is suspended, or at least significantly reduced, memory traces and images are allowed to arise from *chitta*. The mental field is cleared enough so that material from the unconscious may be more easily observed. In other words, the unknown or unconscious mind is allowed to come forward bringing fantasies and past experiences that appear vividly and in full color. This is what happens during the hallucinatory experiences of sensory deprivation. But it also occurs during the meditative process. In the latter case, however, involvement with the images and fantasies is not cultivated. One acknowledges the fantasies or hallucinations but learns to step around them. The unseen influence of this part of the mind is eliminated when it is brought into awareness. Then it can be successfully navigated and higher levels of consciousness can be approached.

The value of sensory withdrawal in bringing unconscious material into consciousness has been well recognized by psychoanalysts, whose patients ordinarily lie on a couch in a quiet office and stare at the blank ceiling:

> The analogy between the experimental conditions of sensory deprivation and the structure of the psychoanalytic treatment situation was observed by many....

the reduction of sensory input appears to facilitate access to unconscious material....

The emergence of primary process material or regression in the experimental situation can be utilized constructively by the subject....for either problem-solving or the achievement of creative syntheses of experience. [6]

Researchers in this area go on to point out that writers, artists and scientists have often sought out isolation and restricted environments in order to work more effectively.

When the external world is not intruding, it is difficult to avoid coming to terms in some way with the inner world. A spiritual teacher tells of meeting a political activist who was sent to prison. He was amazed at his personality change. There was an air of calmness and serenity that hadn't been evident before. When he enquired about how this might have come to be, he was told that it resulted from long hours spent in solitary confinement.

THE SENSE OF "I" (AHANKARA)

We have seen that *manas* has a very limited ability to organize behavior. It does not provide for the delay of gratification, planning or the preservation of the integrity of the organism except through rote habit or when emergency action of the instincts comes into play. *Manas* does not carry a sense of self-awareness. It is tied into nature and the flow of phenomenal events. It automatically takes in sensory data and responds automatically on the basis of habit or instincts.

But a sense of "I" lends the ability to separate the self from the flow of events and to think of oneself as an individual entity. This *I-ness* is called, in yoga psychology, *ahankara.* In Sanskrit *aham* means "I am." *Ahankara* does not instinctively flow with nature. It makes possible the question: "What's in it for me?" and lends the ability to say, "These are mine." By creating such barriers as "mine" and "thine," it separates self from others. Thoughts are no longer merely images flashed on a screen. They are "my thoughts."

In the infant, the sense of "I"—"not I" is of such a nature that it is incomplete and easily overwhelmed. When something flashes on the screen of *manas,* the infant identifies with it. He is it, although we often imagine that he sees the world as revolving about him. Actually, he has taken on *its* characteristics. He has no stable, continuous characteristics to lend it. In this sense, he has no center at all. His "mental body" changes from moment to moment with the changing face that is offered by the world. In a less extreme form, this state of mind can also be seen in the older child when he is sick and irritable. At one moment he wants one thing, at the next moment another. Before he can be brought the toy or the snack he's said he wanted, he's changed his mind again. He petulantly pushes it away and asks for something else. *I-ness (ahankara)* is shifting from moment to moment.

At these moments, integration is temporarily lost. This is also seen in children when they are overwhelmed by emotions that change dramatically from one moment to the next. They become so absorbed or identified with the activity of the moment that they may do harm to themselves—walk into a busy street, for example. Since children have little consistent center of integration within, nature provides a temporary "center" outside in the form of parents. For some time parents provide a concern for the *I-ness* of the child. Moreover, they also make necessary decisions for the child, whose discriminative capacity is still undeveloped. They help to regulate his behavior, gradually relinquishing this responsibility as the child develops his own sense of integrity and judgment.

Until there is some stable center of integration, the mind of the child shifts from moment to moment. For this reason he is very "adaptive" — he can accommodate to many situations since he carries little identity against which to judge them comfortable or uncomfortable. He can change his *I-ness* with ease, but he has little ability to integrate or to sustain any consistent mental consciousness. As his awareness becomes better defined and more stable, this sort of "adaptation" decreases.

Western psychology tends to see development as culminating in the formation of a consistent, unvarying *I-ness*. It is thought that this is reached in post-adolescence when one achieves a stable identity. Keeping certain aspects of oneself outside of awareness (repression) is assumed to be the price that one pays for this developmental achievement.

However, yoga psychology emphasizes the lack of unity that exists in the sense of "I" even at this "adult" stage of development. Even a "mature ego" is seen as only relatively integrated. It still varies to some extent from moment to moment. It still struggles to keep out of consciousness those memories and impulses that could contradict its self-image. In yoga psychology, the potential for evolution is thought to extend far beyond the ego. The capacity of the human being for growth and integration has been found to be much greater.

Ahankara, or "I-ness" and the Western Concept of Ego

Ahankara, which we have called *I-ness*, is often translated *ego*. This is confusing since the term *ego* is used in so many different ways in modern psychology, none of which are equivalent to the yogic *ahankara*. In the Western layman's mind, the word *ego* is associated with such terms as "egotistical," and "ego-trip"—with behavior that demonstrates an exaggerated sense of self-importance. But among psychologists and psychiatrists, ego has a rather different meaning.

For example, Freud and later psychoanalysts saw the ego as arising out of the undifferentiated matrix of impulses, instincts, perceptions and motor apparatuses of the infant's mind. The nature of this mass of functions, they said, was to act impulsively and more or less reflexively in an attempt to gain immediate pleasure. However, that part which was in contact with the outside world developed an appreciation of the demands made by the environment and came to act as a sort of mediator. It came to provide a compromise between the internal wishes and impulses and the demands and requirements of the external world. This "executive" of the mind is called the *ego.* Initially, then, the ego was thought of as that agency in the mind which defended the individual against being overwhelmed by internal wishes and impulses or by demands from the external world. It was thought of as an aspect of the mind that protected the integrity of the "I" through the use of various defense mechanisms.

As more was learned about mental functioning, however, psychoanalysts realized there was more to the integration of behavior and the coordination of mental functions than defensive maneuvers. Many positive integrating abilities of the mind came to light and the concept of ego was expanded to include such "conflict free" functions as perception and language. Gradually the functions attributed to the ego were increased and extended to such a degree that the concept itself became greatly altered, losing its original precision. It remained, however, defined largely in terms of social adaptation. Ego meant a certain range of *I-ness:* that which is functional and productive within the context of the demands made by one's culture.

Ahankara is a broader concept than ego. It encompasses a whole spectrum of *I-ness,* from that which underlies the lowest animal's efforts to maintain its integrity through the range of normal ego development and, as we shall see, even beyond that. However, *ahankara* is also more restricted in the functions it encompasses. It is not an active decision-making, thought-

producing agent like the Western psychology's ego. It is simply
the boundaries of *I-ness.* It is the line that separates "I" from
"not-I." It is the property of individuation. In yoga psychology,
it is *manas* which produces thoughts. It is *buddhi* which makes
decisions. All these, however, are included in the Western
term *ego.*

Even though *ego* implies a certain range of *I-ness,* some
writers on psychology in the West have talked about the early
stages of ego-development where *I-ness* is poorly defined (e.g.,
Sullivan, Klein, Laing). Erikson and, to a great extent, the
humanist psychologists such as Maslow even talk about more
advanced stages of ego-development where one can "lose himself"
momentarily in experiences that transcend the sense of individual
identity. But, in all cases, the term *ego* carries with it a certain
minimal, culturally defined sense of "I." *Ego* implies certain rules
of operation. It thinks logically and sequentially. *Ego* means
"I" in the everyday, ordinary sense: it is the adaptive, competent,
common-sense self that operates in the world of competition and
achievement.

When an attempt is made to extend a way of thinking about
the mind based on this range of *I-ness* to dealing with states which
are less developed or more evolved, difficulties arise. The terms
seem to break down. It is in discussing the earliest stages of the
infant's development or the more severe psychoses that psychologists become most obscure. The extension of the concepts based
on a study of the ego range of *I-ness* to deal with these areas is
problematical. Similarly, the extension of ego-oriented concepts
to deal with states of meditation or transpersonal experience has
been necessarily unsuccessful, so that religious thought and psychology have found communication awkward and have been
unable to find a common meeting-ground.

Modern psychology is organized around the concept of a certain
level of *I-ness* (ego) as a basic given. Psychology is the study of
the mind and this is ordinarily taken to mean the mind of the
separate, individuated person. When this mind enters states where

its individuality is abandoned, or separateness outgrown, it ceases to be "mind" in the usual sense of the word, and the concepts of Western psychology are found to be inadequate.

The mind of the infant is difficult for us to appreciate. In speaking of the work done by psychologists on the earliest levels of development, Robert White says: "Much of the work on these concepts has been cast in language that presupposes the distinction [between self and other] even very early in life, perhaps because it is so difficult for adults to imagine how things would be if experience were undifferentiated in this fundamental respect."[7] We find ourselves unable to grasp the nature of the experience in which the undifferentiated infant is immersed. Existence in a state where there is no coherent self-concept is mind-boggling. If *I-ness* were so drastically diminished, then it follows that the "not-I," the world, would also be totally different. To imagine oneself not being oneself in a world which is not the familiar world is more than we can manage!

Those psychologists who have ventured into this area often find themselves misunderstood. Their writings are understandably difficult. The concepts of Melanie Klein, Harry Stack Sullivan and other theorists who have attempted to conceptualize the experiences of egolessness have usually been either misinterpreted or simply dismissed as incomprehensible. In a similar way, those experiences which involve transcendence of the ego voluntarily to attain states of consciousness where *I-ness* is more encompassing than the limited, personal identity, have also been the subject of misunderstanding. They have ordinarily been rejected as improper subject matter for psychology. Branded "mystical," they are most often thought of as representing some variety of psycho-pathology where contact with reality is lost. At best they are relegated to the fields of theology or parapsychology, fields usually excluded from Western science. Thus *ego,* in Western psychology encompasses a certain range of *I-ness.* This range defines the limitations of the concepts of twentieth century psychology. Beyond these limits they become ineffective or at best awkward and unwieldy. Venturing further, the psychologist has found himself lacking effective conceptual tools with which to work.

The restricted range of *I-ness* implicit in the term *ego* is, then, the hidden limitation in this concept. But when the *I-ness* involved in mental functioning is conceptualized separately, it no longer need cripple psychological theory. When *I-ness* is realized as a distinct property of the mind and no longer tied to a particular level of organization (ego), then a wide range of variation in it can be studied. This permits the psychologist to extend his field of inquiry downwards into the pre-ego levels experienced by the infant or the psychotic and upwards into the states of consciousness experienced by those involved in such disciplines as meditation. *I-ness* can then be dealt with outside that range designated by *ego*.

Concepts as they appear in yoga psychology are only one specific example of their application. Their meaning is broader and deeper. Psychology and philosophy in Indian thought are so mingled that they cannot be easily separated. The study of the human being is considered to be compatible with the study of the universe—both its phenomenal nature and its existential meaning. The microcosm is thought to be merely a reflection of the macrocosm.

Ahankara, therefore, is a characteristic of all stable structures. It is the quality of definition and consistency. Even a rock has a sense of *I-ness,* from this point of view. It has stability and an identity that endures over time. Although this *I-ness* seems drastically different from that which exists in the human being on the mental plane, actually each of these is a part of the continuum of *I-ness* which spans all of the sheaths or bodies which we've discussed.*

* A similar point should be made about the notion of *sattva* (equilibrium, clarity), *rajas* (unrest, activity) and *tamas* (inertia, dullness). While these are three basic qualities or tendencies into which mental content can be analyzed, they are also the gunas or "elements" of which all the phenomenal world can be seen as composed. Individual differences, whether they be on the material, energy, mental or other level, are seen as reflecting a different proportion of these three basic ingredients or qualities.

BUDDHI

There is also a spectrum of stages of *buddhi* that parallels the evolution of *I-ness*. *Buddhi* or reason evolves in a series of steps as personal growth takes place. This occurs in tiny increments. There are innumerable such stages. However, for the sake of convenience we might look at three basic ranges of *buddhi's* development as they are conceptualized by Aurobindo.[8] First there is a crude, perceptive discrimination which simply reacts to the impressions coming onto the screen of *manas*. It is a primitive kind of judgment, deciding that something is good and pleasurable or that something is bad and distasteful. It is still very much subject to the influence of strong memories, emotions or instincts and its response is most likely governed by these unthinking powers. Here reason is subservient to circumstances in the environment, to urges, or to impulses.

Beyond this elementary understanding which influences most of our lives, there is a more sophisticated range of *buddhi's* development. This more mature *buddhi* is associated with the power of reasoning and using intelligence to arrive at a plausible, stable concept of reality and a coherent philosophy of life. It is basically pragmatic, involving an intellectual framework which permits purposeful and rational organization of activities. Providing a rational, commonsensical sort of will, based on what is expedient and serviceable for functioning in the external world and what is compatible with acceptable standards of conduct and behavior, it is this level of *buddhi* which can select or assemble a set of ethical standards for morality. It can decide on a set of aesthetic values—an idea of what is beautiful and what is ugly—and can construct a coherent network of opinions, as well as a reasonable notion of what one's purpose should be. It is relatively highly developed and predominates in people who are genuinely cultured and educated.

But beyond this there is a further development, the highest

*buddhi** which concerns itself disinterestedly with the pursuit
of pure truth. Its decisions are uncompromising and cut through
all illusion, even that which is considered socially acceptable and
ethically admirable. It increasingly reflects the immutable and
transcendent laws of nature and the universe, which are those
simplest and most unifying principles that bring meaning to life
and coherence to understanding. It is said, "Few, if any of us,
can use this highest reason with any purity, but the attempt to
do it is the topmost capacity of the inner instrument."[9]

Aurobindo speaks of *buddhi* as though it goes through a
process of differentiation, becoming more evolved with each
step. But in the more traditional yogic view, *buddhi* does not
evolve, it is simply *uncovered.* It exists already under the
encumbrances of cruder and less mature functioning. The
"crown jewel of discrimination" lies within, awaiting only
patient, careful cutting and polishing to reveal it in all its
brilliance. We have described three principle stages in the
evolution of *buddhi.* But it is clear that these are arbitrary
points in the course of its development which have been selected
for the purpose of description. Between them lie innumerable
intermediate stages. The pure *buddhi* appears in a gradual
manner like the statue which is "uncovered" by the sculptor as
he chips away pieces of marble.

But the question which arises at this point is: what is responsible for the movement from one level to the next? How is it that
buddhi's criteria for judgment are altered?

At any moment *buddhi* may take one of two possible courses.
First, it may give in to the pressure of impulses and yield to the
influence of habits or emotions. When such emotional or
impulsive urges are strong, we say that they overwhelm the more
reasonable faculties of the mind and gain an upper hand. Concern
for overall welfare is abandoned. In this case we might say that

---

* In Buddhist literature, as well as in other Eastern Scriptures, the word *prajna* has
often been used to denote the highest *buddhi,* the state of *buddhi* that accompanies
complete enlightenment.

the memories or sensory impressions that appear on the screen of *manas* in themselves dictate the course of action. They serve as a sort of motivation. In fact, habit and instinct predominate. *Buddhi* does not so much make a decision as it forfeits its right to do so. It has not been sufficiently evolved to assert itself, so accedes to less rational motivation.

But another option is open. *Buddhi* may assert its authority over the realm of impulse, instinct and habit and choose some different course of action. Acknowledging the existence of these lower motivations it may make a decision which is relatively independent of impulses or past programming. *Buddhi* has some capacity to remain detached from the influence of memory traces and sense impressions. It has, at least potentially, the ability to choose. Since it is by definition the decision-making function, it can decide to permit influence by some memories and not others. By maintaining a detached, observing attitude toward the other memory traces, it can allow them simply to pass away and dissipate. *Buddhi* can decide to step outside the chain of cause and effect. It can decide not to remain caught up in that cycle of action and reaction determined by previous programming. By using its full potential it acquires the property of "will." This sort of performance by *buddhi* is characterized as "pure reason" or "pure *buddhi*"* in yoga psychology.

If *buddhi* fails to exert its potential power, and accedes to the influence of impulse and emotions, then evolution, at least for the moment, comes to a halt. The motivations which operate then are those which characterize lower levels of development as observed in the infant or in animals. Past impressions, for example, are allowed to determine one's response to a given situation. This in turn creates new memories or impressions essentially identical to the old, only even more heavily weighted and more deeply imbedded in the unconscious *chitta* or memory

* This has been compared[10] to the distinction between pure and practical reason made by Kant.

bank.   This impression will then return again later having an increased valence and more powerful influence.   In this way, preferences become desires and desires become addictions.   By acceding to impulses, *buddhi* allows them to become strengthened. And a certain way of seeing and responding to the world becomes ingrained.   This consolidates one's position at a certain level of development, making it more difficult to develop past it.

On the other hand, each time *buddhi* chooses to step free of prior programming, it becomes stronger.   It is *buddhi* alone, of all the functions in the mental field which has this capacity to select a course of action which can lead to further growth.   It is apparently for this reason that the function of discrimination and judgment has been conceptualized as independent in yoga psychology.   It is singled out for special attention because it is of singular importance in the conceptualization of a psychology which is growth oriented.*

Buddhi and Conscience

Buddhi's capacity to decide not to fall in with the cause and effect of previous programming is a major focus in yoga psychology.   Attention is directed here because a sharpened *buddhi* provides the most direct tool for promoting growth.   It is the most efficient, productive way of disentangling oneself from psychological problems.

On the screen of *manas* appear numerous images.   Some reflect past experiences which were pleasant, and carry the impulse to repeat these.   Others represent unpleasant experiences,

---

* For example, *buddhi* plays a key role in shaping identity.   By choosing to act on one memory or stimulus rather than another, *buddhi* can bring into focus a certain definition of *I-ness,* since involving oneself with a memory or a stimulus will strengthen the definition of *I-ness* in whose terms it is cast.   Standing on this base, *buddhi* can then make a new decision which brings yet another I-ness into focus.   Gradually, through the innumerable subtle decisions that go into a few minutes' thought, one's sense of himself can be shifted in a directed way.

the memory of which leads to avoidance of similar situations. Among the memories bubbling up from the bed of *chitta,* are the evidences of past conditioning and programming, for example, parental prohibitions. Within this melange of images and impressions is the substance of conflict. The impulses that result from different images are necessarily contradictory. They push and pull one in opposing directions. Such contradictions are reconciled with difficulty, if at all. More often than not they are simply pushed out of awareness (repressed).

In yoga psychology, attention is directed mainly toward *buddhi's* ability to extricate one from this mass of conflict and contradiction rather than to the intricacies of the conflict itself as it occurs in *manas.* Interest is in the decision-making capacity as it functions in its "pure" fashion. *Manas* is studied only in order to differentiate it from *buddhi. Buddhi* must be trained and polished if it is to develop the ability to separate itself from the effects of these influences. The bubbling up of a past parental prohibition in yoga psychology is of interest only in so much as it must be distinguished from the voice of *buddhi.* This misleading or distorted "conscience" must be distinguished from a pure one *(buddhi).*

However, in Western psychology the emphasis is different. Attention is focused more directly on the workings of *manas.* There is a great deal of interest in how the various impulses interact. Mental conflict is a major subject of study. Much of the theory of psychotherapy and psychoanalysis has evolved around the study of "intrapsychic conflict." The concept of a "healthy ego" has grown out of an attempt to find some comfortable and satisfying way of reconciling the contradictory and conflicting impulses that dominate the activity of *manas.*

For this reason certain categories of past memories and impressions have been separately conceptualized in psychoanalytic theory as the "superego." This is made up by parental prohibitions which, though deeply ingrained in the memory, may be in opposition to what seems realistic or what is comfortably gratifying. This superego is often equated with "conscience." This is unfortunate, since the guidance of the early superego is often unreliable, being based on unreasonable notions of right and wrong that were learned from the parents. Though these may have been appropriate for a child, frequently they are no longer useful for the adult. Calling this early superego "conscience" has often led to a tendency to mistrust that inner voice which is called *buddhi* in yoga and an unwillingness to follow its lead and let it evolve. Instead, attention is confined to a more rational and logical assessment of events. The sense of exploration, of opening oneself to new possibilities, is lost.

When the punitive superego is equated with "conscience," then conscience is seen as working in opposition to the more rational, reasonable interests of the ego. This orientation seems to have contributed to a general distrust of all spontaneous and intuitive promptings. The ego and logical reasoning is seen as a bastion of rationality that stands against the more irrational promptings that come from a "punitive conscience." From this perspective any notion of following the voice of a higher, inner reasoning becomes suspect and is likely to be regarded as moralistic or superstitious. "Conscience" is equated with a puritanical kind of morality which interferes with freedom and prevents, instead of promoting, growth. When one is involved in the struggle to break free from irrational restrictions, such a "conscience" can only be seen as an ogre which should be purged from the personality. One of the goals of psychoanalytic psychotherapy is to "trim down" the punitive conscience or superego. An attempt is made to bring it more in line with the interest of the ego and eliminate its harsher, more irrational opposition. To a certain extent, then, ego and superego become integrated.

However, such integration is never considered complete. The superego remains the stronghold of certain social prohibitions which can never be entirely reconciled with the goals and interests of the ego. It is seen as an internalization of socializations which are introduced into the environment of the child in order to provide for a painful but necessary social order. In his *Future of an Illusion,* Freud indicates that there is an inevitable and uncomfortable struggle between the interests of the individual and the interests of society. "Every individual is virtually an enemy of culture."[11] One must resign himself to the conflict that this brings. There is the implication that one cannot grow and expand his identity to the point that his interests and those of society are the same. It is assumed that they must remain in opposition to one another to some extent, although one of the aims of therapy is to minimize this.

Within the context of yoga psychology, however, it is understood that higher levels of consciousness eventually lead to a point of view where one's own interests are not in conflict with the interests of others. In fact, as consciousness approaches a unity, as we shall see, the concerns and needs of all people become identical. What is good for the individual is part of an overall evolutionary process which includes those around him.

Buddhi and Beyond

As we enter the realm of higher consciousness, we come to a place from which the mind can be observed. We depart from that territory where yoga and Western psychology overlap. The yogic *buddhi* is a structure that grows in strength with the unfoldment of the personality. It is the discriminative power that permits one to see through the tendencies of the lower mind that lead to anxiety and mental anguish. But *buddhi* is both part of the mind and "above mental events."

As *buddhi* becomes more evolved, it increasingly separates itself from the activities of *manas.* As it develops its capacity for making decisions that disregard the impulses and impressions flowing through *manas,* it becomes increasingly independent of them. As a result, a level of *I-ness* evolves from which one can witness mental events without being involved in them. Eventually there emerges a kind of vantage point which exists above and beyond the hectic activity of the train of thoughts. This provides a point of observation, then, from which the mental plane can be seen.

The realm of this pure *buddhi* is conceptualized in yoga as constituting the fourth level of consciousness, that which lies beyond the body, the energy and the mind. This is the level beyond that verbal, mental activity which we call "thinking." Awareness ceases to be limited by word-thoughts. This "supra-mental" level of "pure reason" or "intuition" or "wisdom" is where *buddhi* functions unimpaired by the distractions of sense impressions or the preoccupations of a narrow, personal egoism. Where *buddhi* is more evolved, the "mind" is transcended.

At higher levels, as we shall see, eventually even *buddhi* will give way to more purely reflective states. These levels beyond *buddhi* are difficult to deal with, since modern science has no terms in which to describe the phenomena experienced there.

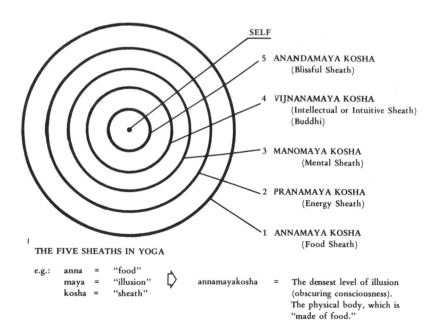

SELF

5 ANANDAMAYA KOSHA
(Blissful Sheath)

4 VIJNANAMAYA KOSHA
(Intellectual or Intuitive Sheath)
(Buddhi)

3 MANOMAYA KOSHA
(Mental Sheath)

2 PRANAMAYA KOSHA
(Energy Sheath)

1 ANNAMAYA KOSHA
(Food Sheath)

THE FIVE SHEATHS IN YOGA

e.g.: anna = "food"
       maya = "illusion"   annamayakosha =   The densest level of illusion
       kosha = "sheath"   (obscuring consciousness).
                                                       The physical body, which is
                                                       "made of food."

THE HIGHER SHEATHS OR "BODIES"

To complete our understanding of mental functioning as it is described in yoga psychology, we must briefly acknowledge what lies beyond the mind and higher *buddhi*. When integration is complete, consciousness is expanded to the point that judgments are no longer necessary. Awareness is global but all is regarded dispassionately with no need to classify the phenomena of the world into "good" or "bad" categories. Neither fear, aversion nor addiction to gratifications persists. This is said to result in a feeling of great release, a peaceful joy that is usually described simply as "bliss." This global "witness" consciousness is called the "blissful sheath." Beyond this even such a global awareness of the phenomenal world ceases. Consciousness exists in a purity that is indescribable. It is "consciousness without an object."* This is called in yoga, the Self,† or *Purusha*.

For the present, we wish merely to note that these highest levels of consciousness play an important part in yoga psychology, making the objective study of *buddhi* possible. From such a perspective, the mind is the object rather than the subject of consciousness.

Consciousness resides in the Self rather than in the mind. The Self *uses* the mind as an instrument of knowing, just as one might use a microscope.+ The key to difficulties in living, according to yoga psychology, is that we identify ourselves with the

---

* A contemporary treatment of this subject is given by Franklin Merrell-Wolff.[12]

† This is not at all what is understood by the ego-related term "self" in the West. This yogic Self (spelled with a capital "S") is a level of consciousness far beyond the mental plane of ego-consciousness.

+ That there is a tendency in Western psychology to return to such a point of view is evident in such current therapeutic techniques as outlined by Assagioli in *Psychosynthesis*,[13] where the practices suggested seem to be taken verbatim from the ancient formulae of the Vedantic school, viz.: "I have a body, but I am not my body;" "I have an emotional life, but I am not my emotions or feelings;" "The 'I' is not the mind." "I am I, a centre of pure consciousness."

instruments rather than the consciousness which is using them. Yoga psychology sees development as a process by which one identifies with each successive instrument until he develops the discrimination and distance to observe it.

CHAPTER FOUR
BUDDHI

"Quite other than this sheath that consists of the mind and interior to it is the intellectual sheath that consists of understanding. This is encased in the mental sheath and has the same form. The one is filled with the other. The first has the likeness of a man, and because it has the likeness of a man, the second follows it and itself takes on the likeness of a man. All the gods revere this understanding. It does not identify itself with the other sheaths and does not yield to the passions of the body."

Taittiriya Upanishad, II. 4

chapter 4
BUDDHI:
GUIDE THROUGH THE UNKNOWN

When we depart from the realm of the mind, we leave the familiar world of words, of verbal thoughts and common-sense logic. Above this lies a consciousness which is more personal because it cannot be easily talked about and described, and because it must be learned about through direct experience. However, in another sense it is less personal because it is not so limited to the restricted, ego-oriented consciousness of the lower mental level. It begins to escape the personal limitations of domination by the sensory-motor mind and its preoccupation with sensory data from the material world. Because this is a departure from concerns for self-preservation and maintenance, it opens the way to a consciousness that has been called "transpersonal." In the mental field it is *buddhi*, the power of discrimination and understanding, that holds the key to the development of this supramental consciousness. Its decisions can lead gradually but effectively out of the entanglement with *manas* to a new plateau where there is serenity and freedom from anxiety and fear.

We shall see now how it is that *buddhi* can guide one from ordinary waking consciousness through the inner world of the unknown mind to the goal of a more evolved, mature awareness.

WHAT IS CONSCIOUSNESS?

In a recent review of research on the psychology of consciousness, Robert Ornstein emphasizes the fallacy of assuming that personal consciousness is a perfect mirror of some external reality. He points out that man is aware of only a tiny bit of what is usually called "reality."[1] The human's sensory systems are not even capable of receiving many energy forms. For example, the spectrum of electro-magnetic waves extends from less than one billionth of a meter to more than a thousand meters. Yet the range of vision, that which can be seen, is only a small portion of this.* What is "seen" by infrared photography, for example, lies outside our range of vision and some animals such as dogs can hear sounds that are beyond our hearing.

Our usual waking consciousness, as we have seen, is principally a product of the functioning of the sensory-motor mind. The limits of this consciousness are the boundaries of the ego-level *I-ness*. It is outwardly oriented, involving action, and seems to have been evolved primarily for the purpose of ensuring individual survival. From the variety of sensory inputs and the information they present, a multi-leveled process filters out that which is related to survival. It is from this that we construct or create a consciousness which will permit us to maintain the integrity of the "I."

---

* That between 400 and 700 billionths of a meter.

We take the chaos and make sense out of it. Our notion of the world "out there" is based on how we select and process incoming data. This is a personal system which varies from one individual to the next. Our agreement on what "reality is" results from our similar limitations: for example, physical traits and common cultural training. Our eyes are restricted to the same spectrum; our conceptual categories are conditioned by common languages and traditions. Learning to take in and handle information in similar ways, we arrive at similar notions of "what reality is." But alternate ways of constructing reality are also possible. A well-known passage from William James emphasizes this:

> Our normal waking consciousness, rational conscious-ness as we call it, is but one special type of conscious-ness, whilst all about it, parted from it by the filmiest of screens, there lies potential forms of consciousness entirely different. We may go through life without suspecting their existence; but apply the requisite stimulus, and at a touch they are there in all their completeness, definite types of mentality which proba-bly somewhere have their field of application and adaptation. No account of the universe in its totality can be final which leaves these other forms of con-sciousness quite disregarded. How to regard them is the question—for they are so discontinuous with or-dinary consciousness....At any rate they forbid a pre-mature closing of our accounts with reality.[2]

CONSCIOUSNESS AS A FILTER

We saw earlier how information coming into the mind is flashed onto a screen called the "lower mind" or *manas*. This information is picked up from the outside world by the senses, which serve as a sort of scanning device. However, many things are filtered out. The senses are turned to take in only certain stimuli while ignoring others, just as a radar antenna is set to pick up only certain signals from the outer world. This protects *manas* from being overwhelmed by limiting the quantity and intensity of data that comes in. But there is also a process of selection. Certain inputs are chosen and others ignored, according to the area of concern outlined by the current self-definition *(ahankara).* On this basis some stimuli are accepted as "meaningful" and interpreted in such a way as to fit with the "I's" current notion of "reality." Other stimuli which cannot be made to fit and do not serve the purposes of the "I" are rejected. When the radar of the senses is pointed towards the external world, the way in which incoming data is selected and filtered determines to a great extent what is present in the conscious mind at that point. In this fashion then, a "waking consciousness" is created.

There is another aspect to this scanning mechanism. Not only can it reduce the quantity of incoming data desired, it can also turn in different directions to focus on different things. An attractive scene may "catch one's eye." An interesting comment can cause him to "prick up his ears." The scanning device of the senses turns and tilts, aiming in first this direction and then that.

This is an action which, at least potentially, can be coordinated by higher structures. However, it is not always done with the purposefulness and deliberation that indicates coordination from above. Certain customary ways of scanning the environment are simply the result of habit. Although originally the result of an instinctual urge or a decision by *buddhi,* through repetition they come to be carried out almost automatically. For example, one may have a habit of staring out the window while he eats breakfast rather than reading a newspaper. Getting in the car, he absent-mindedly turns the radio dial until he finds his favorite program. One person may customarily look at the clothes of a new acquaintance; another notices his posture or speech. Our sensory scanner is governed much of the time by habit and comes to operate in a nearly automatic way. In this fashion, "scanning habits" often determine the content of our waking consciousness, changing it from moment to moment. They play a key role in shaping the state of the mind. Despite the fact that such habits were often formed casually, and for no particular reason or purpose, they persist, essentially unnoticed, automatically and aimlessly shaping and re-shaping our conscious minds from moment to moment.

But more than the momentary waking consciousness is affected by such scanning habits. The content of the unconscious mind is also greatly affected. Much of the information that is brought in by the senses is never acknowledged consciously. It is stored directly in those areas of the mind that lie outside normal awareness. Under hypnosis one is able to recall details about his surroundings of which he had not seemed aware at the time they were happening. Some information, then, while "meaningful" to the "I," cannot be comfortably handled by waking consciousness. It is filed away reflexively in the storage bank of the unconscious. One "hides it from himself" so to speak. Such experiences tend often to be those which are emotionally charged, too "hot" to be held in awareness—so they are dropped into the unknown mind.

Moreover, even those things which are consciously acknowledged leave lasting imprints in the unconscious. A television drama depicting violence may leave an indelible mark on the impressionable child, but less striking sights and sounds are also taken in, quietly and continuously, slowly transforming the inner world throughout life. Though the habits of scanning and attention that determine daily routine input may seem trivial and the stimuli may appear "meaningless," by virtue of their quantity they become important. The huge bulk of the contents of *chitta* is accumulated through processes that receive little notice from psychologists. Yet consciousness is enormously affected in this slow, undramatic fashion. Much of the process of meditation and the discipline of yoga is aimed at transforming awareness through a gradual but persistent reshaping of such seemingly innocuous habits of attention.

MEMORY AND REPRESSION

So there are various ways in which the mind disposes of that data which it does not retain within immediate awareness. Some of this is simply tucked away in memory stores and is easily retrievable. The waking consciousness is created by eliminating from awareness (dissociating) certain thoughts, experiences and memories that are not compatible with that consciousness that is being constructed. This "selective inattention" operates to exclude those items of consciousness that are tied to emotional experiences which the person would not be able to integrate comfortably.

> Joan walks into a group of friends who are discussing the fact that her fiance has been openly dating two other girls. When they notice that she is behind them, they stop in embarrassment. But Joan begins to chat casually about various things, wondering to herself all the while why her friends are looking at her in such a strange way. She has managed "not to hear" the conversation which would have shattered her illusion of security, just as she has managed "not to perceive" other evidences that her relationship with her fiance had been breaking down.

Even data which is consciously perceived can be "stricken from the record" so that it's in the unconscious but not available to memory. The elimination of such emotionally charged experience from retrievable memory or "repression" is a key concept in psychoanalysis. The field of awareness that results from repression is obviously constricted placing further limits on the available fund of information and crippling one's ability to choose. The result has been characterized in a rather exaggerated fashion by George Groddeck: "Human intelligence is nothing but the stupidity acquired through repression."[3]

In contrast to psychoanalysis, which emphasizes the role of

repression in forming the unconscious, yoga psychology sees the imprints left by the constant input of everyday sensory impressions as being equally important in building the unconscious mind. The relatively neutral, undramatic impressions that are constantly taken in during one's daily routine existence, make up the bulk of the mind's content—both conscious and unconscious. Psychoanalysis emphasizes repression because its interest is in how mental illness originates. Yoga psychology, however, is more interested in providing a way of understanding even the well-adapted mind so that development will not be limited to what is currently considered "normal."

THE UNKNOWN MIND

Notions about how normal waking consciousness is constructed and maintained are not so very different in yoga and Western psychology. Processes of filtration, selection and repression are common to both. Moreover, in both the East and West there is the notion that a large part of the mental field customarily lies outside awareness. These ideas are basically the same. But there is disagreement about exactly what it is that is *excluded* from ordinary awareness. Contrasting ideas about what lies outside ordinary consciousness constitutes the major difference between yoga and modern psychology. In the West this is an unknown territory because it, by definition, lies beyond what is known. It is assumed to contain the instincts and bits and pieces of what would not fit into one's ego-level reality.

But in yoga psychology this territory is not unknown. Those who formulated the yoga system of psychology did so by virtue of having familiarized themselves experimentally with these inner spaces. Meditation developed as a technique for entering these areas and discovering just what lay there. The result is a systematic and detailed conceptualization of the "unknown mind."

Modern psychology has progressively approached these realms, and has also begun to evolve some concepts and techniques to deal with them. Freud and Jung were perhaps the foremost of those who ventured into this "unknown" or "unconscious" mind.

The Exploration of the Unconscious in Psychoanalysis: Its Limits

What has been filtered out as a result of selective inattention and repression is salted away in that huge mental reservoir called by psychoanalysts the "unconscious." When there is a great deal of repressed emotional material in the unconscious, the person's attempt to operate in the world will be impaired. Although such material has been banished from the waking consciousness, because it "wouldn't fit," it continuously threatens to intrude on that narrow definition of reality which could not contain it. Its very existence poses a constant problem for the ego-level consciousness. It must be kept safely out of sight.

Yet its very existence means one is not functioning as a totality: he will be pushed and pulled by influences operating outside his awareness. *I-ness* is restricted to a narrow field and the decisions of *buddhi* are limited by having only this as a frame of reference. Psychoanalysis developed as a therapeutic method for transcending such a limitation by bringing some of the unconscious material into awareness. The analyst and the patient together attempt to observe the flow of mental events through the patient's consciousness. This is done by means of the patient's verbalizing what he can of a chain of associations. As each thought comes into awareness, the patient attempts to describe it, trying to be completely honest and to omit nothing.

The patient not only talks. He must at the same time *listen* objectively to what he himself is saying. As he does his best to verbalize what comes into his mind ("free associates"), both he and the therapist observe the flow of mental events. From this they begin to make some inferences about what is going on in the unconscious mind.

If the analysis is to succeed, the patient must permit at least a small part of himself to participate in this observation and inference. This part of himself is sometimes called the "observing ego." If this work is successful, the observing segment of the ego grows in strength and ability, ultimately (by the time treatment is terminated) to carry on the job more or less alone without the help of the therapist. As more material is integrated into the personality, the result is a broader field of awareness and more effective functioning. In yoga psychology we would say an expanded level of observation has led to a new level of control and integration.

When psychoanalytic therapy succeeds in expanding the under-developed ego enough for it to be able to operate more effectively in the world, more often than not the patient considers himself "well" and is ready to end treatment. There is often little interest in the evolution of states of consciousness or levels of growth and maturity that lie beyond what is comfortable and adaptive. For this reason, psychoanalysis and most of modern psychotherapy might be called "deficit" or "illness-oriented,"* when compared to yoga psychology which is more "growth-oriented." Certainly modern psychotherapy has arisen mainly out of the attempt to help persons who are identified as patients—people whose ability to deal with their environment is severely limited.

Its emphasis is on the *analysis* of conflict, on probing and uncovering the roots and origins of the pathological process.

---

* This is, of course, not always true. Psychoanalysis has, to some extent, expanded to work with development beyond the merely adaptive to include the treatment of non-patients. This is especially true in the case of the "training analysis," which is intensive psychotherapy for the therapist himself. The purpose of this is to acquaint him with aspects of himself which were previously unknown to him, contributing to his own personal growth, as well as providing a basis in personal experience for his understanding of patients. Though this constitutes only a small proportion of psychoanalytic therapy it is done by the "training analysts" who teach and take the lead in formulating theory. This has inevitably led to an expansion of the perspective of psycho-analysis and an attempt to adapt its techniques to promoting growth beyond the socially-defined norms of "mental health."

Sometimes this is done through a reconstruction of the patient's psychological development, at other times it is based on an analysis of how he operates "in the now."* Yet in each case it is the negative, the sick or maladaptive aspect of the person which receives the most attention. Often the work on such *analysis,* while helpful to some extent, may divert attention from the importance of *synthesis:* the integrative, and growth-producing processes. This is underscored by Assagioli, who has more recently attempted to move therapy in the opposite direction, emphasizing synthesis. In contrasting his approach† which he calls "psychosynthesis" with the usual emphasis on psychopathology, he says:

> This pathological approach has, besides its assets, also a serious liability, and that is an exaggerated emphasis on the morbid manifestations and on the lower aspects of human nature....Moreover, many important realities and functions have been neglected or ignored: intuition, creativity, the will, and the very core of the human psyche—the Self. [4]

Nevertheless, some of the patients who are undergoing traditional psychoanalytic therapy come to sense that in the process of learning to observe the flow of free associations lies the potential for further growth. They seem to realize intuitively that if one such level of observation is possible, there must be others beyond it For example, why can't that part of the mind which observes the chain of free association, the "observing ego," itself be observed? If the cultivation of the observing ego freed

---

* A current example is "Transactional Analysis" where present interactional patterns are examined so that they can be modified.

† Though he does not clarify to what extent he arrived at his techniques through professional training and personal experience, or to what extent he learned from other traditions, Assagioli includes certain methods of inner dialogue that are identical to ancient Eastern practices. These are, of course, combined with other approaches, some of which are common to other schools of therapy and some of which are peculiar to himself.

one to some extent from anxiety and confusion, then wouldn't the development of a level beyond that expand one's horizons even more? In this way, many continue their therapy, working toward further evolution.

However, even when analyst and patient are interested in opening doors to development beyond the merely adaptive, certain difficulties are inherent in the analytic method. For it is based on the patient's verbal description of his thoughts as they flow through his mind. But much of the content of consciousness is not easily put into words. Thoughts fly by too quickly for all to be captured. Besides, many are simply indescribable. In addition, it is impossible to verbalize everything, there is just too much. This greatly limits the analytic technique and clearly makes it unsuitable for exploring those levels of consciousness that extend beyond the mental, verbal plane.

Even such schools of modern psychology which accept the concept of an unconscious attempt to study it on the basis of observing behavior. In the case of psychoanalysis the behavior is verbal. This is only different in degree from the approach of experimental psychology, where observable behavior, whether it be emotional or verbal, is the basic source of data. Behavior is an external phenomenon, and any study of it must remain different from the direct observation of consciousness that is carried on in introspection. In this sense, modern psychology has not developed a viable discipline of introspection, and all of Western psychology is basically behavioristic:* "There are two roads to all knowledge. One can experience the world as an object or experience it directly, know it endopsychically.... Indian culture has brought the subjective method...to completion, while our occidental culture fosters the method of objective knowledge."[5]

* It should be noted that early in the history of experimental psychology, Wundt, in Germany, initiated an organized attempt to study the mind through introspection. Of course, these introspectionists still relied on verbal report of their experience as a source of data, so they might still be technically termed "behaviorist."

Because modern psychology approaches the unconscious "from outside" through inferences made by observing behavior, it has naturally focused on the emergence of material that relates to the origins and development of the individual, externally-oriented and adapted "ego." Though both the Eastern and Western methods begin with the mental arena and both aim to explore the unknown realms of consciousness, in psychoanalysis and most of modern psychodynamic theory, the exploration of the inner world is thought to lead only to an increasingly detailed knowledge of the personal past. "The deepest layer of the unconscious cannot be other than the psychic reflection of those early biological events which group together under the designation of embryological development."[6]   In psychoanalytic theory then, the limit to inner exploration can only be the earliest stages of the individual's history. There is no notion that such an exploration can lead into areas beyond the personal.

This is reflected in the metaphor which Freud uses to describe the mind. He compares it to an iceberg—with only a small portion, the conscious part, being visible. The rest, the bulk of the mind, is submerged beneath the surface and out of view. But an iceberg is cold, isolated, floating free from any connection or grounding. This seems to reflect a basically depressive perspective, an assumption that the human being is irretrievably separate, isolated and alone. As we shall see, yoga psychology has a different orientation.

The Collective Unconscious: The Discovery of the Transpersonal

In contrast to Freud and his followers, Jung seemed to grasp that there was something more to the unconscious than its personal aspects.

> For Freud...the unconscious is of an exclusively personal nature....A more or less superficial layer...is undoubtedly

personal....But this personal unconscious rests upon a
deeper layer, which does not derive from personal
experience and is not a personal acquisition but is
inborn.[7]

Jung found universal patterns and images in his study of the
world's mythologies and religious symbols as well as in the
dreams of his patients. He felt that this indicated something
beyond the child's history and upbringing. He called this the
collective unconscious:

> I have chosen the term "collective" because this part of
> the unconscious is not individual but universal; in
> contrast to the personal psyche, it has contents and
> modes of behavior that are more or less the same
> everywhere and in all individuals. It is, in other
> words, identical in all men and thus constitutes a
> common psychic substrate of a suprapersonal nature
> which is present in every one of us.[8]

Jung believed that this collective unconscious offered a guide
for the ego's[*] integration of the personality. He felt that dream
symbols were the "essential message carriers from the instinctive
to the rational parts of the human mind." [9] These messages came
in terms of symbols which appear in all cultures. These universal
symbols Jung called "archetypes." Well known expressions of
the archetypes are found in myths and fairy tales. For instance,
the prince who comes to awaken Sleeping Beauty is a classic
example of the "hero archetype."

The archetypes from the collective unconscious supply symbols
to the ego, guiding and motivating it. These charged symbols
"seep into the ego" causing the ego in some cases to identify with
them and act them out unconsciously, and in other cases to see

---

* Jung uses "ego" as more or less synonymous with "normal waking consciousness"
while in Freud's terminology "ego" has both conscious and unconscious components.

them in the external world.[10]   Jung felt that dreams acted in this fashion to restore balance in one who had overdeveloped some aspect of himself.   For example, the man who was overly aggressive and masculine might be found to have his dreams pervaded by a feminine archetype.   This, through its subtle influence, would help to balance his life.

According to Jung, the unknown side of oneself comes to light through creative intuition and in the production of art and other creative work, as well as through dreams. If this information is heeded, then one can integrate into the ego the separated-off parts of himself and begin to become a more mature individual. The ego takes this information and uses it to expand itself. The integrating tendency for this lies in the collective unconscious, where the archetypes are found. This collective unconscious is a primal, prehistorical world of instinct.   It is an underlying substratum of biological, instinctual tendencies which date back to man's earliest development when his "psyche was still close to that of the animal. This immensely old psyche forms the basis of our mind, just as much as the structure of our body is based on the general anatomical pattern of the mammal."[11]

Jung felt that it was in this primitive psyche where one could find "the ground plan lying dormant" for the specific direction that his personal development would take. Thus he found himself in the curious and paradoxical position of asserting that man's highest integration and creativity is guided by his most primitive level of being, the "instinctual" collective unconscious. This does not fit comfortably with a theory of growth and evolution.

The Self in Jungian Psychology

According to Jung, the primitive instincts of the collective unconscious contain the seeds of what one can and will become. It is this which shapes the future and determines the particular individuation of a person.   This integrating tendency in the collective unconscious expresses itself as an archetype which Jung calls "the self." This self represents the ego's potential wholeness. But for him, the bringing together of opposites which makes one "whole," invariably produces a kind of tension. Therefore, although Jung's "self" tends towards a kind of wholeness, it is not like the Self of yoga psychology, a state of peace, tranquillity or perfection. It is instead a coexistence of opposites.[12]

In fact, the ultimate outcome of personal evolution and how it can be attained is not clear in Jungian psychology, though we are told that, "The ultimate goal of Jungian psychotherapy is to make the symbolic process conscious."[13]

> To be able to recognize the archetype, to see the symbolic image behind the symptom, immediately transforms the experience. It may be just as painful, but now it has meaning. Instead of isolating the sufferer from his fellow humans, it unites him with them in a deeper rapport. Now he feels himself a participating partner in the collective human enterprise—the painful evolution of human consciousness—which began in the darkness of the primordial swamp and which will end we know not where.[14]

For Jung the self remains an integrating tendency hidden in the collective unconscious. It comes to light only by means of archetypes sending messages to the ego through dreams and symbolism and yet it remains in the darkness of the unconscious never directly known. It can only be known indirectly through dream symbols, hunches and so forth. It is not the knower. One must depend on the ego as the basis of his consciousness. It is the knower. It is the ego which integrates the information coming from the self. The self can only be known objectively and at a distance, through inference. Consciousness can only be a property of the ego. Jung said: "No consciousness can exist without...an ego....Consciousness needs a center....We know of no other kind of consciousness, nor can we imagine a consciousness without an ego."[15]

He did not carry his exploration far enough to find that the "ego," this "normal awareness" could be increased and modified so repeatedly that it becomes radically different from ordinary consciousness. He did not realize that the potential for growth was so great that its outcome could depart far enough from the familiar world of the ordinary ego to be completely incomprehensible to it.

The notion of an altered state of consciousness which would provide a perspective beyond the usual waking consciousness was not, in Jung's view, possible. One had to rely on ego-waking consciousness to assimilate what bits and pieces of the collective unconscious it could through hints from dreams and symbols. From this point of view, one's only hope is to trim down the unconscious enough in this way so that it doesn't completely swamp him. For Jung saw very clearly that if too little of the unconscious is integrated, aspects of it can become overwhelming— even those archetypes which are potentially most helpful. He said if the unconscious:

> ...contains too many things that normally ought to be conscious, then its function becomes twisted and prejudiced; motives appear that are not based upon true instincts, but that owe their existence and psychic importance to the fact that they have been consigned to the unconscious by repression or neglect. They overlay, as it were, the normal unconscious psyche and distort its natural tendency to express basic symbols and motifs.[16]

Jung recognized that it was only through the integration of repressed material that one could escape being pushed and pulled by invisible influences from the unconscious. He demonstrated in his work with patients that such integration led one to become more aware, more creative. But he said that reducing the load of repressed material allowed "instincts" to express themselves more clearly. This seems to be more than simply a semantic matter, for the instinctual side of man's nature, and his higher nature apparently were not clearly distinguished in Jung's psychology. They were lumped together in the collective unconscious and expressed themselves in a mingled way through the archetypes.

This contrasts with the view of yoga psychology, where instincts are seen as a lower form of consciousness, more primitive than the ego level. They lie on one side of the ego level, while the states of higher consciousness lie on the other. In yoga psychology, there is a level of consciousness beyond the ego level that comes eventually into being as awareness is progressively expanded by making more and more of the unconscious conscious. It comes into full flower when the unconscious is finally fully known.

But Jung, like Freud, had no idea that the full integration of the unconscious could be accomplished. He didn't know it was possible to bring the entire mind, including that which he called the "collective unconscious," into awareness.

Jung is often considered an advocate of Eastern psychology. Many of his concepts (e.g., "self," *mandala*) were in fact taken from oriental sources, though he drastically changed their meanings. He wrote introductions to the translations of a number of important Eastern books. However, a closer analysis of Jung's writings reveals that he actually regarded Eastern concepts as manifestations of his "universal archetypes" and saw them in the context of his own thought. His "self" is, in fact, quite different in many respects from the "Self" of Indian psychology. In certain important ways Jung found himself unable to step outside the preconceptions of his Western point of view; his inability to conceive of a state of consciousness apart from his concept of the ego led him to interpret yoga in the ego-oriented terms of modern psychology.

For him, the "higher voice," came, strangely enough, from a primitive, instinctual collective unconscious. No wonder then that one could not experience it directly: he would be swallowed up—plunged into an instinct-dominated world where he would quickly lose his bearings. Jung said: 'It must be reckoned a catastrophe when the ego is assimilated by the self." [17] To him, departure from ego consciousness could only mean insanity, psychosis. This frightening preconception colored his whole notion of what yoga was about:

> The past masters in the art of self-control, the yogis, attain perfection in *samadhi,* a state of ecstasy, which so far as we know, is equivalent to a state of unconsciousness. [18]

Actually, in yoga psychology, *samadhi* is the highest state of consciousness, the culmination of many years of arduous training. In the traditional teachings, it is clearly distinguished from *ecstasy,* which is the result of an abrupt and largely involuntary immersion in an aspect of the inner world (unconscious) which has been incompletely integrated into awareness. One is "possessed by" ecstasy. *Samadhi,* by contrast, is systematically approached, and after sufficient training, can be entered and left at will.

But Jung seemed unaware of this distinction. He equates *samadhi* with ecstasy and thinks it identical to "a state of unconsciousness:"

> It makes no difference whether they call our unconscious a "universal consciousness;" the fact remains that in their case the unconscious has swallowed up ego consciousness. They do not realize that a "universal consciousness" is a contradiction in terms, since exclusion, selection, discrimination are the root and essence of everything that lays claim to the name "consciousness." [19]

To him, the highest states of consciousness attained in yoga could only be seen as "loss" of the ego's consciousness: a frightening prospect.

Such a misconception about Eastern disciplines is not unusual:

In a recent interview, Stanley Keleman, a well-known bioenergetic therapist, was asked, "I take it you would object to the influx of Eastern spirituality which encourages us to let the ego die, give up the delusion of individuality...?" He replied, "I think all that stuff is dangerous and misleading. Look, it's very easy to be a cosmic being, to sink into Unity."[20]

He assumes that the only route to escape from the limitation of the ego is a regressive one. One must "sink" to a feeling of unity. Yet he notes, as though in passing:

> One of my teachers...taught me a powerful lesson:
> 'You never kill the ego, you only find that it lives
> in a larger house than you thought.'[21]

He realizes that the path of evolution must include a gradual expansion of a sense of *I-ness*. But he is not aware how far this can go. He has had no occasion to discover that eventually this can lead to an escape from the confines of egoism.

The process of meditation is a private one. The expansion of awareness that evolves is not won on the playing field of external behavior alone. It may be evolved quietly and internally. To the casual Western observer who is unfamiliar with such practices, only one conclusion is possible: the meditator is "sinking into an undifferentiated state." The subtleties of inner exploration are not easily apparent to one who is oriented toward the materialistic, external criteria of modern science.

In his theoretical writings Jung gives the impression that his knowledge of these deeper layers of the unconscious comes from the study of myths and symbols and the reports of his patients. However, a reading of his autobiography, *Memories, Dreams, Reflections,* suggests that Jung's own periodic encounters with involuntary alterations in consciousness may have played a major role in shaping his theories. These episodes seem to have been for him, an abrupt and even disturbing departure from his "ego consciousness." In any case, he did not have the benefit of a systematic program of inner exploration which would permit him to integrate the experience of these phenomena and go on beyond them. Instead, he saw them as separate from his "ego consciousness," messages from the collective unconscious, and perhaps a bit threatening. It would be "catastrophic" to be "swallowed up" by this and the ego could only assimilate so much of it. Therefore, huge areas of the inner world remained cut off from direct, experiential exploration by Jung.

It was for such reasons, perhaps, that Jung stuck so insistently to the normal waking-consciousness as the only possibility. The "reality" that results from the usual way of filtering incoming data was the only one he knew. As far as he could understand, the state of *samadhi* consisted of losing consciousness, not expanding it. For him, clarity of consciousness was possible only within the limits of the ego. The reality structured by the ego was the only "reality" possible. The possibility of experiencing a state of consciousness that lies beyond the bounds of the ordinary ego was ruled out:

> We must look for a different solution. We believe in ego-consciousness and in what we call reality...Our European ego-consciousness is therefore inclined to swallow up the unconscious and if this should not prove feasible we try to suppress it. [22]

What the limited ego cannot assimilate, it denies and represses. Those bits and pieces of the data of experience which point up the inadequacy of our notions of "reality" are pushed out of sight rather than remaining in view to serve as inducements to reorganize our way of seeing our world. They are stuffed into our already overcrowded unconscious. Here they add to our psychological burden and accentuate our susceptibility to anxiety and mental disorder.

Jung's work was very valuable in emphasizing that there was something to the unknown mind beyond its *personal* aspects, though he did not acknowledge that one could experience it directly. He ventured far enough into the unconscious mind to find that there was something more than darkness there. He said, "What our age thinks of as the shadow, an inferior part of the psyche, is more than something merely negative."[23] He grasped that therein lay the possibility of a knowledge and awareness that transcended individual limitations.

But he mistakenly assumed that all material from beyond the personal field comes from the same place. It was all "biological, prehistoric and...archaic."[24] He lumped the instinctual level of the psyche together with the integrating tendency of the higher consciousness. They were both outside the normal ego consciousness and beyond the personal unconscious, so they were assumed by him to be identical. This combination of the most primitive and the most advanced consciousness he called the collective unconscious.

Dealing with them together fit with the world view and preconceptions of his culture. The ego was seen as the culmination of the development of consciousness. The primitive, instinctual collective unconscious gives rise to it.

In the thinking of his time everything was either instinctual or learned. What could not be explained in terms of learning and personal history could only come from one place, the instincts. He says that archetypes are "an instinctive *trend,* as marked as the impulse of birds to build nests or ants to form organized colonies."[25]

> "Instincts are impersonal, universally distributed, hereditary factors of a dynamic or motivating character.... there is good reason for supposing that the archetypes are the unconscious images of the instincts themselves, in other words, that they are *patterns of instinctual behavior.*"[26]

But there are difficulties in this approach. If the collective unconscious, through the formation of archetypes, guides the ego in its integration and development, from where does it attain this wisdom and sophistication? How can a more primitive, archaic level of man's psyche organize and guide a more evolved one?

Jung's archetype which pushed one towards a more complete differentiation of his individual personality, the "self," was an individual thing. Though an archetype from the "collective" unconscious, and universal in the sense that each person has one and the symbols in which it is expressed show certain similarities, it is not "transpersonal" in the sense in which we use that word. Being made up of a combination of the primitive mind, higher consciousness and influences from an incompletely explored personal unconscious, it would obviously be different for each person. It was unique, "occurring only once in time." [27] But in yoga psychology, "transpersonal" consciousness indicates something quite apart from this.

Collective vs. Transpersonal

As personal evolution advances, one comes to find that his consciousness has more in common with that of others who have developed themselves. As the sense of "I" expands, personal definitions of I-ness increase until they eventually overlap. Then they become "transpersonal."

People who function at the level of the sensory-motor mind (manas) exist more in a state of disparity. When the mind flits from one subject to another, the pattern of impressions is vastly different from one person to another. At that level man is very different from his fellow man. One person may be concerned with sensory stimuli that relate to sex, another with those related to food. The attention of each is drawn towards these desires through paths that are quite different from one another. At this level, disparity is predominant and concensus and agreement are reached only with difficulty, necessarily through compromise, with its inherent struggle and conflict.

But as consciousness expands, it reaches levels where more is held in common. In terms of yoga psychology, the consciousness of an evolved person is similar to that of another person functioning on the same level, whereas the consciousness of two people who are dominated by *manas* is quite different.

At the highest states of consciousness, as described in yoga, experience is not only similar, it is shared. In other words, we might think of the hierarchy of consciousness as similar to a pyramid. At the base there's a wide area where diversity exists. But ascending through different levels of the hierarchy we begin to approach others who are clinging to the same step-wise fashion. At the peak of the pyramid all paths must come together and the consciousness and perspective that is gained there is identical. This is not a "loss of consciousness" nor slipping back into an undifferentiated state. From this point any part of the surrounding area can be viewed clearly.

As the ego level of *I-ness* is transcended, for instance, and the diversity which is a property of that level is dropped, then the impediments to experiencing a non-personal, encompassing consciousness begin to fall away. Higher consciousness is experienced, then, as "above" the personality, though the personality remains intact below to serve as its tool. For this reason, those who have attained a higher consciousness may continue to be quite different from one another in their outward behavior, even though their underlying consciousness has become identical. This contrasts with the attempt to gain identity through altering the ego or the grosser aspects of the personality. Social conformity, uniform behavior and uniform dress are, in a sense, polar opposites of the unity that is experienced through advanced awareness.

MODELS OF THE UNCONSCIOUS

In his work with dreams and myths, Jung uncovered evidences of a transpersonal level of consciousness but did not think of it as being—even potentially—shared. He had not completely broken away from the Freudian model of the isolated iceberg. The consciousness of each person was still irrevocably separate and individual though the archetypes that led him to his unique individuality were similar to those which guided others. In each case, they arose from the submerged "collective unconscious." It was instinctual and biological and for this reason was a common substrate in all human beings. But the archetypes taking shape here were different in each case. Even Jung's most encompassing integrative archetype, the "self," which is often thought of as "universal," is in fact different in each person, though universally present.

Without quite realizing it, Jung unearthed evidences from dreams and symbols of a common base which transcended separateness. He inadvertently uncovered along with the primitive part of the mind a higher level of consciousness. This was quite distinct from the limited waking consciousness which he was trying to use to understand it. It was much vaster than the ego-consciousness into which he was trying to integrate it. It was much more evolved than the instincts with which he confused it. Actually, he was combining two kinds of contact with awareness beyond the personal: that which can be experienced by dropping back to domination by the lower mind *(manas)*, and that which results from moving forward to expanded consciousness.

Like many an explorer, he had discovered something the vast implications of which he could not entirely grasp. He had sighted the shore of a new territory but tried to describe it in terms of the old world. Like Columbus, who called the natives of the new world "Indians" because he expected to arrive in India, Jung tried to understand the transpersonal in terms familiar to the limited ego: he called it "instinct." But just as the discovery of America was not diminished by the misconceptions of Columbus, Jung's discoveries are not invalidated by the inadequacies of his theory. His bringing to light of the collective unconscious remains an epochal landmark in modern psychology.

The Personal Unconscious: The Great Barrier

So we have seen that at the grossest levels of mental functioning there is a great deal of disparity. There is a tremendous variety of contradictory pulls by the instincts and sensory stimuli so that a person is drawn first this way and then that. In order to create a coherent personality out of this mass of diversity it is necessary to select out portions and "repress" the rest. This gives rise to the segment of mind that we call the "normal waking consciousness," which contains much less contradiction. In this way, one is able to function as an identifiable, operational human being in society. But that which is pushed out of view, which is repressed, becomes the "personal unconscious." This is the first layer of the unknown mind. Beneath that lie those levels beyond the personal which Jung brought to light. Beneath* them, in turn, lies the cosmic or superconsciousness.

In entering this unknown world, one will find that the stratification is not initially so easy to discern. Even in the personal unconscious there are glimmers of light from the deeper levels. But essentially the personal unconscious is a stronghold of instinctual derivatives and repressed memories (samskaras). This is the place where habits leave their impressions.

In journeying inward, then, the personal unconscious is "the sandtrap of the mind." It is a pitfall lying between oneself and his goal. It is a sort of obstacle, where one can be sucked into the quicksand of instinctual urges or waylaid by the memories

---

* Here "Beneath" is intended to mean "deeper." Unfortunately this figure of speech is awkward, since one often says that "higher" consciousness results from going "deeper" into oneself.

of past experiences. These past impressions have been weighted down in the unconscious by the energy with which they were invested *(karma)*. They present one during his inward exploration with nearly irresistible enticements. They give rise to rapturous fantasies and enticing memories. They are the Sirens of the internal sea, luring one onto the rocks of entanglement and confusion. Or they present him with aspects of himself which were repressed because they were unacceptable: the dark shadows of the psyche with which he had not been able to come to terms. These aspects of the personality may lurk in the darkness of the unknown mind, assuming horrible, threatening proportions.

So the unconscious is a dark world populated with seductive Lorelei and grotesque monsters offering only glimmers of light from the higher consciousness to guide one through.

Psychosis and Mysticism

The dark world of the personal unconscious is a barrier which must be conquered by the inner explorer who wishes to reach the higher levels of consciousness. In the course of his explorations during meditation, he must gradually work his way through this dangerous territory.

The secret of success is twofold. First, there must be careful preparation. By gradually training the body so that it can relax, and gradually minimizing the distractions of poorly organized nervous energy, the mind can be more detached and observant, impartially witnessing the mental flow. With the sensory input reduced, past impressions bubbling up from *chitta,* the memory bank, begin to appear before the inner observer. Here will come to light the repressed material which caused the borders of *I-ness* to be narrow and restricted. Little by little these repressed memories, these embarrassing bits of oneself must be gradually acknowledged and incorporated into his self-concept, enlarging the sense of *I-ness.*

If the management of input has been wisely arranged so that a minimum of dissonant and disturbing material has been taken in, then this inner exploration has a chance of going well. This is the meditator's way of arranging for a fairly comfortable or at least tolerable journey for himself through the inner world. What he has put into his unconscious through his daily activities—his casual reading, his television viewing, his friendly conversations, his emotional outbursts, his business or professional activities—will all await him when he turns inwards.

His other tool is a one-pointed attention fixed unwaveringly on his goal, which is a level of consciousness that lies beyond the personal unconscious. If his will is unshakable, he can avoid being pulled into involvement with the alluring images in the personal unconscious or into struggles with those which threaten his narrow *I-ness*. If his attention is focused fixedly on his destination, which lies beyond the personal unconscious, he may be able to successfully traverse it.

Some who enter this world of the unknown mind do not fare so well. A psychotic is one who has lost his way. Entering with no previous preparation, he finds a writhing cauldron of devils, evil spirits, and grotesque monsters which quickly engulf him. His sense of *I-ness* is too limited to encompass this and it is for this reason that such negative memories and images were banished to the unconscious in the first place. Moreover, he does not have a strong will to sustain him in his journey. Since *I-ness* varies from moment to moment, there is no consistently defined goal, and the will wavers. With an especially hectic path to travel and without a determined guide, the traveler becomes mired down in the personal unconscious, lost in a world of madness.

Psychic Phenomena

Research on parapsychology reflects what can occur when the ego is momentarily transcended. Brief contact with a world beyond the personal leaves the ego puzzled. Telepathy, for example, is inexplicable in terms of the ego's notion of "reality." The boundaries of *I-ness* are temporarily interrupted to allow contact with something outside the "I" which cannot be encompassed by it. When this contact is terminated, the boundaries are restored much as they were before. There is no evolution of the "I" as a result of this experience. Contact with phenomena and perceptions outside the "ordinary reality" is accomplished by suspending, at least momentarily, the usual "I-consciousness." Some "mediums" are even unconscious during the time they supply information from a trance-like state. This is a state of "ecstasy" as we have defined it earlier. It is essentially a sort of delirium. When the ordinary waking consciousness is stopped, the usual filtering of sensory data ceases. When input is no longer "censored" to maintain a predetermined "reality," *manas* is open to a much greater range of information. The underlying base of primitive consciousness, *chitta,* is permitted to come into view. The instinctual underpinnings of the mind have freer play. Jung's collective unconscious is plugged into *manas.*

But this underlying pool is, according to yoga psychology, open to influences that have been blocked off by ego-consciousness. The intermingling of energies, of "psychic prana" is here more diffuse and global. Individuality at this level is not discretely outlined. This is the primordial pool out of which the individual mind has differentiated. At this level there is access to information beyond the field of the ego's consciousness. This is the merging of undifferentiated consciousness that permits mother to be "aware" of a child's needs, that allows "extrasensory perception" of the sort that is usually seen. This kind of "telepathy" is in yogic terms called "instinctual telepathy," or a "psychic experience." Its basis is primitive. It is not a result of a highly differentiated and evolved consciousness.

Because of the fact that *I-ness* has not been gradually expanded to gain access to this contact, the personal consciousness is still

largely unknown. The material it contains is not integrated and the
impulses and tendencies it creates continue to operate outside
awareness. For this reason, the "information" from those who
report "psychic experiences" is notoriously unreliable even when
they are sincere and honest. There is a large admixture of
distorting influences from their personal unconscious. The
psychic's prophecies may occasionally be sensationally accurate,
but often they are embarrassingly wrong. For this reason in
research on telepathy and clairvoyance, positive results can
usually be established only through statistical studies. Even the
most successful subjects have enough failures to throw some
doubt on their abilities so that an experimental evaluation is
generally necessary to establish beyond doubt that there is more
than chance involved.

It is not difficult to understand why psychotics sometimes
report "psychic" experiences. Their fragile sense of *I-ness* results
in abrupt—and often unwanted—contact with areas beyond the
personal. A patient, for example, who has formed a very close
relationship with his therapist may come to demonstrate a
supernormal sensitivity to the therapist's inner states. At times
he may even be able to describe correctly the thoughts going
through the therapist's mind. However, just as often his notion
of what the other is thinking is completely erroneous, being
clearly a matter of projecting his own thoughts and feelings.
His perceptions may be called psychic or extrasensory but they
contrast with a higher transpersonal awareness by remaining
contaminated with the coloring of his own unintegrated personal
unconscious.

At moments the psychotic reverts to the sort of total identification with his sensory impressions that characterizes the infant,
having very little *I-ness* to interfere with his becoming one with
the objects of his perception. We might say that the psychotic
has a "poor grasp of reality," meaning that his ability to make the
usual selection of stimuli which creates ordinary "reality" is not
developed. His capacity for tuning the sensory scanner and

choosing the stimuli which will create a culturally acceptable interpretation of the external world is weak. Without such deliberate selection and observation, he is likely to receive data that other people have tuned out. Information may appear on the screen of *manas* which would ordinarily be eliminated.

This is likely to happen since his focusing on the object or the other person is so intense; his sense of oneness with others may permit him to momentarily open channels that are normally kept closed. In the view of yoga psychology, the phenomenon which occurs during ordinary cases of extrasensory perception involves this sort of mingling of *manas* with the object on which it is intensely focused, or with the *manas* of another with which it is entangled.

Although the psychotic may happen upon such psychic perceptions during his drastic shift from one massive identification to the next, he is ill-equipped to benefit from such information. His real need is for development and integration on the most basic levels which will provide him a base from which he can gradually resume his personal evolution. He must pass through the level of ordinary ego before he can begin to explore truly transpersonal levels of consciousness and contact.

In yoga it is traditionally accepted that when through inner discipline one learns to step, with full awareness and control, outside the limits of the personal reality of the ordinary ego, he can see from a perspective that is no longer limited by time, space and causality. These are seen as merely self-imposed forms whereby one is "enabled to apprehend in the relative sense." [28] When the constructs that shape ordinary reality are no longer limiting one's view, then awareness of events occurring in other time/space contexts is said to be available. But the accurate perception of some future event, for example, when it is involuntary and does not result from such a systematic mastery of higher consciousness, is not considered worthy of much attention. An "extrasensory perception" which comes as an involuntary flooding of consciousness is not highly valued in the context of yogic

training. It is of passing interest, however, since it indicates that
one is beginning to open himself to new areas of awareness, just
as catching a glimpse of an illustration while leafing through a
book may suggest that one has found a text on the subject he
wished. But such a glimpse is no substitute for a systematic
reading and study of the complete work. In the traditions of
yoga, any "supernormal" phenomenon or "power" that operates
outside control is regarded as essentially useless and potentially
a waste of time. Focusing one's attention and energy on it can
become a serious obstacle to further movement along the path
of growth and evolution.

Dreams

Jung often felt that dreams were able to warn one of disasters
which lay in the future. He reports the dream of a man who had
a "morbid passion" for dangerous mountain climbing. "He saw
himself stepping off the summit of a high mountain into empty
space." Despite this "warning" he continued his climbing. Six
months later while descending through difficult terrain, he "stepped
off into space" and fell to his death. This and other such examples
led Jung to conclude that "dreams may sometimes announce
certain situations long before they actually happen." [29]
He pointed out, however, that dreams may also mislead one.
He was taking into account the role played by the monsters who
people the personal unconscious and who can act in opposition
to the conscious ego. He said that "a benevolent agency is
sometimes at work and sometimes not. The mysterious hand may
point the way to perdition. Dreams sometimes prove to be traps,
or appear to be so." He tells the story of the Delphic oracle that
told King Croesus that if he crossed the Halys River he would
destroy a large kingdom. "It was only after he was completely
defeated in battle after the crossing that he discovered that the

kingdom meant by the oracle was his own." [30] If the unconscious contains too much repressed material, as Jung said, its influence becomes distorted and twisted and it can operate against the ego. [31]

In yoga psychology, a dream can be understood as a combination of derivatives from the personal unconscious as well as some contact with a field beyond the personal which has not yet been integrated into awareness. For this reason it can both communicate intuitions, such as knowledge of something that is happening elsewhere, as well as represent personal problems and psychopathology.

The dual nature of the unconscious, unknown world is thus aptly represented by the dual nature of the dream. It carries evidences of both the personal psyche as well as that field that lies beyond it. It can tell us about our psychopathology or it can bring us awareness of phenomena beyond the limited self.

The way in which Freud and Jung worked with dreams illustrates the difference in their approach to promoting growth and evolution. Jung concentrated on the messages which the dream brought from the collective unconscious. From the point of view of yoga psychology, we would say that he used dream symbols, art and myth to make available the awareness gained through alternate modes of consciousness as it could be used for the purposes of integration. But this awareness came from a state of consciousness that could not be directly experienced. So in working with dreams, Jung would often interrupt the patients' chain of associations. He was critical of Freud's practice of allowing the patient to free-associate and of his technique of following the stream of ideas set off by a dream symbol. Jung felt that following one's thought could only lead him away from the "message" that the dream carried and into his own personal complexes and problems. He was less interested in the details of the personal unconscious than in the messages which deeper integrating levels might send. He felt that when these were integrated, personal problems would clear up as a matter of course.

The Observing Ego vs. Integration Through Archetypes

Freud's method by contrast, was to examine the personal pathology and attempt to resolve it. In his work with dreams, the dream symbol served as a starting point for a train of thought that would inevitably come back to the patient's repressed conflicts making them ever more obvious to him.

His method was to meet the personal unconscious head on and systematically bring it into awareness. His efforts were directed toward cultivating in this way the "observing ego," that piece of the person which stood back and watched and listened as he described the thoughts going through his mind. This provided the new level of observation from which the unconscious material could be viewed in relation to the ego's field of awareness. From here the two could be integrated, expanding the ego and reducing the amount of troublesome material hidden in the unconscious.

Thus in Freud's theory is implicit the idea of higher levels of consciousness. His technique demonstrates that there is a perspective from which one can observe the ego. This suggests, of course, that there may be a potential for even higher levels of observation. That these have not become evident in Freudian analysis seems partly due to the fact that the method limits further exploration. The world of the ego is verbal and the technique of psychoanalysis is verbal. Though the theory implies the importance of developing a hierarchy of levels of observation, its methodology prevents it from going further than a still verbal "observing ego."

Meanwhile, Jung denied the possibility of developing a hierarchy of levels of consciousness. Distinct, step-wise states of consciousness which could be experienced were not part of his idea of evolution. His therapeutic efforts were directed, not so much at developing "an observer," but rather in learning to attune the waking consciousness to the messages and hints that came from another level of integration which was not directly experienced.   Nevertheless, Jung's method did open him to evidences in religious symbols and in dreams of what was, in fact, a truly transpersonal consciousness, a rich source of information that could not be available to Freudian psycho-analysis which was oriented toward the personal unconscious.

Yoga psychology offers a perspective from which these two theories can be integrated. Its concept of a hierarchy of consciousness is more extensive than Freud's, extending beyond the levels of functioning which can be described verbally to include the more transpersonal areas of consciousness explored by Jung as well as those which stretch far beyond.

Yoga psychology also emphasizes a facet of psychological function largely ignored by both schools of psychotherapy: the effects of mental habits, e.g., what we have called scanning habits, on the mental makeup. In psychoanalysis, patients analyze the unconscious but there is no actual training in how to regulate input into the unconscious. In yoga psychology, however, it is recognized that although the unconscious may be relatively *cleared,* it can quickly accumulate a new load of conflictual material, if one's mental habits and attitude toward his experience are not skillfully managed. Patanjali's system of yoga, while less intricate in its analysis of the personal unconscious than psychoanalysis is far richer in its methodology for maintaining the mind in an uncluttered condition. It offers a variety of techniques for managing input so that emotional and mental problems are minimized, and the exploration and development of more evolved levels of consciousness can continue undisturbed. Because modern psychotherapy has its roots in the treatment of illness, whereas yoga is oriented toward developing beyond ordinary adaptation, they complement one another very nicely. Yoga may provide the concepts and philosophical framework which will enable western psychotherapy to escape its illness-orientation and respond more fully to each person's search for growth and evolution.

A Note on Energy and Repression: Kundalini and the Unconscious

A great deal of energy is tied up in keeping repressed material outside awareness. Work is involved in holding a memory or impulse away from the conscious mind. This energy can be released and made once more accessible when the unconscious material is brought into consciousness. The patient in psychotherapy who is able to bring repressed material into consciousness is usually found to have more energy available. This reduces chronic fatigue and makes work more effective and dynamic. This is usually a gradual process.

Similarly, the person who successfully through the discipline of meditation enters the unknown world and explores the unconscious, bringing it gradually into awareness, experiences an increasing amount of energy that "rises up" and becomes available to him. In yoga psychology, this "raising of energy" is symbolized by a rising serpent which is called *kundalini*. *Kunda* means a bowl or basin and the *kundalini* serpent is said to be coiled up in the basin formed by the pelvis. Here it is traditionally and metaphorically said to be "sleeping," intoxicated on the energy it is sapping from one's potential supply. As the process of meditation continues and the unconscious is gradually made conscious, then *kundalini* "rises"; the energy it was absorbing is released, and one feels an upsurge of vitality.

CHAPTER FIVE
THE BLISSFUL SHEATH

"Quite other than this intellectual sheath that consists of under-
standing, and interior to it is the sheath that consists of bliss.
This sheath is encased in the intellectual sheath and has the
same form. The one is filled with the other. The first has the
likeness of a man, and because it has the likeness of a man, the
second follows it and itself takes on the likeness of a man."

Taittiriya Upanishad, II. 5

chapter 5
THE SECRETS OF SLEEP

We have seen in previous chapters how current psychology emphasizes verbally oriented concepts. How can observation and control be extended beyond this realm, into the exploration of other "states of consciousness"? If the area to be explored lies beyond the verbal then clearly our approach cannot be based on discourse and discussion. Nor can it result from reports from others. It must necessarily base itself on personal experience. Each of us must make his own inward exploration.

But exploration of what? Two areas immediately suggest themselves. One is the control of "involuntary" processes, the constant regulation that takes place outside the domain of our normal waking consciousness. The other is the wordless state our consciousness enters during the depths of dreamless sleep. These are the frontiers of the inner world—the lands that lie beyond the familiar territory of words and thoughts. Recently in the West, biofeedback research has catapulted the psychologist into some of these unmapped territories. The control of internal physiological functions has been made possible in the laboratory. In the process of working with biofeedback, subjects have discovered internal cues, wordless inner maneuvers, which enable them to bring under their control what was thought to be impossible. Meanwhile, sensitive equipment has led to more thorough studies of the many and mysterious worlds of sleep—the unknown spaces we enter during the night, from which we return with no memory.

As scientists enter these areas, they are finding to their surprise that they are not completely uncharted. All along the way they find evidences of previous explorers. Eastern sages— yogis, Zen masters and Sufi "wise men"—had long ago turned inward to conquer the unknown world within and plant their flags firmly on the most distant and serene shores. Their disciplines and their methods, which before seemed mystical or bizarre, are beginning to take on new significance, to have a new impact and relevance.

Besides such everyday phenomena as deep sleep and the regulation of internal organs, other such apparently inconsequential matters like the control and focusing of attention are gaining new interest and relevance in modern psychology. Each of these areas, it now appears, is of crucial importance in the movement into and through the world within. The keys to the conquest of inner space it seems, were always at hand.

PASSIVE VOLITION

In Chapter I we described the experimental control of migraine headaches through biofeedback training. Shifting of the blood flow away from the head seemed to be accomplished by increasing the flow to the hand, "warming it." Patients have, however, often had difficulty in learning to raise the temperature of the hand.

After a week of being unable to produce a response on the temperature meter, one patient became "furious with the machine" and felt like smashing it, like "throwing it out of the window." He gave up trying to "make" it go up and, surprisingly, it immediately began to respond. Giving up the willful effort to influence vascular response seemed paradoxically to bring control. After ten days of this practice he could increase his hand temperature when he chose, without further need of the meter.[1]

Another patient tried willfully to increase temperature in her hands with no success. She also became frustrated and began to "give up." Just as she gave up in despair, the temperature in her hand rapidly climbed five degrees Centigrade. Her response was euphoric. "It seemed she could 'feel' the difference between the states associated with decreasing and increasing temperature. The feeling of giving up in this case seemed to be associated with detachment and objectivity, and the meter immediately responded."[2]

This paradoxical sort of gaining control by giving up strenuous effort is often reported by those participating in such experiments. Subjects in biofeedback training discover that the more they *try* to produce a particular effect, the less successful they are. Trying leads to tension and frustration. When they relax and observe the changes in the instrument recording the biofeedback effects, they find that they become successful in controlling internal processes and even brain waves. This kind of control is linked to tranquil detachment and the term "passive volition" has been used to describe it.

> Passive is synonymous in this context with detached, objective, non-emotional, non-anxious....Active volition is "turned off"....One of the...trainees who had suffered from migraine headaches for over forty years went through several stages of increased amelioration, terminating in an unusual degree of control through passive volition. Upon sensing an incipient migraine

attack....She merely focuses on serenity and says to the
blood in her head, "Go back down," and continues her
activities without further concern. Anxiety, or trying to
force the blood to "go back down" (active volition),
seems to be accompanied by a physiological change
opposite to the one desired....[3]

In the Menninger experiment where Jack Schwartz was demonstrating control over bleeding and pain by passing a needle
through his biceps, he explained that "he never forced his body
to do things by will-power, but *asked* if it would agree to it....
he asked the 'unconscious' if it would be willing to do it again
and he had to wait for the answer." The researcher notes the
similarity between this "asking the unconscious" and the concept
of "passive volition."[4] In his work with the control of alpha
waves, Swami Rama similarly indicated that he adopted a
passive, relaxed state of mind, imagining "an empty blue sky,
with a 'white cloud' sometimes coming by." Using this process,
he was immediately able to produce seventy per cent alpha waves
over a five-minute period.[5]

Moving to a state in which volition is "passive" rather than
"active" seems to involve moving to a state in which thinking is
organized non-verbally, using images. For example, the use of
images is employed in treating some patients with psychosomatic
problems. A woman who had nervous spasms of the large
intestine was taught to imagine she was "moving a warm blanket"
over the abdomen to relax the colon.[6] Here images are used to
give the body instructions. Thinking is done with pictures rather
than words.

The manipulation of spatial figures characteristic of this level
of functioning is also familiar in artistic endeavor. Here, too,
images are used to free one from the restrictions of verbal thinking.
Images enable the artist to go beyond verbal logic and express
intuitions and understanding that are normally not available.
Jung capitalized on this fact, getting his patients to paint and

draw in order to gain access to their higher integrative tendencies. There is a sort of spatial logic that guides the use of picture thinking that transcends the narrow verbal reasoning of the ego. It is the first access to a level of observation and expression that extends beyond the materialistic thinking of the ego-state. In yoga psychology, this is just the first hint of higher levels of consciousness. But it is very important in that it gives one some notion that there are other kinds of awareness that lie beyond the usual verbal thinking.*

Researchers have suggested that when one wills a certain physiological change while maintaining a tranquil, detached state of mind, the body responds in the way that is being visualized.[7] In the move to this new level of control, the decision-making power has become more refined. There is a shift to a "passive" from "active" volition, accompanied by a shift in the use of and manipulation of images rather than of words and ideas. This new way of controlling physiological processes brings what was before unconscious within the scope of a higher perspective. The conscious and a portion of what was before unconscious are now simultaneously held in awareness. By definition, then, a new level of integration has appeared.

Brain Waves and Higher Volition

Beta waves on the EEG correspond to normal waking consciousness while alpha indicates a more relaxed, tranquil state. The consciousness correlated with theta waves, which are even slower than alpha, is characterized by a dream-like or "reverie" state during which one is immersed in a world of images. It has long been known that these dream-like states (called "hypnogogic

---

* The use of a non-verbal exercise as an introduction to the exploration of higher consciousness is beautifully described by Eugen Herrigel, a German philosopher who studied archery under a Japanese master, in a little book called Zen and the Art of Archery (Vintage Books, New York, 1971).

experiences") play some part in scientific and artistic creation. The chemist Kekule, who discovered the ring structure of benzene, was dozing lightly when he observed the atoms dancing before his eyes. They fell into rows, twisting like snakes, and when one of these snakes "seized hold of its own tail" he awoke in a flash and working from this image developed the ring structure of benzene.

With such anecdotes in mind, research was initiated which would train students to produce this kind of experience through the induction of theta waves in a biofeedback setting. By watching the biofeedback machine which reflected the percentage of alpha and theta waves, the trainee learned to voluntarily enter this state. The results showed an increase in images during the alpha and theta practices as well as another, unforeseen, result: There were an "unexpected number of self-integrative experiences." One subject reported that, "It seems that last Saturday night something happened to me. Something clicked and I've felt different ever since. I'm calmer and I feel more inner peace. I just kind of slipped into a state of mind and I haven't left it much since...." As a result of these experiences one student described the following change: "I'm able to let myself get out of the way and enjoy things more." Others reported "feelings of greater involvement in whatever they were doing," seeing things in perspective, and feelings of detachment from such tasks as writing papers which now "just seem to fall together."[8] A number of archetypal images (such as those which had been described by Jung) were also reported. This state of reverie and image-oriented thinking seems to involve a level of functioning which gives rise to increased integration within the personality.

At the "ego" level of functioning, much of the internal world is not included in the definition of *I-ness*. For this reason its volition is exerted by overriding and subduing. At this level of functioning the internal milieu must be coordinated by its own set of instinctual, unconscious governors, since any attempt to control one aspect of this system without an understanding of the whole, risks throwing the entire system out of balance. The body cannot be manhandled. It cannot be forced beyond its limits to serve the narrow purposes of the ego's limited "I." What Proscauer called "living too intentionally" is associated with uncoordinated use of the internal organs or "psychosomatic disease." At the "ego-level" of development the unconscious mind easily gets into power struggles with the body or with parts of the personality which are outside its awareness.*

Only when a higher level of integration comes into play can this struggle within be consistently avoided. Otherwise the attempt to control can produce only inner conflict. From this perspective it is clear, as pointed out by Assagioli, that:

> will does not produce results by means of sheer force
> (as the "Victorian" conception of the will maintained),
> but through the regulation and harmonizing of the other
> psychological functions, which it "steers" toward the
> chosen goal. [9]

Integration through Meditation

Just as the ego can become involved in struggles with the body, it can also become involved in struggles to control thoughts. For example, there is a traditional story in yoga about a student of meditation who went to his teacher and asked, "What should I think about when I meditate?" The teacher replied, "You may think about anything you wish as long as you do not think about monkeys." The student went home to meditate, but during his session he found to his dismay that the more he tried to keep the thought of monkeys from his mind, the stronger and more

* This is related to the psychoanalytic concept of the immature ego struggling with repressed impulses. In the course of therapy, these repressed or unconscious aspects of the personality are brought into view and integrated into the personality through growth of this ego. But the possibility of extending the ego's conscious control into those areas of the unconscious where physiological processes are regulated has not been explored in psychoanalysis.

overpowering it became. This example illustrates that when the ego is trying to suppress thoughts, the thoughts become more intense. Like the earlier example of temperature training in biofeedback, the result is just the opposite of what is desired. The example of "thinking of monkeys" illustrates to students an improper approach to meditation—attempting forcibly to exclude thoughts from the mind. The more effective approach is to allow the thoughts which come to pass through one's consciousness without becoming involved in a struggle with them.

One of the most common mistakes made by beginners in meditation is that they *try* too hard to achieve a goal. They use their "ego-will," their "active" volition in an attempt to force relaxation. Their very effort makes calming the mind impossible. By assuming a more passive volitional attitude, that is, by using a relaxed approach, the result, e.g., calming the mind, follows naturally. The meditation teacher helps the student to learn this new approach to controlling the agitated mind by continually stressing the necessity of maintaining a calm, detached attitude while observing his mental processes.*

When one turns inward to explore the inner space during meditation, he will encounter the stream of thoughts which is flowing through the lower mind *(manas)*. These thoughts parade before him as though on a stage. It may happen that he finds one of them to be either attractive or repulsive. If so, as his attention centers on it, the parade stops for a moment and the thought begins to enact its little drama. Objectivity, the neutral stance of *buddhi,* is lost.

It is for such reasons that in yoga meditation, the student is given a mantra, a special sound, on which he focuses his attention.†

---

* In the Burmese satipatthana school of Buddhist meditation, this is called "bare attention": the ability to attend to thoughts without either condemning them or becoming too enamoured of them.

† Other systems of meditation may use other objects to serve a similar purpose of focusing attention: e.g., in Zen meditation attention is often focused on the breath. In yoga, a visual image may also be used.

This provides a base from which he can observe without becoming drawn into the drama of thoughts parading before him. It constantly leads him back toward objectivity and non-attachment. As he becomes less involved with the parade on the stage these thoughts begin to fade into the background. The mantra thus draws him toward a higher state of consciousness.

From the point of view of yoga psychology, the thoughts that stream into consciousness arise from the bed of chitta. Metaphorically, this may be described as bubbles rising to the surface of a lake. When such thoughts and memories surface in the conscious mind, they can be allowed to burst and dissipate. This will occur as long as the rising thoughts are observed impartially and without attachment. But when one becomes entangled with a memory, it acquires new energy. Involvement with a thought in this way gives it more "weight." Then, when it is finally released from attention by the conscious mind, it sinks once more into the bed of the lake, rather than bursting and disappearing from the surface. Its power in the unconscious mind is enhanced.

It is *buddhi* which decides to energize and strengthen a thought in this fashion or to allow it to dissipate and disappear from the unconscious.   Through *buddhi's* discriminating capacity those thoughts and memories which contribute to the evolution of consciousness can be retained and strengthened. Those which hinder growth can be allowed to evaporate and disappear. For example, the thought "I am hungry" could lead to "I wonder what's for dinner" or perhaps to "I should check to see if there are enough groceries before the store closes." If the initial thought is allowed to pass by, such involvement doesn't develop. Those thoughts which lead outwards toward entanglement with the distractions of material, physical preoccupations are given up during the meditative process. Those thoughts which spiral inward, leading to deeper introspection and enhanced awareness are solidified: "This is my time for meditation. I'll think about other things later." Or: "I will just observe."

The more *buddhi* performs this function, the more sensitive and effective it becomes. Through observing the results of different thoughts it comes to judge more astutely which are helpful and which are not. This ability eventually spills over into life outside meditation. *Buddhi* says, "I don't want to listen to this argument. It's just filling my mind with static that I'll have to clean out later!" It begins to learn to select its stimulus field.

The conscious mind then serves as a sort of "gatekeeper" for the unconscious. What it focuses on returns to the unconscious to have renewed and strengthened effect on the total mind. What it allows to pass out, dissipates, losing its influence and disappearing from the inner world. In this way the content of the personal unconscious can be slowly transformed, leaving a cleaner, clearer path to the higher levels of consciousness.

The use of the mantra is one method that is particularly effective here. It is prescribed for the student by his teacher from the vantage point of a state of consciousness that is more evolved. The mantra is selected for the student's particular mind and its peculiarities. It gives him something to "hang onto" so as not to be pulled into thoughts he doesn't wish to reinforce. Moreover, when he concentrates on it, it is itself strengthened and weighted, sinking into the unconscious. In this way it gradually fills the unconscious with itself, displacing and replacing distracting thoughts. In this way *chitta*, the memory bank, is eventually filled with mantra.

Because the mantra is an expression of a more evolved consciousness, it offers a unique link with that higher level. For this reason, it not only makes the path to higher consciousness clearer by replacing interfering thoughts, its gradual incorporation pulls consciousness toward that state. When *chitta* becomes filled with mantra, the bubbles that arise are not disturbing. They are merely memories of the mantra. Then, instead of distracting from the movement toward higher consciousness, they assist.*

* For a fuller explanation of the nature and function of mantra, see *Yoga Psychology, Vol. 1, A Practical Guide to Meditation,* by Swami Ajaya.

ATTACHMENT AND ANXIETY

When consciousness is dazzled by the attractive qualities of one of the thoughts parading before it across the mental stage and abandons its position of objectivity, becoming caught up in the performance, this is described in yoga as "attachment." During meditation, the thought of owning a car may lead to fantasies of how envious friends might react. The result is a loss of objectivity. The thought, rather than bubbling to the surface, bursting and evaporating, is reinforced.   The dissipation and discharge of troublesome memory traces ceases.   Instead, this one is re-weighted, and dropped back down.

The tendency to become drawn into thoughts and fantasies and the difficulty in disentangling oneself from them not only disrupts meditation, it can have a disastrous effect on one's outside life as well.   The reweighted memory traces will rise again during one's everyday life to influence behavior.   They are the raw material of which daydreams are made as well as the impetus for many of our actions.   Once the fantasy of the impressive automobile gets out of hand, one may feel an irresistible urge to act on it.   Although not financially able, he will hurry to the car dealer, sign a contract and go deeper into debt.   There follows worry about meeting the payments, concern about losing the car and preoccupation with the tarnished image he would present to his friends if this happened.   Now he is thoroughly caught up in his attachment to the automobile and his anxieties may show themselves in many ways.   Any tendency to develop psychosomatic problems such as ulcers, insomnia, or elevated blood pressure will be accentuated. Or he may experience an aggravation of such symptoms as restlessness and uneasiness.   Just as one can become caught up in the thoughts parading through the mind, he can also become entangled with the objects passing him in the world.   When this tendency to become attached or "addicted" to objects carries over into various areas of life and the pattern is repeated with other objects and in personal relations, tension and anxiety may become pervasive. A possessive entanglement with people is a frequent cause of such fear and anxiety. For example, a young person who depends on her boyfriend for a sense of her own self-worth may be unable to give up her relationship with him when it is appropriate to do so. She becomes clinging and his efforts to withdraw make her anxious and afraid. In yoga psychology, some version of this sort of "addiction" or attachment is seen as the underlying basis of all anxiety.

Anxiety is that mental-emotional state experienced when there is apprehension about either losing something that one craves or being unable to get it. Many such attachments exist outside awareness. Though one may acknowledge, on being questioned, that he is attached to ordinary possessions such as his house, his car or to his family, he normally doesn't think in such terms. Nevertheless, some underlying concern about losing these objects may play an important role in creating the anxiety he experiences. But ordinarily he remains unaware of what it is "that he is anxious about." As long as one is "addicted" to objects or people, feeling that he must have them to maintain the security of the "I," a vague but pervasive anxiety is likely. To the extent that one remains more flexible and psychologically independent of possessions and other persons, anxiety is less. Relationships are more mutually rewarding when they are free of feelings of addiction and dependency. In both yoga and modern psychotherapy a primary goal is the overcoming of such attachments with the development of a broader, more detached perspective from which to view them.

In psychoanalytic therapy, for example, the technique of free-association is used to allow the parade of thoughts to become "visible." As the therapist and patient listen to this chain of associations, from time to time it becomes clear that the patient's ego is becoming drawn into one of the thoughts, and involved with it. This "resistance" to the flow of associations gives the ego away and reveals where its attachments lie. This may happen, for example, when an image comes along that the ego relies on for self-esteem. There will be a halt in the flow of associations as the cherished ego embellishment is defended and justified, or while the ego identifies with, and luxuriates in it. In such cases detached observation clearly comes to a standstill. This can be seen by both the therapist and the patient and through this process, the nature of the ego's attachments is learned and eventually resolved. The therapist serves as a sort of anchor in the objective, detached position, reminding the patient when necessary that he has slipped from his role as observer and has been seduced into entering one of the dramas on the mental stage.

In yoga meditation the flow of mental events is also observed, this time privately, while the mantra serves as one's anchor to detachment. But again the parade is stopped when awareness becomes dominated by the sensory stimuli, memories, instincts and impulses that are flowing through the lower mind *(manas).* To the extent that one can free himself from entanglement with this train of thoughts and observe them, there is an opportunity to learn about and come to understand the foibles of the lower levels of functioning which must eventually be coordinated and integrated. That level of awareness which observes is that which will control and synthesize the opposing tendencies it sees.

In both cases, in psychoanalytic therapy and in meditation, the aim is to avoid becoming involved with any of the thoughts which are flowing past. The aim is *not,* however, to struggle against such entanglement. When the entanglement occurs, this is where the work is done. It is by observing such occurrences that the higher integrating capacity can extend its field of awareness and coordination. In yoga, as *I-ness* or *ahankara* expands and a more detached and objective *buddhi* develops, there is less entanglement in attachments. This is reflected by a decrease in anxiety.

RESEARCH ON THE REDUCTION
OF ANXIETY THROUGH MEDITATION

According to yoga psychology, anxiety stems from attachment. Since meditation is a process for reducing attachment to thoughts and objects, we might expect that those persons engaged in meditation would, at least temporarily, show some reduction in anxiety. In fact, recent research studies on persons while they are mentally remembering a mantra* "demonstrate a set of physiological responses that parallel what is usually taken to represent an unanxious state": sweating decreases, breathing slows down, and although less oxygen is used, there is a decrease in the amount of metabolic wastes in the blood. The brain wave pattern shows an increase in alpha activity, which is associated with calmness. There was also, in certain cases, the appearance of theta activity on the EEG. This theta activity would suggest the attainment of a state where reverie and imagery are prominent. It suggests that a state of consciousness beyond the usual ego level is beginning to appear. [10] The psychophysiological changes produced by meditation seem to be the opposite of those seen in the "fight or flight" reaction. This "alarm" response is similar to what can be seen in anxiety syndromes or psychosomatic disorders. It was hypothesized that the practice of meditation would be useful in reducing such reactions. To test this, thirty meditators and thirty non-meditators were placed in an anxiety-arousing situation by showing them a film which vividly depicted maiming accidents. Physiological and psychological measures indicated that when subjects meditated before being

---

* In yoga, repeated remembering (mental repetition) of mantra is called japa yoga. One version of this which has become popular in America is called "Transcendental Meditation." This has become sufficiently widespread so that it has been possible to statistically evaluate its effects, something not usually possible with the more advanced and difficult meditational techniques. The use of mantra is a small part of the more comprehensive system of raja yoga. Since Transcendental Meditation is not actually an exclusive or unique method we would expect that results of research on it would be generalizable to the practice of mantra meditation by beginners throughout the yoga tradition.

shown the film, they returned to a less emotionally aroused state more quickly after viewing the accidents.* [11]

Meditation also seems to have certain effects that are longer lasting. Some of these changes are similar to the ones described earlier in those students trained in theta production through biofeedback. Persons who practice mantra meditation have been found to show evidences of increased integration in their life activities. For example, one study reports that eighty-three percent of a large group of drug users practicing this kind of meditation gave up the use of drugs. The subjects made such comments as, "All aspects of my life have become better: in school, at work, my interpersonal life—everything." [14]

In another research project, one hundred and thirty-eight experienced meditators were compared with fifty-nine subjects about to begin meditation and thirty-nine non-meditators. It was found that besides showing "significantly less usage of all drugs, including alcohol, cigarettes and even coffee....meditators reported general increases in positive mood states, and....they live in a less stressed, more regular life style than the typical American." [15] Elsewhere, psychological testing to measure "self-actualization" was administered to a group of fifteen students before and after two months of "transcendental meditation" (mantra meditation). In contrast to a control group, they showed statistically significant changes in the direction of increased self-actualization on a widely used personality inventory. Meditators scored higher on scales measuring "inner directedness,"

---

* Those who were experienced meditators also responded to threat with less subjective anxiety. They seemed to anticipate and to adapt to stress better than non-meditators. [12] In another study using breath rather than mantra as the object of concentration, twenty-six children in the third grade of a school in a disadvantaged urban area were taught meditation and practiced twice each week for eighteen weeks. When compared with non-meditators, the meditators were "less test anxious as measured by the Test Anxiety Scale for Children." The researcher suggests that they may have achieved this "by shifting attention from anticipated dangers associated with failures of achievement to the moment by moment flow of ongoing...experience." [13]

"spontaneity," "acceptance" and "self-regard." [16]   Subsequent
research has tended to confirm and replicate these findings. * [17]

Some of these studies taken individually have inadequate
experimental and control situations or use questionable tests of
the variables they purport to measure. Replication with better
research designs is clearly needed. The question of what extent
entering into a new value system and to what degree the actual
practice of meditation contributes to the effects noted has not
been adequately explored.   Taken as a whole, however, the
results of these studies are remarkably consistent. They suggest
that even for relatively inexperienced persons meditation produces
a state of calmness reflected by decreased arousal, the appearance
of alpha waves, and a tendency toward personal growth.

SCIENTIFIC EVALUATION
OF HIGHER MEDITATIVE STATES

During the usual waking consciousness, the mind jumps
quickly from one thought to another. It is, in a sense, distracted
by the many sights, noises, smells, etc. of the outside world, and
the multitude of memories and recollections from inside. The
rapid flashing of thoughts on the screen of *manas* is reflected in
the brain wave pattern (EEG) by a rapid, irregular pattern of
jerky waves. These are called beta waves. Alpha waves, on the
other hand, indicate a more tranquil mental state.† The thoughts

---

* A study of students who were learning to be counselors also suggests that
self-actualization increases with the practice of Zen Meditation. Counselors who
practiced meditation over a four-week period also improved significantly in their
empathic ability.   The experimenter concludes that the practice of meditation
"holds far more potential for personal growth...than we have previously supposed."[18]

† It should be noted that brain wave patterns are only *correlates* of the various
states of consciousness. The correlation is not perfect, and while monitoring the EEG
is useful as a research tool, it cannot be assumed that every person who produces theta
waves for example, is experiencing the same sort of consciousness.

are slower, less frantic; the EEG pattern is more regular, rhythmic and less rapid. The mind is relatively calm and peaceful. But a sudden noise or flash of light will interrupt the alpha rhythm. The EEG of a person in an alpha state will then return immediately to faster, more jerky activity. Alpha is normally stopped in this way by noises or bright lights. One's serenity is disrupted and his quiet detachment lost. We might say the foothold he had in a comparatively advanced consciousness slips, and he topples back into the preoccupations of the ordinary level of awareness and the distractions of the lower mind. One is not startled by every sound and light. If a piercing noise is repeated, the mind gradually becomes accustomed to it. When a bell is rung regularly, for instance, the alpha rhythm is "blocked" only the first few times. After that the noise comes to be "expected," and alpha continues undisturbed. "Alpha blocking" no longer occurs.

Zen and yoga meditators who had been practicing intensively for some years, however, were found to depart from this usual pattern of "alpha blocking" in their reactions to sudden stimuli. In one study of Zen meditators, alpha was blocked *every* time the light was flashed.[19] They didn't "learn to ignore it," so to speak. Though the mind was in a calm alpha state, their awareness of the world was in a sense heightened. Zen meditation is a process of learning to live in the present moment. Thus the world is always new and unique. Every sound is a "new sound." Every repetition of a sound interrupts the alpha flow as though it were the first. Thus in the experiment, one moment's experience did not dull the vividness of the next. No expectation about the future developed. Apparently, each event was experienced as unique in a way that recalls the fresh, open innocence of the child.

A similar openness to each sense impression was seen in advanced yoga meditators. But in their case it was observed when they were *not* actually sitting in meditation. There was alpha blocking with each stimulus, as though it were new, during their "normal waking consciousness." They seemed to have carried their sense of immediacy and their ability to live totally in the present outside the meditation session. But, these evolved yogis presented a totally different picture during the period when they were actually meditating. At that time there was no response even to the first noise. It was as though it had not been heard. The brain wave pattern was not interrupted at all. There was no "blocking." The world of sensory impressions seemed to have been totally cut off from awareness. They were, apparently, practicing the "voluntary sensory deprivation" (called *pratyahara*) which we discussed earlier. Sensory input had been blanked out to allow an undisturbed exploration of the inner world and the ascent to higher states of consciousness. [20]

Some of the Zen meditators seemed to be involved in a more inner-directed experience than others. Out of the twenty-three Zen disciples studied in the above mentioned work, three of them, those who had been practicing the longest (twenty-one to forty years) showed a predominance of theta rhythms in the EEG towards the end of their meditative sessions. As we have noted, theta rhythms seem to be associated with a state of reverie, an inner exploration which moves through a world of images rather than words, to approach higher levels of consciousness and integration. These three priests who showed increase theta waves were also those selected out of the group by their masters as the most advanced. [21]

It would appear, then, that the movement from beta to alpha to theta states on EEG may correspond to a shift to progressively higher states of consciousness in meditation. The ability of an advanced yogi to move in and out of these states at will was demonstrated in research done at Menninger's with Swami Rama. In several preliminary sessions he experimented with the brain wave machine, learning which wave pattern was associated with each of the levels of consciousness he had mastered during his training in the Himalayas. After that he was able to produce at will the EEG pattern requested. "In one five-minute period of test, he produced theta waves seventy-five per cent of the time."

He commented that what he experienced at this time was a
"very noisy" inner space where all the things he had wanted to do
or he should have done, but did not do, etc. were tucked away.
In the terms of modern psychology we would say he had entered
a state of consciousness from which the "personal unconscious"
was accessible to awareness. [22]

Although moving successively from one stage of consciousness
to the next seems to bring an increase in awareness, control and
the ability to integrate, it would seem, paradoxically, that each
successive stage is characterized by less arousal of the central
nervous system. It is traditionally thought that the appearance of
alpha waves corresponds to an actual decrease in the activity of the
brain. Alpha waves reflect a lowered level of cortical excitatory
states.* With further synchronization and slowing of the brain
waves, cortical arousal decreases further and the theta pattern
appears. It would seem then that the evolution of higher consciousness brings a state of diminished arousal in the brain. In
meditation, the jerky rapid beta waves are replaced by the slower
alpha, and as meditation becomes deeper, theta waves begin to
appear.

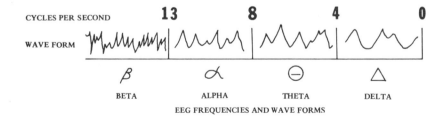

CYCLES PER SECOND   13   8   4   0

WAVE FORM

β α $\ominus$ $\triangle$

BETA   ALPHA   THETA   DELTA

EEG FREQUENCIES AND WAVE FORMS

* There is a review of a large body of literature on this point included in the article
by Kasamatsu & Hirai, *op cit.*

We might then wonder what happens at what is usually considered the stage of lowest nervous system arousal, the *delta* stage on the EEG. This is customarily seen only during the deepest stages of sleep when there seems to be the least central nervous system activity. During these periods even dreaming stops. The brain and even "the mind" seem to be more at rest. There are occasional reports of mental activity by patients awakened from this delta stage of sleep, but it has been suggested that this mental activity reflects transient passage through intermediate stages during the process of awakening. Patients wakened more rapidly seem to report less of this. Though there has been a great deal of research[23] on this, exactly what happens during delta sleep remains elusive. If decreased arousal means higher consciousness, then to be consistent, one would have to suggest that the delta state, which appears during dreamless sleep involves an even higher level of consciousness than theta.

SLEEP AND HIGHER CONSCIOUSNESS

Modern sleep researchers say that sleep includes two distinct states.[24] One is associated with dreaming and is identified in experiments by the observation of rapid eye movements (REM's). The other state, which seems less related to dreaming has often been called "deep sleep." There are no REM's and the brain wave pattern reaches its slowest rhythm. During a night's sleep one usually alternates between these two states, moving from a dream state down into deeper sleep and then back again. Such a cycle will ordinarily last about ninety minutes.

In many ways, dreaming is the most "aroused" of the sleep phases. The eyes begin to move rapidly and the mind seems busy with the imagery of the dream world. A person awakened at this point will describe scenes of life-like events involving persons and places that are reminiscent of the waking world. During this state, the heart rate becomes irregular, seemingly influenced by the dream events as it would be during the day by shifting situations and circumstances. The pupil opens and closes as though reacting to what it "sees" and there are sharp fluctuations in penile erection. The whole body seems on the verge of activity when it is compared with dreamless sleep.*

The dream state seems to be the crest in the sleep cycle, that which lies just below wakefulness. The waking person will ordinarily slow his brain wave rhythm only to the alpha state, whereas during dreaming the still slower theta waves are seen. As dreaming progresses, theta becomes more pronounced. During this time it reaches its maximum. The eyes begin to move jerkily with the REM's (rapid eye movements) which seem to indicate that the mind is busy with the imagery of the dream world. But this doesn't last all night. Gradually, after a half hour or so, the brain waves become even slower and the eye movement comes to a halt. Sleep now becomes "deepest" and the EEG moves into the delta range. During this period if one is awakened, he may have trouble orienting himself. It may even be difficult to rouse him. He's usually not aware of having been dreaming and may report little mental activity of any kind.

If the deep sleep is allowed to continue, it reaches a certain depth and then the process reverses. The EEG begins to speed up again, the waves become faster and the eye movements reappear. Now, once again, when the sleeper is awakened, a dream is interrupted and he is able to describe it. The sleep cycle has made a full swing and returned to dreaming. During a night's sleep this cycle is repeated a number of times. Each time the dip into deeper sleep is a bit less and the "peak" into dreaming sleep is a bit higher. With each cycle more time is

---

* The only exception to this is an overall *decrease* in muscle tone in the dream state, whereas there is a comparative *increase* in muscle tone in dreamless sleep. It is almost as though the muscular system must be "out of gear" during the dream state—otherwise the little muscle "twitches" that accompany dreams would become violent threshing about in the bed, making sleep quite impossible!

spent in dreaming and less in deep sleep. After the first five
or six hours most of the deep sleep is finished. When a need is
felt to sleep longer than this, what this really seems to indicate is
a need for more dreaming.

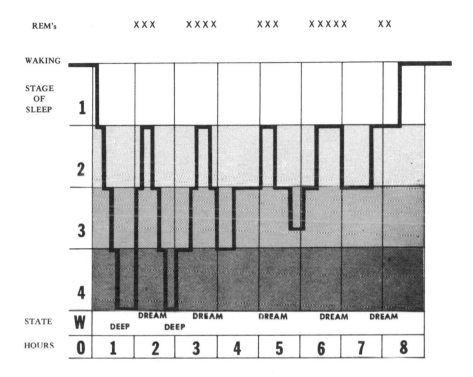

THE SLEEP CYCLE AND STAGES OF SLEEP

People vary a lot in their sleep needs, which probably means
they vary in their need for dreaming.[25] This may be related to the
quantity of the personality that is cut off from waking consciousness (repressed). When a huge portion of oneself is not integrated
into awareness, more time must be spent in dealing with it separately, in dreams. The personal unconscious, when it is larger,
requires more hours of one's sleep. Our understanding of this has
grown through the study of patients who have repressed much.

Their waking consciousness is restricted and narrow. But their personal unconscious is swollen with repressed material and they are "always tired." They require lots of sleep. The acute psychotic, by contrast, may require little sleep. His repression mechanism has broken down; his unconscious floods his conscious mind. He hallucinates vividly. Dream state and waking state have merged so sleep requirements often drop, because dreaming is no longer required. However, for most people, the dreaming state seems very necessary. Experimental subjects have been awakened each time dreaming began, allowing them to sleep but eliminating the dream phases of the cycle. After a few days they became increasingly nervous and upset. They began to be suspicious. In such cases the content of the personal unconscious begins to press into the waking consciousness. The world of images demands attention. The exiled portion of the personality insists on its share of the mind's time.

When a person undergoes successful therapy, the parts of himself which were relegated to the unconscious become reintegrated into his waking consciousness, and sleep requirements often become less.[26] Frequently, students who begin to practice meditation find the same to be true. Allowing the unconscious to come forward, permitting the thoughts to parade past on the inner stage, seems to substitute for dreaming. Moreover, as the thoughts are brought in this way, within the scope of the waking consciousness, the amount of repressed content in the personal unconscious gradually decreases. The need for any kind of dreaming is then less. Yoga teachers frequently find that their students who practice meditation regularly report needing an hour or two less sleep each night. But the amount of deep sleep required seems to vary little from person to person. It comes mainly during the first hours of sleep, so even those who "sleep little" get the usual quota (see diagram on previous page).

More advanced yogis sometimes practice a special kind of sleep called *yoga nidra.* They go voluntarily and deliberately into the deeper levels of sleep and stay there, eliminating the dream phases. The normal sleep cycle is not present. Only dreamless sleep is experienced. In this way, it is necessary to sleep only two or three hours a night. They apparently no longer need dream time and, moreover, have discovered some way to go directly to the delta stage, by-passing the usual lighter levels. Yet even for many advanced yogis, the need for dreamless sleep remains. Why is this? What basic requirements does it satisfy? Whereas the role of dreaming has become increasingly understood by modern psychology, the function of deep sleep has remained a mystery.

Dreamless Sleep and the Highest States of Consciousness

Freud suggested that dreaming sleep satisfies the need for coping with the personal unconscious and its repressed material. Jung went a step beyond this explanation and said that it gave glimpses of something more universal, something that could serve to integrate. Yoga psychology clarifies this even further: Dreams not only allow us to cope with the inner world of repressed material. They also put us in contact with the beginnings of higher consciousness. The world of images encompasses the personal unconscious and the beginnings of the transpersonal. The dark world of repressed conflict is brightened at moments with rays of light from a more evolved level of consciousness which is the true ruler of the world of inner imagery.

The waking consciousness is ordinarily restricted by the limitations of the narrow ego. Higher consciousness cannot be assimilated by it. So the mind works in shifts. It "leads two lives." It dwells in ego consciousness during the waking state. During dreaming sleep the cut-off aspects of the person, both negative and positive, come into prominence. The function of dreamless sleep becomes less mysterious and can be understood more easily when sleep is seen from this perspective. In yoga psychology the role of the delta state has long been recognized. It is the time when consciousness can leave its lower levels and reside in its true center. It is when the inner world can be suffused with the full light of the highest universal consciousness. The ego state of waking consciousness drops away. Moreover, the personal aspects of the unknown mind are temporarily abandoned. The memories, the problems, the troubled dream images are left behind. All the limitations of the personal unconscious are drowned out in the full light of the highest consciousness.

Of course we bring back no memory of this when we awake. The understanding of our usual consciousness is too frail to accommodate such a universal awareness. We only know that we awake from this deepest sleep refreshed and revitalized. Troubled dreams may cause us to toss and turn and wake feeling "more tired than before."* But the deeper stages of sleep leave us renewed, feeling once more "whole." Like sleep walkers carrying out a secret mission, we have, unbeknownst to ourselves, established contact with our innermost center. We are ready to face again the frenetic confusion of the world of attachments and worries.

The *Mandukya Upanishad*† says of this state which lies

---

* Sleeping "too long," probably means an increased proportion of dreams in relation to deep sleep.

† In the voluminous literature that is available today in modern and ancient psychology the *Mandukya Upanishad* along with its *Karika* (explanatory comments) is said by the yogic scholars to contain the most highly sophisticated description of the four states of human consciousness, viz.: waking, dreaming, dreamless sleep and *turiya.* The fourth state *(turiya)* which lies beyond the other three, is described by the great yogis as a state of constant awareness. Gaudapadacharya, grand guru of the famous Shankara is traditionally recognized as the codifier of this psychological/philosophical system. In Sanskrit literature, especially in Vedanta, the *Karika* is considered to be unique among the works on meditative psychology, standing as it does on its own strength, dependent on neither assumptions about God nor any other support. This book is a model of succinct, concise writing. It might be thought of as the very foundation of Vedanta psychology. Highly evolved yogis teach their students this particular book after teaching the *Kathopanishad, Ishopanishad* and several other Upanishads as a preparation. Though simple and straight forward, it is extremely profound and laden with meaning, so that an understanding of it is usually impossible for those who have not been properly prepared.

beyond waking consciousness and dreaming sleep:

> The third aspect of the Self is the Universal Person in
> dreamless sleep—*prajna*....He experiences neither strife
> nor anxiety, he is said to be blissful....*Prajna* is the
> Lord of All....He knows all....The sphere of *prajna* is
> deep sleep in whom all experiences become unified
> or undifferentiated, who is...a mass of consciousness...
> who is full of bliss...who is the path leading to the
> knowledge of the other states.[27]

But this universal state is split off. It is experienced separately.
It is not remembered. The waking consciousness—even the
dreaming consciousness—are too limited to cope with it. It
remains unknown, a four-hour mystery that takes place each
night, hidden between our dreams leaving occasionally just a
hint of "other-worldliness."

Though this way of understanding dreamless sleep seems very
foreign to Western thinking, the Upanishads go even further.
They describe a fourth state. It is still more advanced than the
third. It is what results when the expanded consciousness is
brought back from dreamless sleep into dreaming and waking
consciousness. This is considered more evolved than the third
state because it is the result of a massive reintegration. The
universality of deep sleep is carried over into the other levels of
consciousness. One maintains the all-encompassing awareness,
the serene and universal consciousness constantly. He maintains
contact with the brilliant light of cosmic awareness while also
remaining in touch with the usual levels of waking consciousness.
This "fourth state" is called *turiya*. It is the perspective from
which all can be observed, controlled and integrated. It brings
total awareness of all the compartments of the mind, all the
lower levels of consciousness.

For example, the dream state becomes totally accessible. A
yogi who is approaching this highest state of development can
maintain consciousness during the period that would normally be

dreaming. This explains how he might be able to practice continuous deep sleep; how he would be conscious enough of the sleep cycle to enter it where he wished and stay as long as he needed. It also implies that one could maintain awareness of the external world even while in the delta stages of sleep. If consciousness is truly integrated, then from the vantage point of this higher level both the dreamless sleep and the external world should be perceptible. This contradicts all our customary ways of thinking about deep sleep, of course. It is normally assumed that one is totally oblivious during this deepest level of the sleep cycle, that he can be aware of nothing around him.

In an experiment done with Swami Rama at the Menninger Foundation, this usual conception of delta level sleep was found to be inadequate.

> After producing theta waves, the Swami said he knew exactly how the inner states of awareness were arranged in respect to the brain wave frequency bands. Then he said, 'tomorrow I will consciously make delta waves for you.' I replied that I doubted that he would succeed in that because he would have to be sound asleep in order to produce delta. He laughed at this and said that I would think that he was asleep but that he would be conscious of everything that occured in the experimental room.
>
> Before this test he asked how long I would like to have him remain in the delta state. I said that 25 minutes would be alright and he said he would bring himself out at that time. After about five minutes of meditation, lying down with his eyes shut, the Swami began producing delta waves, which we had never before seen in his record. In addition, he snored gently. Alyce, without having told Swami that she was going to say anything (she was in the experimental room observing him during this test) then made a statement in a

low voice, 'Today the sun is shining, but tomorrow it may rain.' Every five minutes she made another statement and after 25 minutes had passed the Swami roused himself and said that someone with sharp heels had walked on the floor above and made a click, click, click noise during the test, and a door had been slammed twice somewhere in the building and that Mrs. Green had said—and here he gave her statements verbatim, except for the last half of the fourth sentence, of which he had the gist correct though not the words. I was very much impressed because in listening from the control room, I had heard her sentences, but could not remember them all, and I was supposed to have been awake.[28]

Yoga nidra can be considered "semi-*samadhi*" in which the consciousness remains in an active state while the body, nervous system and brain remain completely relaxed. This might be thought of as voluntary, fully conscious sleep. The sleeper remains alert, observing himself sleep. It is said that those who know the techniques of *yoga nidra,* by slowly increasing the duration of their meditation have reached the point where they no longer need the kind of sleep that most people require. Advanced yogis consider spending eight hours in sleep a waste of time. Gandhi made a practice of determining before he went to bed exactly how long he would sleep—averaging about two and a half hours. Napoleon Bonapart apparently had a somewhat similar ability. It is said that he often slept while on horseback, but that he was always fully alert the moment the occasion demanded it.

This recalls the ancient Indian saying that a yogi should sleep "like a dog naps": fully alert, though completely relaxed. His sleep is under his control. Ordinary sleep is, by contrast, a state of deep inertia. *Yoga nidra,* on the other hand, is a deep meditative state, which approaches *turiya,* the state beyond

waking, dreaming and sleeping. *Turiya* is considered to be the
most highly evolved state of consciousness *(samadhi)* and is
attained through the persistent and systematic practice of meditation. In this state, yogis claim that the mind does not need to
express itself at all through the use of the brain. The mind or,
more correctly, consciousness, is withdrawn deliberately from
the functions of the central nervous system. Though this may
sound preposterous from the perspective of current Western
ideas, in Eastern psychology the mind and brain are seen as
totally different and are clearly distinguished from one another.
The mind controls the brain. The brain is a physical instrument
of the thoughts, emotions and desires.

> It is true that the mind usually functions in ordinary
> persons through the nervous system and brain cells,
> just as electricity functions and is manifested through
> wires and electrical apparatus. Yet one can not
> conclude that the electricity and the wires are identical.
> Similarly, the mind in its functionings, conscious or
> otherwise, cannot be identified with the instruments
> through which it works or has expression. [29]

This writing from the point of view of Indian psychology,
maintains that, in the superconscious state, "the mind can
function without the help of the nervous system." [30] Though
this is clearly at variance with presently accepted notions of
mind-body interaction, its implications bear examining. Modern
psychology's concept of the relationship between psychological
and physiological functioning is at best fuzzy and we cannot deny
that it needs further clarification.

Yoga sees consciousness and the nervous system as fully
separable entities. During *turiya* the central nervous system
(which is part of the physical sheath) is said to be in a state of
even less arousal than during dreamless or delta sleep. If this
were true one would expect EEG activity to be minimal. This
would be in line with our previous observation, that at each stage,

moving to a higher level of consciousness is accompanied by a decrease in arousal of the brain. Though we would expect some activity in the lower, more primitive centers of the brain to persist in order to maintain the functioning of the body, if what the yogis claim is true, the higher cortical centers should be essentially at rest. The brain wave pattern should be nearly "flat." In fact, the activity of the central nervous system during the state of *turiya* has not yet been studied by modern science. Confirmation of the yogic hypothesis would clearly have profound implications for our basic understanding of the relationship between mind and body.

From what we have seen thus far, the levels of consciousness usually associated with beta, alpha, theta and delta waves seem to form a continuum. Beta is related to the most outward and materially oriented level of experiencing. It is the "lowest" in terms of yoga psychology, whereas delta corresponds to a much higher state of consciousness. There is perhaps a highest level where brain waves would be even slower and barely detectable. Consciousness dwells in each room successively at regular intervals; so long as it is unable to dwell in all simultaneously. Until integration of the different parts of the inner world is achieved, they are experienced separately. Modern psychology accounts for this in the language of instincts: we have a sleep "need," a dream "need," a "need" for dreamless sleep.

Yoga offers a systematic approach to gradually integrating these levels so that man can become a unified whole, so that the anxiety and mental disturbance that occur in the lower levels of body and mind can be dissolved in the understanding of higher levels of integration. This is accomplished in the simplest way: the modes of consciousness that are already part of daily life, but experienced separately, are brought together. Our fragmented existence is integrated. The consciousness of the "outer world," of the dream world and of the dreamless state are pulled together and seen simultaneously from the height of an unlimited non-verbal plane of awareness that can accommodate all of them.

CHAPTER SIX
"THE SELF"

"Beyond all Sheaths is the Self."

Taittiriya Upanishad, II. 6

chapter 6
PSYCHOSIS TO MYSTICSM: JOURNEY TO THE SELF.

As we have seen, Eastern thought is based both on the appreciation that man has the potential to attain states of consciousness that are increasingly advanced, and on the experience of those who have disciplined themselves sufficiently to enter such states. It also maintains that much of the mind ordinarily lies outside one's awareness, an idea which finds its counterparts in the Freudian notion of the personal unconscious and the Jungian concept of the collective unconscious. These different areas of the unknown mind that ordinarily lie outside awareness are experienced independently in dreaming and dreamless sleep. The gradual expansion of one's waking consciousness to include more and more of these areas leads to expansion of one's self concept and drastic alterations in his concept of reality. As this continues, there is a recurring process of metamorphosis, consciousness becoming "higher" or more evolved. As far as yoga is concerned, it is this process of expanding awareness that underlies psychological growth, and this is the essence of psychological development.

Although he is sometimes limited to suppressing behavior that is disruptive or destructive through the use of tranquilizers or electroshock therapy, for example, the psychotherapist is usually interested in re-instituting the growth process. If this is his goal then he must not only understand the process of growth and evolution but also be able to identify the obstacles that can interrupt progress along this path. If he is to help, the therapist must have a clear grasp of the traps and pitfalls that lie along the way and that can bring to a halt the natural, joyful process of exploration and self-discovery.

From the perspective of yoga psychology, it is the clinging to a familiar, and hence relatively secure, concept of reality that is seen as the most basic obstacle to the process of growth. When one refuses to let go of a narrow and limited way of seeing the world and other persons he becomes locked into a sort of repetitious pattern. The sense of exploration and discovery ceases and the process of growth grinds to a halt. Stagnation sets in, and one's emotions, thoughts and social relations take on a feeling of sterility and emptiness. Any of a variety of psychopathological syndromes may begin to emerge in such a case.

The more severe and unresponsive cases of "mental illness" are simply a more entrenched holding on that continues despite many confrontations with reality that make the clinging seem bizarre and out of place. In yoga psychology there is less interest in distinguishing between the person who has clung to his entrenched patterns to the point of bizarreness and the person who is neurotically or even what we would call "normally" clinging to a narrow construction of "reality." In each case, there is an acceptance of a limited definition of reality which Patanjali calls *avidya* or "ignorance." *Avidya* means "absence of *vidya*." *Vidya* is that knowledge or wisdom which penetrates *all* superficiality and illusion.*

A stagnated and limited version of reality implies, by definition, a stagnant and narrow definition of oneself. This limited self-concept is called *asmita.* In Patanjali's system, *avidya* and *asmita* are called *kleshas,* or "causes of misery." They are five in number. Besides 1) *avidya* and 2) *asmita,* he lists: 3) attachment *(raga),* 4) aversion *(dvesa)* and finally 5) the fear of death.† From the perspective of Patanjali's psychology, these are the cause of all fear, anxiety and depression. Even when they may not be operating with enough strength to produce what we would recognize as psychopathology, they are nevertheless what is preventing the average person from realizing his capacity for higher consciousness. In this way the *kleshas* are both obstacles to growth as well as sources of suffering.‡

Yoga contrasts with modern psychotherapy in that it was not developed as a system for treating the disabled, but rather as a training method for the able. The range of growth that is focused on is different. Psychotherapy concentrates primarily on the areas of growth that lie just before the ego. Yoga is interested primarily in development and growth beyond the ego. The training of yoga is geared to those who have already worked their way through the

---

* Patanjali writes, then, from an absolute point of view. The Yoga Sutras are not like a modern text book on psychotherapy in that the deficits in psychological development which the Sutras describe are not overcome when one reaches what is normally regarded as maturity. They are, rather, written as a guide to the expansion of consciousness to its ultimate, and Patanjali's remarks about *avidya* are worded so as to be applicable to one's limitations, no matter how much reduced they may be, no matter how far along the path of personal evolution they may occur. Even one who is actively moving along this path is still a victim of *avidya.* He is completely free of it only when he reaches the highest state of consciousness.

† For a thorough and authoritative treatment of the *kleshas,* see *Yoga Philosophy of Patanjali.* 1

‡ The elimination of the experience of dukkha or pain is a central focus in both Buddhist and Samkhya psychologies. The *Samkhya Karika* along with its commentary presents the essential teachings of Buddhist psychology on the causes of pain and its removal through a more profound understanding of the way in which the individual fits into the context of nature and the universe.2

more massive attachments to the point of a "dissatisfied nor-mality," those who are searching for avenues of further growth despite the fact that they are, in the eyes of society, well adapted and acceptably productive. Those who we in the West would call mentally ill are, in the Eastern tradition, in the class of those who have not yet learned to concentrate the mind, and are therefore unable to benefit from yoga training. The everyday frustrations, disappointments, and experiences of the world are seen as their teacher, slowly encouraging the development of their higher mental capacities much as nature nurtures the plant which grows in the wild. The world is seen as their mental hospital, the field of experiences which provides situations where realistic response is necessary or suffering is more acute. Through the lessons learned in this way they are led gradually but inevitably to feel their way toward more mature and less disturbed functioning. As a system of training, yoga shows little interest in tracing the intricacies of those extreme psychological disturbances that must be overcome before the training can begin. The contrasting approaches of yoga and modern psychology to assisting the growth process might be clarified by an analogy: a plant is *trained* by directing its growth in certain ways—through tying up limbs, trimming or turning it to use the "pull" of the sun to direct its growth. But signs of illness must be watched for too, and *treated* (therapy) as necessary with water, soil and fer-tilizers. Both training and therapy have their place in the cultivation of growth. Our purpose here is to look at what happens when the concepts and techniques of yoga training are blended with the theory of psychopathology and the practice of psychotherapy. It would seem worthwhile to look at the synergistic relationship that might result from a synthesis of a deeply profound system and theory of growth beyond the normal (yoga) and a highly developed theory of illness (psychopathology) and its system of psychotherapy to attain normality. The resulting integration might be called *yoga therapy*. The traditional distinctions between "sick" patients coming to a psychiatrist to be made normal, and prepared students seeking a teacher in order to become enlightened is today breaking down. Many who don't think of themselves as "patients" are seeking out encounters in search of growth beyond what is considered normal. At the same time, many of those whom a psychiatrist might label psychotic or neurotic are now turning toward yoga and meditation for help. As the practice begins to shade over into the area of the other, the integration of yoga and psychotherapy becomes even more promising.

Modern psychologists and psychotherapists have studied the growth process as one moves from emotionality and mental disturbance to the "adapted ego." They are now struggling to conceptualize growth as it extends beyond the ego. Yoga psychology also includes conceptual models of growth and evolution. However, its emphasis is in the attainment of more advanced states of consciousness, rather than recovery from emotional imbalance. We have tried, especially in this chapter, to synthesize these two approaches, identifying and conceptualizing as clearly as possible the process that underlies movement from one level of growth to the next throughout the continuum. We have attempted to tease out the common denominator, the basic experience that comprises each step of growth, regardless of where along the path it is occurring.

From the perspective of a broad and comprehensive theory of growth and evolution the complementary relationship between the approach of yoga and that of modern psychology can be seen. Though they focus on growth at different points along the spectrum, each has something constructive to contribute. We have tried to outline and conceptualize the process of growth and evolution in such a way as to demonstrate this complementarity.

THE PROTOTYPE OF ATTACHMENT

Pleasure and Pain in the Infant

In yoga psychology attachment *(raga)* along with its contrary, aversion *(dvesa)*, is considered the key to understanding how the process of growth can come to a halt. Attachment is said to result from the experience of pleasure. The orderly process of growth necessitates repeatedly letting go of one type of gratification and the urge to repeat it, in order to open oneself to the new. When one clings to the memory of previous pleasures and the attempt to recreate them, his behavior pattern becomes repetitious and his creativity suffers. Freud used such terms as "fixation" and "repetition compulsion" to capture the flavor of this phenomenon. In yoga psychology this is called simply "attachment" *(raga)*.

The way in which personality is rooted in attachment is most easily seen during the earlier stages of development. The infant becomes "one with" whatever happens to flash on the screen of *manas* because he has developed no stable, enduring sense of "I" which persists from one moment to the next. His fragile sense of himself breaks down constantly and he experiences a feeling of oneness with whatever he is relating to. *I-ness* varies in the extreme. He is anything and everything. At the same time, it is this same distinction between pleasure and pain that is probably the most clear-cut and developmentally important discrimination made by the infant.

The experience of pleasure and the experience of pain come to be associated with certain objects and certain situations. In this way two categories of phenomena, "good" and "bad" emerge. There is little *I-ness* to provide a reference point during these shifts. Therefore, the pain is all-encompassing, as is the pleasure. There is no modulating influence. Pleasure is not simply pleasure. It is ecstasy. No pleasure can compare. The pleasure experienced at future levels of development is not likely to be so total or intense.

However, if the pleasure is ecstatic, the pain experienced is equally extreme. It is excruciating and unbearable. Pain at this point is not merely pain. It is terror. While a good experience gives the infant a feeling of security and warmth, the experience of pain totally shatters his fragile sense of "I" and seems to turn the world upside down. The "I" which had experienced pleasure is not simply subjected to pain. It is annihilated. It disappears. It is replaced by a new "I" which knows only the suffering of the present moment. This experience of massive pain and pleasure remains as the basic substratum on which later mental development is built. More mature categories and discrimination will evolve out of this. But this is the origin of likes and dislikes, of desires and repulsions, of addictions and fears. It is the prototype of all attachments and aversions.

In its first grasp at I-ness, the infant's choice is very simple: ecstasy must be preserved, pain must be avoided. When the "I" has its limits first drawn, it takes up its residence in the "good" so to speak, and life becomes a struggle to maintain this and to prevent the shattering experience of pain. Maintaining life seems to mean maintaining pleasure. This is the most massive example of "attachment." This is the earliest version of what will become increasingly refined and sophisticated. Later on, the search for objects, for relationships, for mental images that reinforce the sense of I-ness becomes more complex, more subtle. But at its base this search originates in the infant's desire to prolong and preserve the primal state of pleasure.

The developing child has not only painful situations and threats to ward off in the outside world, but he has also negative memories with which to cope. When a negative memory or a negative perception enters his awareness, he finds his security and peacefulness threatened and develops an aversion (dvesa) toward it. Because his sense of I-ness is still tenuous, whatever appears on the screen of the lower mind (manas) has a very dramatic effect. One solution to this dilemma is to attribute these negative thoughts and impressions to something outside. When a past impression bubbles up that is negative in coloring, the child thinks of it as coming from someone else. "Someone" thought something bad, said something bad or did something bad. It wasn't him.

> Mary, who has just begun to talk, turns over her glass of milk. When her mother scolds her, she says, "I didn't do it. Sister did." But sister vigorously denies this and brother steps up to support her. Little Mary is forced to realize that she herself did this thing and must accept the scolding.

The bad impulses, the bad thoughts, the bad actions are *projected* onto someone else. In this way the sense of *I-ness* and security are maintained. But as the sense of continuity over time becomes more sophisticated and the notions of reality more consistent, the world can no longer be reorganized from moment to moment to make it compatible with one's projections. Brother and sister will not take responsibility for one's faults. Mother insists on punishing one for being bad. The fragile, new "I" can no longer maintain the delusion that it is all good. A sense of being immersed in total pleasure cannot be preserved. This definition of "I" has failed.

When the infant's bottle is taken away, he responds by crying angrily. To the extent that this is successful, the belief that he can control his surroundings and maintain a state of constant pleasure is confirmed. However, the world will not always provide what he wishes. His angry tears sometimes prove inadequate. Their failure forces him to "give up." It simply doesn't work. Pain and helplessness are brought forcibly into awareness. The failure of the "I" as it was, sets the stage for its being redefined. If the process is successful, a more mature concept of oneself with more realistic limitations and capabilities is created. This is the prototype of the experience of giving up attachments. As a result, the lines of *I-ness* are redrawn and one little step in the process of growth has occurred.

This experience is not limited to early development, but is

repeated over and over again through the long course of personal evolution. The child, the adolescent and the adult go through this same process: attempting to maintain the attachments characteristic of a certain level of *I-ness;* finding that this ultimately fails; and experiencing a sense of loss and disappointment. After the loss and disappointment are experienced, attachments are finally relinquished. *I-ness* becomes redefined and restructured. A more comprehensive grasp of oneself and of the world results. With time and the accumulation of more experience, each new "I" in its turn will be found to be lacking. Its limitations must be experienced and understood. It must be relinquished for a more inclusive and less restricted identity. The course of evolution is made up of innumerable such steps. Each one reorganizes and expands the identity to some degree as a result of changing the pattern of attachments. *I-ness* is no more than the sum of one's attachments. It is defined by the totality of those objects, persons and thoughts with which he is entangled. This is the stuff of which one's identity is made.

I-ness and Habits

The yoga concept of attachment is similar to the Western idea of addiction: the addict is overwhelmed by the desire for his drug. If he can't get it, he loses all rationality and objectivity and becomes intensely emotional. He is dependent on it and is unable to do without it. In yoga, the same concept is extended beyond the more extreme cases. On close examination, one can be seen to be addicted or attached to many of the objects, thoughts and persons around which his life is organized. Dependency and clinging are the hallmarks of such addiction or attachment.

Objectivity also is lost when one becomes swayed by fear or aversion. When an object, person or mental image provokes an avoidance reaction, the attempt to escape can become so engrossing that all sense of perspective is lost. Detachment disappears. In yoga psychology, aversion and attachment are considered to be two sides of the same coin. Ultimately, each fear or aversion will always be found to result from an underlying attachment. In both cases one loses his distance and becomes involved to such an extent that the ability to observe the situation and learn from it is lost.

When there is an extreme wish for gratification or a marked feeling of either fear or distaste, then the memory trace resulting from the experience will be one heavily charged with energy. Rather than being a relatively neutral memory, it will be laden with feeling and will leave a deep mark in the unconscious memory *(chitta)*. Later, when it reappears in the conscious mind, it will bring with it the charge of feeling or emotion and will carry the power to push and pull one further into a blind involvement with desire or aversion. When such highly charged memory traces bubble up from *chitta,* the memory bank, it is very easy to become entangled in them. Such a memory or past impression *(samskara)* usually leads to action. It is so compelling that one either becomes involved with it in his thoughts or begins some course of action motivated by it. This, of course, reinvests it with additional energy. In the terms of yoga psychology, it is "weighted with more karma." As a result, it sinks back down to the bed of *chitta* with more impact, making a deeper and heavier impression. It will therefore rise next time with an even more compelling push toward action or thought.

As long as such *samskaras* or past impressions go through this cycle of rising, being automatically invested with energy because of their compelling character, sinking and rising again, they are habits. As long as the pattern persists, one's thoughts and behavior continue to be governed by them. If, through an act of will or determination, the *samskara* is ignored, it will not be reinvested with energy. If detachment is maintained and no thought or action is allowed to follow from it, it will not be reweighted. Eventually, as it rises repeatedly and gets no additional investment of karma, it loses its power to motivate and is dissipated. In this case we say that a "habit has been broken."

When there is a consistent constellation of such past impressions or *samskaras* that arise and motivate one's thoughts and actions, a characteristic pattern of behavior and thought patterns results. Characteristic mannerisms and characteristic ways of thinking are maintained by effects of this collection of *samskaras*. This "bundle of habits" together comprises what we call the personality or character. It is the substance of *I-ness*. It is the basis of our uniqueness and individuality. The momentum of these heavily invested *samskaras* which rise, motivate and fall again, gives the *I-ness* its enduring quality. The energy with which they are weighted (karma) is responsible for the momentum that keeps the wheel turning. This momentum gives one a sense of continuity over time. It is responsible for the consistency and solidity of the "I."

Therefore, it is the selective weighting of certain past impressions or *samskaras* that creates the particular pattern of habits which forms the "I." It is a rather arbitrary choice, this decision as to which *samskaras* to invest with energy and which not to. It is through doing one action and not another or becoming involved in one thought or fantasy rather than another that certain *samskaras* have come to be weighted with more karma and a characteristic *I-ness* is created. (The "I" is then, from this perspective, essentially an illusion. If the habits were broken and the *samskaras* allowed to dissipate, this particular "I" would simply disappear.)

It is in this way that attachments come to shape one's self-concept. Identity is a result of impressions to which one is attached. Later, objects or persons to which one becomes attached serve to support and bolster this self-image. The picture of himself that a young man is striving to maintain is reinforced as he steps into his new automobile and drives down the street. His sense of *I-ness* has been bolstered through his attachment to the automobile and the image of himself that it represents.

PAIN AND THE PROCESS OF CHANGE

In yoga psychology the notion of attachment is a central one. Although the magnitude or intensity of attachments may vary from one level of development to the next, their basic nature remains the same. The dilemma of being bound up in attachments is universal. In each case, they provide a major obstacle to further growth and evolution. In yoga psychology, the path of personal development is seen as a step-wise process of evolution. *I-ness* becomes repeatedly redefined, gradually expanding and becoming less fragile. *Buddhi* becomes more sophisticated and shifts its goals to correspond to the gradually changing needs of the "I." It gradually shifts from a preoccupation with pleasure towards a concern with truth and understanding and frees itself from the grip of attachments. The attachments themselves become successively redefined, growing less tenacious and controlling. In this movement, however, one can become "hung up." He can stagnate as the attachments of a particular level of development become more deeply ingrained. When growth stops, from the point of view of yoga psychology, it is then that the person might be termed "sick." Where he is in the course of development is not so important as whether or not he is moving.

Attachment and Anxiety

When the process of growth stops, more and more of one's attention and energy is devoted to increasing his attachments at that level, where he has become stuck. When one's energy and attention is not directed toward loosening and redefining his attachments, then it comes to be channeled increasingly towards multiplying them.   Rather than moving to a new level of consciousness and a new, less compelling set of attachments, he becomes increasingly entangled and enmeshed in those present attachments which define his current *I-ness*.   Evolution ceases and fears and anxieties will inevitably result.

As long as one is immersed in the struggle to gratify a desire or avoid something to which he has an aversion, then neither his urgent need to achieve his goal nor his fear of failure can be seen by him in a clear way.   He is too involved in the fight to wonder why he is fighting.   He doesn't have the distance necessary to see what's driving him.   His understanding of what it is exactly that he fears or craves is murky.   His concerns are not conscious and deliberate.   In such a case we tend to use the term "anxiety" rather than "fear."   To the extent that he is able to step back and observe the situation, his appreciation of what causes him concern becomes more objective.   His understanding is more lucid.   Apprehensions that are observed in such a detached fashion are more reasonable and can be acted on in a more rational, coherent way. Here it seems more natural to speak of "fear" instead of "anxiety."

> Joan, whom we described earlier as "not knowing" about her fiance's dating other women, begins to experience symptoms of acute anxiety.   She is unable to remain at home at night without restlessness, rapid heartbeat, and a feeling of apprehension.   She decides to see a psychotherapist.   In the course of therapy material comes up which suggests that she has misgivings about her boyfriend's involvement with her.   She describes incidents in their relationship which, when looked at objectively in the therapist's office, clearly provide evidence that he is losing interest in her.   As her doubts come more into focus, she is able to face more squarely her concern about being deserted.   Her symptoms of anxiety turn into a *fear* of loss and

loneliness. After further work, she comes to realize that her fear of abandonment is based on a distortion of her self-concept and on an underestimation of her real strengths and the possibilities that await her. She is eventually able to give up the relationship, the fear having, also, in its turn, faded out of the picture.

Anxiety, fear and equanimity lie along a continuum. As attachment is decreased, one's ability to observe increases, he feels a more manageable fear. With further detachment one can respond even more constructively, limited by neither anxiety nor fear.

Impediments to Growth

When growth and evolution stop, anxiety often builds up. In these cases it may help to push one towards taking a fresh look at himself. Just as physical pain becomes a signal that something needs to be done, so anxiety can serve as a motivation to go on with the steps involved in change and development. But there are a number of other factors which operate in opposition to this need to move forward. Change can seem to be a frightening thing, and the fear of giving up a position of relative security may lead one to tolerate the anxiety or cover it over in one of a number of ways. Alcohol, tranquilizers and acting-out are several of the techniques used to cover up or temporarily release tension and anxiety.

The ego always reacts defensively. Any change tends to be seen as a loss of what has been attained up to this time. The nature of *I-ness* is to defend itself and maintain stability. There is an intuitive understanding that it must, in a sense, give up its existence to make way for the appearance of a "new I." Moreover, the present identity has been gained only with significant struggle. It was itself a hard-won accomplishment. To give it up seems dangerous. One might slip back to previous levels where his view was more limited, where he was more subject to the circumstances around him and where he had less control and less freedom. To give up the definition of "I" seems equivalent to losing it. Caution and prudence seem to prohibit this step into the unknown and demand that one hang onto the certainty of what he has.

Since attachments or "addictions" are an integral part of sustaining the self-image, giving them up can become a frightening prospect. To loosen one's attachments seems to mean loosening his hold on the ego. It seems to imply that reality is slipping from his grip. The frantic clinging to attachments can become a matter of desperation. But the grip is a death grip, choking off further growth. When one ceases to grow, his life becomes stale. It loses its quality of vitality and creativity.

Moreover, there are cultural pressures which tend to encourage the development and maintenance of a certain range of *I-ness*. That level of growth which is associated with ego is encouraged by virtue of demands that society places on an individual. He must be able to care for himself and function with a certain minimal effectiveness. In other words, there is a social pressure to develop an effective ego.

In many societies, experimentation with growth beyond this level is not encouraged. In fact, if it involves an investment of energy that detracts even temporarily from one's material productivity, it may be actually discouraged. Investing time or energy into developing oneself beyond the ego level may be little understood or appreciated by a society where economic success and material possessions are the major criteria by which one is judged. Experimentation with higher states of consciousness may be regarded with suspicion or considered wasteful nonsense.

Growth: Apparent or Real?

Each step in growth entails a fundamental reorganization. The new sense of "I" and the new way of seeing the world will not be something that can be imagined in the terms of the old. What can be foreseen and understood in terms of the present level of development does not represent genuine progress. Authentic change always means stepping into the unknown. There is necessarily an element of uncertainty and adventure. But the ego struggles to maintain the familiar *I-ness* and preserve its stability. In its effort to avoid the uncertainty of change, it resorts to a variety of clever tactics. One of its most frequent methods of sabotaging real change is through imitating it. A pseudo-growth is enacted. All the outer trappings of change and metamorphosis are adopted while the essential inner plunge into a totally new and unknown way of seeing oneself and the world is avoided. Meanwhile, there is the conviction that genuine progress is being made.

The bane of every psychotherapist's practice is the sophisticated and clever patient who talks endlessly of his intellectual insight but makes no essential change in his personality organization. He "talks a good game" but clings tenaciously to his little world. He relates endless examples of how he has "finally given up this" or "at last changed that." But each of his pseudo-changes is only a new version of his old pattern. For him, the new remains perennially cast in terms of the old and therefore never really comes into being. For every experience that makes up the transition from one stage of development to the next, there is easily found a counterpart, a pseudo-experience which often passes for the real thing.

Pseudo-growth is often difficult to distinguish from authentic growth. With the best intentions big plans are made to accomplish one thing or to change another. Grand schemes are elaborated for the process of expanding one's horizons. There is a heroic struggle, a great push. There are magnificent fantasies of how great the "I" will be, once all the new changes are incorporated. But all the plans are cast in terms of the present *I-ness*. All the notions of "progress" are based on the present desires and fears. The basic concept of oneself is not about to be relinquished. On the contrary, the whole scheme solidifies it, and extends its power. There is a smug feeling of certainty. It seems as though "it's all under control now"; the process of growth is "understood"; and is well underway.

Disappointment: Therapeutic and Non-Therapeutic

However, the actual process of evolution does not permit such comfortable certainty because change cannot be cast in terms of security. Each step is a step into the unknown. A sense of uncertainty is an integral part of the process. Moreover, each bit of advancement involves a definite and painful experience of disappointment. Shedding the old and moving into the new is a transition that necessarily includes some pain.

In the first place, the frantic struggle to improve oneself must stop. One must admit defeat and "give up." For the struggle is framed in the terms of the present *I-ness* and it is these terms and this notion of oneself which must be relinquished. The grand plan for progress must be abandoned. Its foolishness must be acknowledged and all the frantic effort stopped. The situation is like that of trying impatiently to open a door which is stuck. Angrily tugging on the doorknob accomplishes nothing. Try as one may it doesn't budge. Before a new approach is possible he must first acknowledge that his present effort won't work. He has to sheepishly admit that he has failed. Then he can calmly examine the door and discover where it is caught. After that, a slight lift and a little leverage allows it to open easily.

For true change to occur, the limits of the present *I-ness* must be consciously admitted. Its relative ineffectiveness must be accepted. What's worse, it must be examined in detail, stripped of all its pretense, exposed as it really is. The mask must be looked at honestly, without the benefit of any embellishment. A cool, calm appraisal of one's present state must precede any reasonable, effective change. Moreover, even after one marshalls all his humility, all his perceptiveness, even if he is fortunate enough to grope in the dark and find a new definition of himself, he will still be forced to admit that this has led to only the most modest increment of progress. Only a tiny step along the path of evolution has been made. Evolution is gradual and slow, it doesn't occur in jumps. One must accept that his painful admission of failure, his hard won sense of detachment and his brave step into the unknown have led him to only the most ordinary degree of change—an accomplishment nowhere near the glory which had been imagined in the terms of the old *I-ness.* There are further reasons for the disappointment that recurs at each step along the way. The certainty of the present world must go. It must give way to a very uncertain, as yet unknown way of seeing the world. All of one's devices for reassuring his security have to be given up. Moreover, that which is currently pleasurable, that which is seen as "good," attractive and desirable must be let go in order to step back and see it in a new way. One must come to look at it from an unattached position.

In the terms of traditional yoga psychology, when a desire or aversion is exposed to the burning light of uncompromising discrimination, it loses its ability to grow. It is likened to a parched seed. It cannot sink its roots into the subconscious mind and subtly control one's life. Its ability to give rise to new problems and entanglements is destroyed. The objects of one's most exquisite fantasies, his most private and cherished pleasures will wither when exposed to the uncompromising light of objectivity. Their true nature becomes apparent. They come to be seen as trivial, silly, even somewhat embarrassing. Ultimately they lose their ability to give pleasure: the lover impulsively sought out in the darkness of night may be revealed in the light of morning to be childish, unattractive and anything but romantic. Not only must the pleasurable be examined and re-evaluated, but those objects in the world which are feared or seem distasteful must also be regarded dispassionately. In a similar way, one must come to see as part of himself those aspects of his being that he considers disgusting and repulsive.

> A patient who was just beginning to explore facets of
> his personality which he considered distasteful and
> "dirty" reported a dream which clearly expressed the
> feeling of aversion: he was reaching into a hole in the
> ground where the valve for opening a pipeline was
> located. The recess was filled with murky water and
> dark slime. But in order to open the line he had to
> plunge his hand into the foul depths. Opening a new
> way for himself could only be done by deliberately
> getting into the "dirty" parts of himself which had
> been hidden in his unconscious mind.

Giving up one's treasured attachments or coming to terms with
his defects and dislikes, entails a certain pain.

All disappointment, however, is not an indication that progress
has been made. All pain is not constructive. When one is still caught
up in the struggle to achieve gratification, his efforts to do so will
not always be successful; when he fails, there is a sense of pain
and disappointment. If, however, he has no detachment with
which to observe the situation, this pain and disappointment will
not be of benefit. This happens when pain and disappointment
are not accompanied by any change in the definition of *I-ness*.
There is no new perspective gained. There is no restructuring of
one's notions about the world and himself. Unfortunately, this
kind of pain can be mistaken for the disappointment which is an
indication that some growth is taking place. The two are not
always so easy to distinguish. Subjectively they are both
unpleasant and difficult. Yet their implications are quite
different.

Death and Rebirth

The painful giving up of each self concept, each set of attachments in order to move on, is the experience we most fear. This
apprehension finds its most extreme expression in all of our

concern about death. For to give up the old and step into the unknown is, in essence, to die. Krishnamurti has said:

> You cannot live if you do not die psychologically every minute. This is not an intellectual paradox. To live completely, wholly, every day as if it were a new loveliness, there must be dying to everything of yesterday, otherwise you live mechanically....[3]

In yoga psychology death is seen as one phase in the process of metamorphosis. At each step of growth, we must die in order to be "reborn." This is the essence of life. Resistance to this moment to moment "letting go" is more accurately a fear of life than of death, though our fear of giving up the old comes to be crystalized around our anticipation of the death and decay of the physical body.

> As long as we are frightened of life, we shall be frightened of death. The man who is not frightened of life is not frightened of being completely insecure, for he understands that inwardly, psychologically, there is no security. When there is no security there is an endless movement....[4]

Patanjali lists "fear of death" (abhinivesha) as the last of the kleshas or "causes of misery" (obstacles to growth). This basic, primitive fear of annihilation reflects a hidden yet pervasive limitation in one's freedom to open himself fully to change. The more advanced yoga masters teach that death and decay, like the physical laws of time, space and causality, characterize only the grosser levels of our being. Diversity and change, while dramatic and disturbing at the periphery of the wheel, give way as consciousness shifts towards its center, to that state where there is no movement and no change.

A widely used therapeutic technique in modern psychology focusing on giving up one's false sense of security, replacing it with an increased openness to immediate experience is called

Gestalt therapy. One of the central tenets of this approach is that the well functioning individual is constantly reorganizing his world while the neurotic clings to his particular manipulative routine. Many of the techniques of Gestalt psychology are designed to lead to a greater awareness of the present moment. This may be achieved by asking the person to describe in the minutest detail his immediate experience. He is then confronted directly with the manipulations and ploys he uses to avoid the present. The patient will often become aware of an increased vividness of feeling and perception. In commenting on such a heightened awareness in a woman with whom he was working, Fritz Perls said: "This is what we call in Gestalt therapy, a mini-satori. She begins to wake up, the world becomes real, the colors are bright."[5]

Gestalt therapy seems to have certain similarities to yogic training. Its emphasis is on letting go, on simple *awareness* of the present. In fact it has been called "spoken meditation" by one Gestalt therapist who says, "I encourage the person to become an impartial witness...an observer, one who watches without evaluating—as a way to more objectively see oneself."[6]

This therapeutic approach seems useful in giving up attachments and intellectualizing in favor of an enhanced experience of the present moment. But the letting go and resulting *awareness* which comes about in Gestalt therapy also shows some fundamental differences from the expansion of consciousness characteristic of yoga. For the awareness of Gestalt is primarily in the realm of sensation, emotion and fantasy. It is very much tied to the physical energy sheaths described in the first chapters of this book. In leaving behind attachments to the intellect and to past and future orientations, there is often a tendency to form new attachments to the newly enjoyed sensory and feeling experiences. An immersion in sensory inputs and emotionality can become an escape from intellectual obsessions, substituting for the development of a level from which both feeling and intellect can be held in awareness.

PSYCHOSIS VERSUS MYSTICISM

The Buddhist tradition likens one's reticence to let go of his customary reality to that of a monkey locked in an empty house which has five windows, representing the five senses.[7] Though reassured by the security of confinement, he inevitably finds himself bored. But he cannot escape. The bare walls of the house and the square, limited pictures of the outside world that can be seen through the windows are all that exist. Yet there is an underlying discontent, like that of an animal long confined to a small cage in a zoo.

What the monkey sees is, for him, the only reality. The more he focuses his attention on the inside of the house, the more solid it becomes. The more he looks at the bare walls

and the five windows, the more these impressions become part of his unconscious mind. The more his mind is filled with these impressions, the more they bubble up and the more they reinforce themselves. His limited "reality" becomes even more "real." As far as the monkey is concerned, the house and its windows are the solid, indisputable world of commonsense reality. He is so preoccupied with it that there is not an available moment to see in an alternate way. He is too busy trying to reinforce his own notion of reality. "He never allows a gap. Thus there's no room for inspiration, no room to see other aspects of the situation, to see it from different angles. From the monkey's point of view, the confusion is real." [8] It's as real as a nightmare, which at the moment is very real and terribly frightening.

But what happens when our monkey gets out of his house? What happens when one departs from his customary definition of himself and the world? When one takes the step into the unknown and enters "an altered mode of consciousness," what kind of state does he find himself in? What does he become if he is no longer himself—is the result personal growth and the expansion of consciousness? Or might it be a plunge into insanity?

The apparent similarity between certain euphoric psychotic states and the experience of higher consciousness has been a subject of perennial interest. The psychotic's descriptions of his feelings of oneness with the universe, his sense of having reached an understanding of everything, and his delight with the beauty of the most mundane objects seem intriguingly parallel to descriptions given by highly competent and talented people who have experienced what they call a universal consciousness.

Paramahansa Yogananda, a renowned yogi, describes his experience of "oceanic joy" in the following words:

Soul and mind instantly lost their physical bondage...
In my intense awareness I knew that never before

> had I been fully alive. My sense of identity was no
> longer narrowly confined to a body...People on distant
> streets seemed to be moving gently over my own
> remote periphery....
>
> An oceanic joy broke upon the endless calm shores
> of my soul.[9]

But the description of the experience of a patient in a mental
hospital may seem on the surface very similar:

> I seemed to be filled with a sense of universal benevo-
> lence and constantly bear in mind the text "love your
> enemies"....
>
> At the same time I feel a mystic sense of unity with
> all fellow creatures and the universe as a whole; I am
> at peace with myself....
>
> In a sense I am God. I see the future plan of the
> universe, save mankind; I am utterly and completely
> immortal....the whole universe, animate and inanimate,
> past, present, and future is within me.[10]

This striking resemblance led psychologists and psychoanalysts
several decades back to equate the experience of enlightenment
with the experience of psychosis:

> From our present psychoanalytical knowledge it is
> clear that Buddhistic self-absorption is a narcissistic
> turning of the urge for knowing inward, a sort of
> artificial schizophrenia....the catatonic condition of the
> Hindu ascetics in self-absorption prove quite clearly
> the correctness of this contention.[11] *

Thus, using the familiar state of psychosis which they encountered
in their work as a model, psychoanalysts attempted to explain the

---

* This confusion is not limited to Western psychologists. For example, Indian
physicians were called in to decide whether Ramakrishna (who later became a leading
teacher with an international following) was especially gifted or whether he was insane.[12]

strange descriptions of advanced consciousness of which they had heard reports. More recently, this notion has been turned upside down. "Radical therapists" have on occasion suggested that the psychotic is in touch with a more advanced consciousness than is the ordinary person. Some writers have discussed psychosis in quasi-mystical terms that emphasize its positive aspects.

But the psychotic experience has another facet. It's not always so beautiful; the same patient who described his "mystic sense of unity" above reports the following horrific vision:

> My fears had become in fact so overpowering as to appear to me like certainties...unending horrors awaited me....
>
> I was an appalling sinner, the worst man who ever existed. I had been chosen to go alive through the portals of hell....
>
> Whichever way I turned I could see nothing but devils waiting to torment me....
>
> Paroxysms of fear overcame me and I nearly jumped straight out the window with the idea of killing myself with the broken glass.[13]

This abrupt reversal of the state of euphoria is a key to the difference between the psychotic's experience and that of the enlightened mystic. It reveals that the psychotic's consciousness is fragmented, varying from moment to moment. This contrasts with the expanded consciousness of the mystic that permits him to integrate the diverse and contradictory aspects of the inner world. Between these two extremes lies the whole path of personal evolution during which a stable and pervasive consciousness gradually evolves.

Pre and Post Ego Attachment: Psychosis and Mysticism

Having viewed the process of growth as it can be conception-
alized in yoga psychology, we have seen how a limited sense of
"I" is progressively replaced by a more expanded one. This
process extends from infancy when a fragile and tentative
I-ness is first created through the acquisition and development
of an ego to stages of development in which the ego is transcended. In this context it would appear that the psychotic
and the mystic lie at opposite ends of a long path. If the
stagnation of the growth process is what defines psychopathology,
then the psychotic is clearly the sickest, since this process of
growth has never made much headway. This is most dramatically true in the case of the autistic child, locked in a world of
psychosis, many of whose psychological processes remain at the
earliest stages of development. The chronic adult psychotic also
often presents a picture of one who has forfeited the struggle
for growth, passing his years tortured by threats from within
and unable to play a constructive role in the world.

But an acute psychotic episode may represent an attempt—
however misguided—to break free of one's limitations and come
to terms with aspects of himself that were repressed. From the
point of view of the growth process, such a person should not
be considered "sick" if he is actively reorganizing and evolving.
This point has been dramatically made by R. D. Laing who
has said:

> ....to be mad is not necessarily to be ill....
> If the "ego" is broken up or destroyed....then the
> person may be exposed to other worlds "real" in
> different ways from the more familiar territory of
> dreams, imagination, perception....[14]

Dabrowski in his book, *Personality—Shaping through Positive
Disintegration,* emphasizes that "in order to leave the lower
developmental level and pass to a higher one, the individual

must go through a...disorganization of primitive structures and activities."[15] He says that "even in certain psychotic processes we may observe positive disintegration...revealing intellectual, moral, and social values higher than those before the disease...."[16] But this is only true, he says, in those cases of psychosis which reflect a capacity for what he calls "auto psychotherapy." These cases stand in contrast to those who show no tendency to reorganize in the direction of growth, a state he calls "negative disintegration." Laing, also, while emphasizing the potential of the psychotic experience for restructuring and reorganizing, has suggested that this is a more prominent feature in some patients than others.

Assagioli also points out that those who are going through the steps of self realization, may appear similar to typical psychotherapy patients: "While the troubles that accompany the various phases of self-realization may be outwardly very similar to, and sometimes appear identical with, those which affect ordinary patients, their causes and significance are very different."[17]

Thus, it is important to distinguish between the person who is purposefully dealing with newly discovered aspects of himself, uncovering, reintegrating and growing, from one who has simply turned his back on growth and lapsed into madness. Though on rare occasions, or with skilled guidance, the psychotic episode may prove to be the jolt that shakes one loose from a sterile existence, reinitiating a growth process that will continue, this is not often true. More often the psychotic "break through" miscarries. The flooding of an underdeveloped ego with such a huge amount of alien material is usually catastrophic. It cannot digest, assimilate and integrate so much at once. There are abrupt reversals, disruptive shifts in emotional state and an inability to concentrate the mind. Without the help of an unusually gifted therapist, this situation becomes chronic. The turmoil and chaos tend to perpetuate themselves.

For the gradual process of redefinition that is necessary for personal growth, there is substituted instead a continual merging or fusion with others. The psychotic has slipped back to that point where identification shifts from moment to moment. Like the infant he is once more at one with whatever flashes onto the screen of *manas*. His identification with each object or person is complete, abrupt and overwhelming. He lacks the stability of *I-ness* that is associated with a healthy ego. He has not gradually reduced his attachments; instead he has retreated to a point in development where attachments are the most massive. If his attachments are the most massive imaginable, then it is not surprising that his anxiety would be the most severe, for his feeling of oneness with what is around him changes abruptly. Though his universe is at one instance all benevolent and gratifying, at the next he is plunged into tortures, recriminations and pain. There is no *I-ness* which would lend the capacity to integrate the world experienced at one moment with that of the next. He has no place to stand; there is no observing awareness. There is no part of him which can simultaneously view the disparate worlds that he experiences. So "fear" is too mild a word to apply to his emotions. He is instead plagued by a constant and massive anxiety. The psychotic has never really constituted a stable *I-ness*. What little *I-ness* he has is fragile and tenuous but clung to frantically. Since it is easily shattered, his sensitivity is great. In contrast to one who has taken the steps that carry him along the path of growth, given up his attachments one by one, and exposed his cherished fantasies to scrutiny, the psychotic has refused to do so. His daydream world is not relinquished but cultivated and indulged in. The world around him is distorted in whatever way necessary to preserve his fantasies. If all else fails he withdraws disdainfully into a private universe of hallucination. He will not condescend to the humiliation of accepting limitations, of constituting a limited, but realistic, *I-ness*.

Further along the path can be found the neurotic who is in many ways a caricature of that state in which most of us find ourselves. He has gradually established that bundle of habits which goes to make up a personality. He has accepted the limitations of *I-ness* and safely settled into a routine of reinforcing and acting on the habits which sustain him and give him a sense of continuity and solidity. He clings tenaciously to the narrow and exclusive self-definition he has established for himself. Rigid and restricted, he is constantly afraid to lose his foothold in the organized world which promises him at least some security. No matter how maladaptive his pattern of habits, no matter how much pain his attachments bring, he is unwilling to let go his familiar self-definition and venture around the next turn in the path of personal growth. The uncertainty of what lies ahead is more than he can tolerate.

Still further along the path is the mystic who has patiently trained himself to not only live with the uncertainty of the external world but to relish the feeling of constant renewal that its changes bring. He has learned to continuously give up his prior concepts of self and accept a continual process of changing *I-ness*. He has learned to accept casually the pain associated with admitting his limitations. He has become accustomed to letting go of habits, easily and without apprehension or regret. He has cultivated an inner stance of non-attachment to the external world and to the superficial aspects of himself.

The psychotic, on the other hand, rejects change. He refuses to accept and come to terms with the negative, embarrassing or disgusting aspects of himself. Instead he falls back on the primitive mechanisms seen in a child. He projects his defects onto others. "They are making me feel bad, they are causing me to be unhappy." His pleasure is also like that of the child. It is a fantasied omniscience. He is all-important. He imagines that everyone he passes is conscious of his presence, they envy him, they are laughing at him, etc. He has turned his back on the fundamental process of growth. He has refused to relinquish the primal attachment to pervasive pleasure, and thus suffers the tortures of primal pain. He is at the mercy of whatever stimuli happen to reach him. He is tossed as though at random from world to world.

The mystic by contrast, ultimately exists in a universe which is enduring. The further he goes along his path, the less abrupt are the reversals he encounters. Fewer and smaller parts of himself remain repressed to haunt and threaten him. The shift from pain to pleasure becomes progressively attenuated, since both are increasingly integrated into a constant awareness.

The growth experience is like that of a climber who follows a trail that spirals around a mountain toward its peak. At first each few steps bring a view radically different from the last. Diversity and change are marked. But as he nears the top, the view is more complete, more integrated and less changeable. At the summit the perspective is total and enduring. Consciousness has expanded to become all-inclusive.

The mystic attains this position of serenity by virtue of repeatedly abandoning each bundle of habits that made up his personality at different stages. He turns loose his attachment to them and no longer relies on them for his identity. By virtue of this, the mystic is finally able to locate himself in a position of serenity and calm. There is only consistency from the point which he observes; changes are only superficial. They are around him, they may involve his body, his actions, the external world, but they have no power to disturb his equilibrium. Change is like the spinning of spokes around the hub of his being, visible but irrelevant. He has located himself in the eye of a hurricane where all is calm. From there all can be observed, changes can be seen but they have no effect. He has found a center in himself which is enduring and dependable and offers a reference point from which all experiences can be intelligibly integrated and from which everything can be seen as impermanent.

The psychotic is quite different:

> The psychotic doesn't see things as impermanent. He
> doesn't see things. He *is* things impermanently.

The psychotic has no center. To the extent that he can describe his feelings, he may say he feels "hollow." He is caught in the winds of the hurricane. He has neither located the calm eye at the center of the storm, nor does he know of its existence. Only abrupt and shattering change is known to him. He has not even the relative comfort of the confining and stagnant identity that characterizes the neurotic. He has never acquired an identity. Like the mystic, he is strikingly lacking in the "bundle of habits" that make up a personality. His lack, however, is due to a stubborn refusal to accept the limitations of I-ness, an unwillingness to condescend to being an ordinary, limited mortal. He has not shed the ego-identity, rather he has never acquired it. His need is to develop the ego, which can later be transcended. This is an indispensable transitional stage—one necessary step on the ladder. Trying to jump over such necessary rungs results in a tragic fall.

Dwelling on the intermediate rungs of the ego level can also become an obstacle to growth. Though the overly strong ego can become a problem, many authorities see failure of its development as even more serious:

> My judgment would be that it is easier to master an
> overly developed egoism—for here we have strength
> to work with—than it is to build the necessary strength
> in the too dreamy consciousness. So I should place
> somnambulism, rather than egoism as the first among
> the problems that must be mastered in this humanity
> if it is to progress.[18]

The psychotic and the most advanced mystic seem to lie at opposite extremes of a spectrum which spans the whole of personal evolution. At one end are the most massive of attachments—where pain and pleasure are both excruciatingly exquisite and where identity is fleeting and fragmentary. This is the domain of madness. At the other extreme attachments have been almost completely shed. There is no more of the alternation of pain and pleasure, only a constant and pervasive joy. Identity has been expanded to the point that every part of the universe is part of the Self. This evolutionary path is a basic theme that figures prominently, not only in Eastern psychology and philosophy, but also in modern psychology and psychotherapy, where the perspective has shifted increasingly toward an emphasis on growth and the expansion of consciousness.

In discussing the distinction between these basically different states of psychosis and mysticism with Indian teachers, the reaction most often encountered is one of surprise that the two might be confused. Although the state of psychosis was not in itself of much interest to the ancient teachers, the decision as to whether or not a person was genuinely evolved was of great importance. One must know whom he can safely regard as a teacher, whose advice and guidance is likely to be helpful and whose to ignore. Though the student may not be able to understand all the teacher's arguments, thoughts or motivations, he must be able to evaluate him in some way. In the traditions of yoga certain guidelines are given to help distinguish one who is advanced from one who isn't. In the Bhagavad Gita, Arjuna asks his teacher how can one identify a man who is firmly established and absorbed in the highest consciousness. He is told that such a person is "not shaken by adversity," that he is "free from fear, free from anger."[19] The way the teacher sits is carefully scrutinized. He who is restless with poor posture betrays his lack of control over the body and reveals a dissipated, unfocused mind. The way he walks is observed; whether it indicates hurriedness, a sense of being torn and pressured, a posture of defensiveness, or whether, on the other hand, it reflects confidence, ease and self control. Speech is also evaluated: Is one distracted, wandering, rambling, losing the thread of the conversation? Is he critical and negative in his comments about others? Does he tend to focus on the negative aspects of everything around him, and do his own actions tend toward destructiveness? Does he become angry for no apparent reason,

misinterpreting what others say and do, distorting them so that
they fit his own ideas?

One need not ask the customary question about hallucinations,
bizarre ideas, etc. to distinguish such a person from the mystic
who despite his "strange ideas" presents a vastly different picture.
The traditional observations amount to a pragmatic sort of
descriptive psychiatry. The authentic mystic reflects an inner
discipline—despite the fact that his ideas and behavior may be
difficult to understand. However baffling his speech or actions,
he nevertheless reflects an inner peace—through a relaxed body
and harmonious coordination, and through patience, confidence,
clear thinking and an unselfish attention to the needs of others.

THE EVOLUTION OF CONSCIOUSNESS:
SEPARATION OF PURUSHA FROM PRAKRITI

Discussions of consciousness, especially when they concern
the treatment of mystical states in terms of modern psychology
are often confusing. The confusion arises because the term
"consciousness" tends to be used in two completely different
ways: In modern psychology, it generally refers to "that of
which one is aware." This ordinarily means that level of awareness peculiar to the ego range of development. Consciousness is
usually considered to be an attribute of the ego.

But in yoga psychology, consciousness is said to exist on
various levels, the "ego-level" being only one of those. For one
who has not developed or experienced those higher levels of
consciousness beyond the ego which are inherent in him, their
exact nature remains obscure. In such a case the waking consciousness has not been sufficiently expanded to realize its
potential for these states of broader awareness. They are
experienced only in deep sleep when the usual consciousness is
suspended. In terms of the everyday mentality, then, they

remain "unconscious." But how can consciousness be "unconscious?"

The apparent contradiction results from using the term "consciousness" both in the sense it is used in the East and in the sense it is used in the West at the same time: In yoga philosophy and psychology, a higher consciousness is assumed to exist as a potential in everyone. Ordinary consciousness is seen as a somewhat crude—though, as yet, unevolved—version of this underlying potential. But in modern psychology the ordinary waking consciousness is taken as the point of departure and everything which lies outside its scope is put into the category of "unconscious." Therefore, it is in the Western "unconscious" where the Eastern higher consciousness usually lies undiscovered. We have attempted to clarify this somewhat by pointing out that the "unconscious" is not homogeneous. It contains an area called the personal unconscious, and what Jung called the collective unconscious, as well as potential transpersonal and universal modes of consciousness. Nevertheless, the two different uses of the term "consciousness" indicate a basic underlying difference between the perspectives of modern and yoga psychologies.

In yoga psychology, consciousness is the basic phenomenon. It is the underlying reality. It is the central focus around which the whole yogic conceptual scheme is organized. Human development is not seen as merely the elaboration of a mental structure like the ego. Instead, it is seen as the gradual uncovering of an already present, underlying consciousness. This consciousness manifests itself in such forms as the mental structures, but has the potential of freeing itself from them. With the progressive loosening of attachments, it gradually disentangles itself from the physical and mental forms, which both express it, and, at the same time, obscure and contaminate it.

In yoga philosophy, this underlying principle of consciousness is *purusha*. The long process of individual development is seen as beginning at birth when matter or *prakriti* is infused with

consciousness or *purusha*. *Prakriti* means the material aspect of
the universe. It is the soil in which consciousness can take root.
It is the feminine, receptive principle. It is the mother earth in
which a seed of consciousness can grow, producing living flesh
and active intelligence. The "Earthly Mother," fertilized by
the "Heavenly Father," (consciousness) gives rise to life. It is
prakriti, the material and physical existence, which can embody
purusha or consciousness. *Prakriti* gives *purusha* form.

In the case of individual development, as the infant comes
into being his physical organism acquires the property of
consciousness. This fusion of the principle of matter with the
principle of consciousness sets into motion individual development. During the long process of personal evolution, consciousness
or *purusha* gradually, step by step, becomes aware of itself and
effects separation from its identification with the body, the
material world and their derivatives.

This evolutionary sequence that begins with the fusion of
consciousness with matter and ends with its ultimate separation,
is in some ways reminiscent of that described by Western
psychologists and psychiatrists. They have studied the fusion of
mother and child and the gradual evolution of individual consciousness which separates itself from this union and establishes
its individuality. Such personality evolution seems to correspond
to one segment of the evolutionary sequence described in yoga
psychology and philosophy. It corresponds to a certain limited
range of the step-wise separation of consciousness from its
involvement and identification with the denser, more material
principle.

At each of the levels of consciousness that we have previously
discussed: physical body, energy body, mental body, higher
buddhi and so forth, there is a diminishing degree of density of
prakriti and an increasing degree of purity of consciousness or
purusha. That is, there is an increasing correspondence between
the current level of consciousness and pure consciousness. When
prakriti or the material principle is predominant, at the earliest

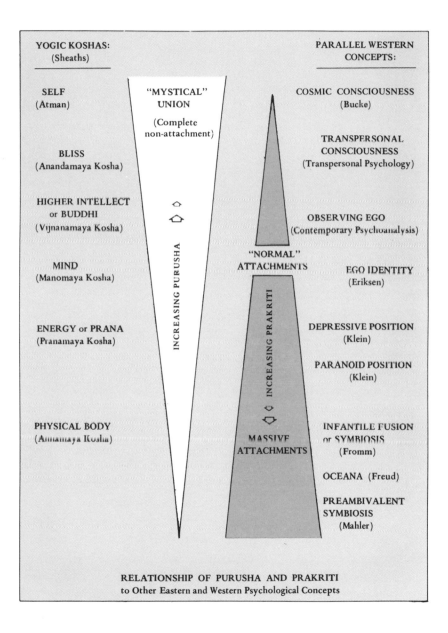

YOGIC KOSHAS: (Sheaths)		PARALLEL WESTERN CONCEPTS:
SELF (Atman)	"MYSTICAL" UNION (Complete non-attachment)	COSMIC CONSCIOUSNESS (Bucke)
BLISS (Anandamaya Kosha)		TRANSPERSONAL CONSCIOUSNESS (Transpersonal Psychology)
HIGHER INTELLECT or BUDDHI (Vijnanamaya Kosha)		OBSERVING EGO (Contemporary Psychoanalysis)
MIND (Manomaya Kosha)	"NORMAL" ATTACHMENTS	EGO IDENTITY (Eriksen)
ENERGY or PRANA (Pranamaya Kosha)		DEPRESSIVE POSITION (Klein)
		PARANOID POSITION (Klein)
PHYSICAL BODY (Annamaya Kosha)	MASSIVE ATTACHMENTS	INFANTILE FUSION or SYMBIOSIS (Fromm)
		OCEANA (Freud)
		PREAMBIVALENT SYMBIOSIS (Mahler)

INCREASING PURUSHA

INCREASING PRAKRITI

RELATIONSHIP OF PURUSHA AND PRAKRITI
to Other Eastern and Western Psychological Concepts

stages of development, matter seems to be "the center of the universe." That is, one's awareness and orientation are in terms of the physical self and world. His attention is focused on material phenomena, where diversity is marked and pleasure is more physical in nature. With progressive disentanglement of *purusha* from *prakriti,* consciousness increasingly becomes predominant.

In the process of personal evolution there is a progressive decrease in the attachments to identifications with persons and objects. The child separates himself from his fusion with mother, first physically and later mentally. He learns to distinguish a stable "I" from the perceptions and memories that appear on the screen of the lower mind. He forms an identity of his own. If he follows an appropriate discipline, he may continue further and sever even those attachments that are inherent in an ego-identity. It would eventually become evident that even the subtlest efforts to extract pleasure or avoid pain from other persons, things or images obscures the underlying pure consciousness.

At each level of development consciousness uses certain vehicles such as body, energy, mind, or the higher *buddhi* to express and manifest itself. Each of these gives it a certain form and consequently certain limitations. They are instruments for consciousness to use. Though these vehicles are increasingly more subtle and refined, they remain by comparison to pure consciousness gross tools in the hands of the user. For development to progress pure consciousness must free itself from each of its vehicles in turn. *In yoga psychology the ego is only one of these possible vehicles of consciousness, whereas in Western psychology the ego is primary and consciousness is a property of it.* Yoga psychology, then, represents for Western thought a kind of Copernican revolution of the mind. It provides a movement away from an egocentric viewpoint.

The perspective provided by the mainstream of modern psychology does not comfortably accommodate a comprehensive theory of growth. It cannot make clear what provides the motivating force for further evolution. A psychology based on the limitations of the ego-level of consciousness can only be pessimistic about the possibility of development beyond those narrow confines. How can the ego get beyond itself? What provides the lift? The dilemma seems to be that of one trying to lift himself by tugging away at his own bootstraps.

Yoga psychology, however, provides a different point of view. Here it is asserted that there is an underlying consciousness which is trying to free itself from the confines of mind. Consciousness is trapped in matter or some refinement of it, but constantly exerts a pressure to escape. There is a basic pull in the direction of growth. Consciousness *(purusha)* tends towards evolution upwards, like the tendency of a balloon to rise. Only matter *(prakriti)* holds it down. When attachments to the denser levels of existence are broken and, like sandbags, cast aside, the balloon is freed and permitted to follow its natural course upward toward a more serene and higher consciousness.*

At each level of development, giving up more attachments further expands the field of awareness and allows a higher consciousness to emerge. As this process is carried to its ultimate conclusion, it leads beyond what can be imagined by the ordinary waking consciousness. It brings one to the furthest reaches of man's potential: a universal awareness. Here there is no longer a distinction between the knower and the known. All is experienced simultaneously as part of oneself

---

* *Purusha* and *prakriti* are sometimes thought of as constituting an underlying duality. This is the position of the Samkhya system of Indian philosophy which includes Patanjali. Here, *purusha* or consciousness is eternal and *prakriti* or matter is co-eternal with it. While the Vedanta school of philosophy and psychology accepts the basic Samkhyan ideas about the nature of the universe, it cannot rest content with the duality of consciousness and matter, of *purusha* and *prakriti*. It insists that all but the highest consciousness (*Brahman*, Self) is *maya* or "illusion." "All that changes is illusory, and the One that is permanent is the only reality, the changeless substratum beneath all appearances."[20] From this point of view matter is said to be in the final analysis a creation and manifestation of consciousness. It is consciousness which gives rise to material phenomena rather than *vice versa*.

It is a universal characteristic of all mystical states
that they cannot be conveyed adequately in any
conceptual formulation. The reason for this is clear
once it is realized that the essence of the mystical
state is a Consciousness that does not fall within the
subject-object framework. In contrast, all language
presupposes that framework.[21]

The State of Pure Consciousness

Plotinus expresses the dilemma one encounters in trying to
describe the states approaching pure consciousness.

You ask how can we know the infinite? I answer, not
by reason. It is the office of reason to distinguish and
define. The infinite, therefore, cannot be ranked among
its objects. You can only apprehend the infinite by a
faculty superior to reason by entering into a state in
which you are your finite self no longer....This is
ecstasy (cosmic consciousness). It is the liberation of
your mind from the finite consciousness...when you
thus cease to be finite, you become one with the
infinite.[22]

This is the blissful state, *ananda* in Sanskrit, that which, as we
saw in the last chapter exists in dreamless sleep and can be
integrated into constant awareness *(turiya)* as growth proceeds.
It is perhaps because of descriptions of such states of bliss,
however obscure they may be, that "it is possible for the typical
egoistic man to desire and therefore seek mystical realization."[23]
Yet in the ancient Vedic teachings this blissful sheath is still
one of the coverings that mask the highest consciousness. This
is attained, according to the Buddhist scriptures by a final
"turning about at the deepest seat of consciousness."[24] Not
only has all attachment to objects been severed, but ultimately

even attachment to subjectivity—to bliss.   Merrell-Wolff, a contemporary author of a remarkable book on the systematic exploration of inner space, reports that this was accomplished for him by "merely the renunciation of private enjoyment of bliss." [25]   This is beyond consciousness without an object, it is now Consciousness without a subject.

The difficulties here for the student are nearly insurmountable for, Wolff continues,

> ...when we deal with the notion of a state of Con-
> sciousness which, in addition to transcending the
> subject-object framework, is also marked by being
> neutral with respect to bliss and its opposite, it
> appears that here we have something that lies quite
> outside the range of either human conception or de
> sire. That, in addition, such a state should have the
> highest superiority and could even be preferred to a
> state of bliss, certainly seems fantastic to say the
> least. Yet I can testify that such is the case.[26]

It is only when the last attachments are broken, even to the experience of bliss, that the highest pinnacle of pure consciousness is reached. There is no longer a further level from which to observe. Patanjali in describing this state says simply:

"Then the seer abides in itself."*

*Yoga Sutras of Patanjali, Book I, Sutra 3.

CHAPTER SEVEN
CHAKRAS

Write the things which thou hast seen, and the things which are, and the things which shall be hereafter; the mystery of the seven stars.

Revelations 1: 19-20

chapter 7
THE SEVEN CENTERS OF CONSCIOUSNESS

THE CHAKRAS: THE INNER PLAYROOM

It should be clear by now that yoga science is very complex and extensive. It includes a science of the body, an understanding of the energy level which governs the body's functions, a study of the mind and higher states of consciousness as well as a whole philosophy of the structure and nature of the universe. This would seem enough to occupy a whole faculty of university professors and medical school specialists. Yet we have said that the major asset of yoga is its ability to integrate all these various disciplines into one meaningful whole. Its beauty is really in its simplicity and accuracy.

But how is it possible to integrate so many diverse areas of science and philosophy? How can all these bits and pieces of understanding be pulled into a coordinated whole? It would seem that yoga like modern science and psychology would break down into a host of different specialties that couldn't communicate and had no common ground. The reason it does not is that its philosophy, its understanding of all these various aspects of the human being, are organized around one's inner experience. The many facets of oneself and his world are coordinated by means of bringing them together within the field of inner life. Here they find their focus and their unity.

If one is to explore the world of inner experiences, his thoughts, his emotions, and learn about himself, he must have some framework within which to do this. He must have a "playroom"—a sort of workshop or laboratory within which he can experiment with experiencing and expressing different aspects of his being and different reactions to the world. The framework provided by understanding the centers of consciousness gives him a place to do this. It provides the student with a structured inner space in which he can play.

The more one studies these centers, their nature, and their interrelationships, the more he comes to understand the difference between various psychologies and therapeutic points of view. He becomes more able to understand and put in perspective different aspects of personality and to grasp in a first hand way what goes on during the evolution of consciousness. Many things can be simplified and understood in a coherent, orderly way by understanding the various centers of consciousness and how they function.

Throughout the course of this book, we have seen how the yoga concept of who and what we are is very comprehensive. It goes beyond the idea that we have only a physical body which is controlled by a vague and undefinable thing called the mind. We have seen how beyond the physical body there are other "bodies" which, though operating on levels different from it, are coordinated with it.

The first of these is the energy body and beyond it lies what

we have called the "mental body." In other words, part of us is
physical, having to do with various systems; muscular, skeletal,
circulatory, respiratory, and so forth. But also a part of us, in
terms of our functional selves, is energy. When we take in food
and digest it, we extract energy which allows us to move around
and do things. It is also energy which allows us to think as well
as perform actions. Though we may characterize energy as
chemical, as electrical or as something still more subtle, it is in
any case always involved along with the material phenomena of
our functioning. A third aspect of the system is thinking. Matter
and energy alone do not complete the picture. Some mental
action is always involved. You might say that there are at least
these three obvious components to our experience.

But, underlying them is a more basic principle, that which we
call consciousness. This is, of course, the basic phenomena in
yoga psychology. Consciousness is sometimes compared to a
light, and the different bodies to lamp shades which cover it.
These shades surround the light, one inside the other, each of
a different color and material. Each shade captures light to a
certain degree and is illuminated by it. Each transforms the
light and modifies it according to its properties. The outer
shades are the densest and allow the least light through. If
we remove each of them in turn, the light becomes brighter
and brighter and is less and less obscured. The physical body,
the energy or pranic body, the mental body, and those beyond,
have each been described in the preceding chapters. Each fits
inside the next and is like another shade illuminated by the light
of consciousness. Each is denser than the one just interior to it.
Or, in the terms of yoga philosophy, each involves to a greater
degree the principle of matter *(prakriti)*. Because of the way
these bodies cover up and conceal the underlying consciousness
(purusha), they are often called in the ancient philosophical
writings "sheaths."

These bodies or sheaths do not each function independently.
There is a connection between them so that they are more or

less coordinated. We have seen, for instance, how the mental body, the energy body and the physical body interact: if one focuses his *thoughts* on the solar plexus, it increases the concentration of the *energy* in that level. This concentration of energy speeds up the action of the digestive organs and improves their ability to secrete enzymes and process food. The solar plexus serves here as a focal point for the interaction between three bodies or sheaths. The solar plexus is a point in the physical body, but it also corresponds to a point in the energy "body" and in the mental "body." This point is thus a center of activity in each of these bodies. It constitutes, then, a sort of nodal point, a point of connection through which the three can interact. It is one of the "centers of consciousness" which provide the links between the various sheaths. The correspondence among the three bodies is best understood by studying experientially these centers of consciousness that serve as points of interconnection between them.

These centers we will describe are seven in number.* They are called *chakras*. Their positions correspond, in the physical body, to points along the spinal cord. The first is located at the base of the spine near the tiny little bone that lies at the lowest extreme of the vertebral column (coccyx). The second center is just a few inches up above that at the level of the genitals (in the region of the sacrum). The third is located at the level of the navel, and is associated with the solar plexus. The fourth center is near the area of the heart. It lies at a point of intersection between a line drawn through the arms and shoulders and one through the trunk. These centers are all in a vertical line when one is sitting erectly. This is one reason for sitting straight during meditation: the centers are aligned. The fifth center is at the base of the throat. The sixth center lies at the point between the two eyebrows, while the seventh and last

---

* A number of "minor," less important centers have also been described elsewhere.[1] To avoid too much complexity, however, they will not be discussed here.

is at the topmost point of the skull, at the "crown" of the
head. The highest or "crown" chakra has to do with the highest
state of consciousness—while the lowest chakras are more closely
tied to the animal or instinct-based side of human nature.*
Developing the capacity to concentrate more energy, attention
and awareness at the higher centers is one aspect of what happens
as one's growth proceeds and consciousness evolves.

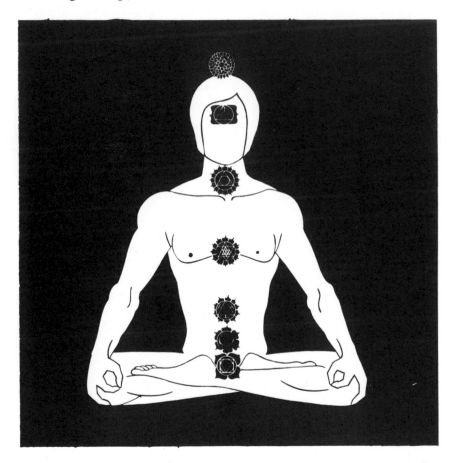

* Though the chakras serve to interconnect the sheaths, the higher chakras are more
closely related to the innermost sheaths—higher (inward dwelling) levels of consciousness—and the lower chakras to the outermost sheaths—lower (outward-going) levels of
consciousness.

The Chakras: Centers of Integration

The word *chakra* itself means "wheel" in Sanskrit. At the
outer circumference of a wheel there is more space, more
material, more diversity, more movement. When one focuses
on the rim of the wheel, it flies by in a blur, like the variegated
world of material phenomena. This outermost aspect of the
chakra relates to the grossest sheath, the physical body and
material world. As one moves inward, the spokes of the wheel
converge, and the dizzying movement slows. The inner aspects
of the chakra correspond to the higher sheaths, energy, mental,
etc. At the center is the center of consciousness—*purusha,* or
Self.

Within each one of these dynamic centers can be seen, in
condensed form, the relationship between certain aspects of the
physical world, the energy system, the mind and higher consciousness. For example, at the solar plexus, aggression, assertiveness, fire, heat, digestion, assimilation and active metabolism,
intermix in a way that cuts across our separate concepts of
what is physical, what is physiological and what is psychological.

Moreover, the interaction between the higher sheaths or
levels of consciousness and the lower level of material phenomena
and external events that is brought into awareness when one
focuses his attention on one of the centers will reflect much
about his particular circumstances, his peculiar place in the
world, and the course of events that comprise his life. Traditionally, these centers are likened to wheels of fortune. In the
carnival midway we find the wheel of fortune spinning constantly while people look on in fascination. We put our quarter
on the numbered space and the wheel of fortune begins to turn.
If it comes out in our favor, we win. We leave with our arms full.
If not, we go away discouraged, or, maybe we try again. Our
fate is decided by the spin of a wheel. Symbolically then, the

idea of the wheel of fortune has something to do with destiny, karma, and the spinning that unfolds the future. Thus, the term "chakras" or "wheels" for these centers of consciousness is apropos, for, like the wheel of fortune, they have a great deal to do with the shape and outcome of one's experience on its various levels. The spinning focus of energy and imagery experienced at each of these points reflects very concisely one's basic nature and contains the seeds of the fortune that awaits him.

Let's take the example of energy again. We each have available a certain amount of energy and it can be directed within our systems in different ways. This energy can be focused in one place rather than another; it can be concentrated in one chakra or in another. The chakras are points where, on the pranic level, energy has its highest concentration and, anatomically, the nerves come together to form their most important centers or plexuses. In medicine it is recognized that within each system there are places where functioning is most vital, places which are most highly energized. This centralization of vital functioning is a characteristic of each of the different systems of the physical body. Moreover, these systems interact with each other at special points. Examples of system interaction points include the cardiac plexus, where a very important network of nerves surrounds the heart; and the solar plexus at the level of the navel, where the control functions of several systems that have to do with digestion and its regulation are more or less centered. Other chakras are associated with the major endocrine glands such as the thyroid, pineal and pituitary. Modern medical research has established that the endocrine glands serve as strategic points of interaction between physiological, emotional and psychological functioning.

From the point of view of yoga, one who is ill is unable to distribute his energy properly through the centers. Poor digestion may mean an inadequate focus of energy in the area of the solar plexus. This means improper control of the bodily functions governed here. Since the chakra is a point of intersection between the various sheaths, mental factors are obviously important, too. When there is a weakness at that center physically, pranically, psychologically, etc., one is susceptible to diseases of the digestive system.*

The Chakras and Symbolism

The chakras provide a sort of central point, an underlying framework, in which a multitude of factors intersect and interact. It should be clear that the experience of these centers is a highly intricate and complex affair. Any attempt to express it in words is certain to prove to be only partially successful. The experience of the centers of consciousness or chakras is a non-verbal one. Putting it into words is really difficult. It is for this reason that the chakras have been described symbolically. Even this, of course, presents problems, especially for the Westerner. The classic symbolic descriptions are framed in the terms of Eastern culture. For instance, one of the best known translations of the literature on the chakras bears the following description:

> ...at the center of the region of the navel, is the lotus Manipura...so called...because, owing to the presence of the fiery Tejas, it is lustrous as a gem...the triangular region of the Tejas-Tattva...has three Svastikas. The red Bija of fire, "Ram," is seated on a ram, the carrior of Agni, the lord of fire. Here is the old red Rudra, smeared with white ashes, and the Sakti Lakini who is Devata of this digestive center is said to be "fond of animal food, and whose breasts are ruddy with the blood and fat which drop from Her mouth."[2]

* Dr. Shafiia Karagulla studied several people whose awareness was developed to the point that they were able to "observe" the energy distribution in these centers. One of Dr. Karagulla's subjects, Diane, was able to use her awareness of the energy movement in these centers to accurately diagnose physical disorders.

Traditional representation of
the manipura (solar plexus) chakra.

The intuitions and understandings of literature, of art, of
mythology, of religious symbolism, of physiology, physics and
metaphysics all come together at a central focus in the centers of
consciousness called the chakras. All understanding is distilled
here. This is what is meant by saying that "the microcosm
reflects the macrocosm." By immersing oneself in this inner
experience, an understanding of the coordination between the
various aspects of oneself and the universe begins to grow.

When one sits quietly, with his eyes closed, and focuses his
attention on a particular center, he may catch a glimpse of a
certain color, or he may have a fleeting impression of an inner
sound, or he may observe that memories and thoughts of one
particular type tend to bubble up into his awareness. If one
focuses attention on the genital center, for example, sexual

thoughts, memories and fantasies begin to appear.

It becomes obvious, then, that each of the chakras has a rich meaning and is vast in its significance. Each center pulls together different aspects of the external and inner worlds into a coordinated, but difficult to describe, whole. Here the relationship between certain objects, colors, sounds and certain inner states (the essence of what we call symbolism, poetry, music and art) is clearly evident. Thus it is that at the solar plexus, where aggression is a central issue, the Ram figures as a prominent symbol, and the goddess is pictured as having blood dripping from her lips and lusting for flesh foods. The color is red and descriptions always include fire.

The descriptions of these centers are not limited to Eastern philosophy or psychology. Since they refer to underlying experiences in all human beings we might expect similar descriptions in many cultures and historical periods wherever man's sensitivity and capacity for subtle inner exploration have been highly cultivated. Thus, for example, we find strikingly similar descriptions of such centers in the Hopi Indian culture. Here five of these seven centers have been identified. When the young Hopi child of seven or eight received his first initiation into a religious society he was taught that:

> The living body of man and the living body of the earth were constructed in the same way. Through each ran an axis, man's axis being the backbone, the vertebral column.....Along this axis were several vibratory centers....[3]

The experience encountered at these focal points can be followed outward into any area of human thought or endeavor. We will focus here primarily on one limited aspect of their implications: We will attempt to present some aspects of their relation to psychology, psychopathology and psychosomatic diseases.

I. THE ROOT (ANAL) CHAKRA: FEAR AND PARANOIA

Survival

The lowest center at the base of the spine is psychologically related to the most rudimentary survival instincts. It is connected with feelings of fear, the instinct for self-preservation and a kind of jungle mentality. Here there is a great preoccupation with physical and bodily survival. This can be seen most clearly in the animal who lives in the wild. The most primitive responses to life threatening situations involve energy at this point. This energy is not normally under conscious control and is to a great extent related to such autonomic responses as flight and fright. This can be observed in the squirrel, for instance, which is always on the lookout. It constantly looks around to see that nothing is going to attack. As soon as it sees another animal or a person, it scurries away. Such alertness and concern about self-preservation is a very common aspect of animal life. The first chakra is related to this very basic and primitive fear of being attacked or injured. On the other hand it is also related to attacking, being aggressive and searching out prey. The animal that hunts and kills another animal in order to eat it is also working at this level where the most basic survival instincts are focused.

Mentally, when a person has his energy centered here he will be concerned about being hurt by others, not only psychologically but in a physical sense. One who has an unregulated focus of energy at the first chakra is constantly afraid of being injured or has a strong tendency to hurt and injure others, to attack another person in some way. The fear involved here is an intense, unreasonable fear of the magnitude that is associated with the role of the hunter and the hunted. It is a total and global sort of anxiety. Threats are not sensed so much as presenting the danger of loss, but rather as potential sources of total annihilation. The massive kind of terror associated with this chakra is seen in psychosis and in patients who are undergoing a paranoid episode.

The following statement about the nature and purpose of life from someone who looks at the world primarily from the perspective of this chakra is taken from an interview by one of the authors with a young man in his mid-twenties. He had been convicted of rape twice, and admitted to a number of brutal physical attacks upon others. At the time of the interview, he was a patient in a maximum security state mental hospital.

> You see, man is like an animal and like a hunter. He stalks the game he's going to kill....I feel that people are stalking me. So while they're stalking me, I'm

stalking them. It's a cycle going round and round. It's
survival of the fittest. I'm being stalked, so I stalk
them, constantly. You see, I'm not going to let anyone
mess me around. Like an animal—if he senses somebody's going to kill him, he's going to try to get you
first. And that's how I feel. That's what life is, just a
game of survival when you get downright basic about
it. I do unto people what they would do unto me.

Each of the chakras is associated with a certain "element."
These are not to be confused with the elements of modern
chemistry which refer to *structure* on the atomic level. In
Indian philosophy all the phenomenal universe is seen as made
up of some combination of five basic ingredients or *bhutas*.
These each contain different proportions of matter *(prakriti)*
and consciousness *(purusha)*. These proportions possess the
quality of solidity (earth), that which is liquid (water), that
which is combustive (fire), that which is like a gas (air), and
that which constitutes the space in which the others exist
(ether). These are neither literally earth, water, fire, etc. nor
merely material, molecular substances. They are "elemental" in
the sense that everything can be analyzed into some combination
of them. They are practical and operational in that all the
phenomenal world can be both understood in these terms and
through them easily related to other aspects of our existence,
such as energy, mind and higher consciousness.

The first chakra is associated with the element of earth. It is
associated with the denser levels of the being, that is, the physical
body and awareness of and attention to the material plane. In
this way it is easy to see how concerns about protection and
preservation of the body and physical existence are involved
when consciousness is centered at this chakra.

It is interesting that anatomically, this center is in the area of
the anus and is associated with the excretion of solid matter from

the body. When animals are observed in frightening situations, it will be seen that defecation is one of the main components of their fear response. If they are intensely frightened, they will defecate repeatedly. Persons who are subject to this primitive, basic fear may begin having bowel problems. If there is a strong underlying fear running throughout their emotional lives, they may develop such illnesses as ulcerative colitis or chronic diarrhea.

Emotionally and psychologically this chakra is concerned with the most primitive fears and the most extreme degrees of pathology. This dichotomy between the attacker and the attacked is related to the formation of the original categories of good and bad. It is at a time when one is beginning to experience these earliest primitive fears that he is beginning to organize his experience into the basic categories of what is pleasurable and what is painful or threatening. This lays the foundations for psychic organization. We have seen earlier how the bad or painful aspect of the infant's environment is what threatens his security. They threaten to overwhelm him and annihilate him. Later on, when his own negative or destructive impulses come up and he projects them out into the world, they also are sensed as threats, as potential attacks. This projection or attitude of paranoia often results when there is a habitual focus of energy at the first chakra. Classically, in psychoanalytic theory, paranoid thinking relates to a fear of attack from behind, which may in some cases be accompanied by fantasies of anal rape.

Becoming Conscious of Latent Fear and Paranoia

In many cases the energy focus at this center is not expressed in an obvious way. While most persons are not blatantly paranoid or consciously concerned with violence and attack, an undercurrent of paranoid functioning may color their emotional lives. Bringing this into awareness is often an important part of any successful process of growth.

As long as one operates from a predominantly paranoid stance, he remains unaware of much of himself. Everything that is negative or destructive is disowned and projected onto people around him. For this reason his destructive impulses are not really under his control. He is simply denying that they are part of him. He sees himself as very loving and kind. It is other people he has to watch out for. They want to hurt him, manipulate him or attack him. This attitude maintains a constant focus of energy at the first chakra. When too much of one's personality is not integrated, but projected out into the world, then he is constantly tossed about by fear and defensiveness. There is no feeling of solidity about him. In the ancient symbols of Indian thought it is said that the element of earth is deficient. He is flighty; he is jumpy; he is undependable. He vascillates from sweetness to viciousness or fearful defensiveness. Of course, the only way out of the dilemma is to bring into awareness the parts of himself that he really hasn't wanted to face.

The Buddhist scriptures tell the story of a farmer who grew the most spectacular crops year after year. He collected the manure from his animals and spread it over the land. Each year the soil was restored and the harvest once more came out to be rich and wonderful. The secret was the manure which fertilized the crops. The farmer's work was to dig out the manure and spread it over the field. A second farmer found such work unappealing. He didn't want to get involved in the dirty side of farm work, so he didn't collect the manure to spread on the fields. After a few years his harvest began to dwindle. His crops no longer grew well. The soil became sterile.[4] Psychological growth is based on the process of continually bringing into awareness parts of oneself that were before regarded as repulsive and unsavory, so that they can become integrated and transmuted.

Though the experience of being dominated by the consciousness and energies of the first chakra may sound rather strange to the average person, there are certain schools of psychology and psychiatry that have dealt with this area. The writings of Harry Stack Sullivan, for example, deal especially with psychotic experience and describe what it's like to see the world from the point of view of this first chakra, to be concerned constantly with the fear of annihilation, and to live in an intensely paranoid world.

Cultural Implications

We can characterize not only individuals and schools of psychology in terms of the chakra on which they focus but cultures as well. Primitive societies which are concerned primarily with hunting and basic survival in a natural environment where survival of the fittest rules, reflect a domination of the anal chakra. In any social situation where law and order breaks down, there may occur a sort of cultural shift and predominant functioning may come to be oriented around survival and the fear of attack: a dramatic example is seen in the old Western movies where the vigilantes ran rampant. Toward the other extreme, an excessive or rigid emphasis on law and order can also betray a predominant influence by the first chakra. In a subtler way this influence can be seen in contemporary Western culture's exaggerated concern with dirt and "germs."

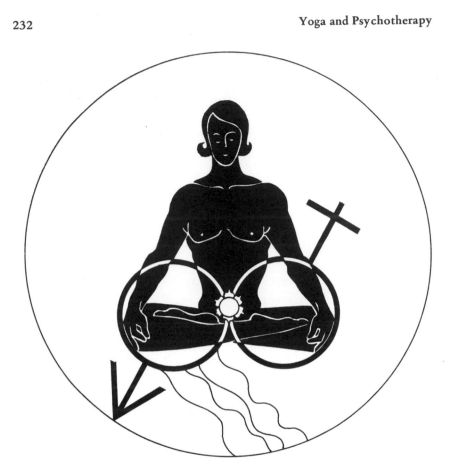

II. THE GENITAL CHAKRA: SENSUALITY AND SEXUALITY

The second center of consciousness is located near the genital organs and physiologically this is where the output of fluids, i.e., control of urination and the expulsion of semen takes place. Whereas the anal chakra was associated with the earth element, this center is connected with the element of water.

Psychologically, this center is concerned with sexual impulses, with lustful feelings, and with an emphasis on sensory pleasure. Whereas the first chakra is concerned with individual survival and self-preservation, the energies at this center concern the survival of the species. Though this is still a biological and instinctual urge, it is less primitive, a little beyond the more basic fear of being annihilated. Its purpose is something beyond simple defensiveness and self-protection. It is responsible for a kind of creativity, albeit one which is still operating on a gross biological level.

A person who has his energy centered in this second chakra will be someone who is preoccupied with sensual pleasures, especially sexual experience. When he meets another person he will tend to regard that person as a sexual object rather than as a companion, friend, competitor or as someone to be feared (as was the case when the first chakra was predominant).

Involvement in sexual acts, however, does not necessarily indicate a focus of energy at this center of consciousness. The young man described earlier who had raped a number of women and who had an extreme preoccupation with survival was asked: "What was on your mind during these attacks, physical pleasure or survival?" In recalling these experiences he said: "Sex is no big thing. It was just done for revenge. You've got to hurt someone once in a while to survive."

Certainly a person whose energy is centered at the second chakra is less crippled and more free than a person who is constantly preoccupied with the fear of annihilation that is associated with the focus of energy at the first chakra.

> When your consciousness is primarily directed toward providing you with the sensation patterns to which you are addicted, you will have more energy than when it was hung up on the Security Center of consciousness.* You will usually be with more people and you will need to sleep less. An individual who is hunting for sex is definitely generating more energy than a person who is worried about his security. In fact, those whose consciousness is heavily addicted to the Security Level

* First chakra

will probably have dropped off to sleep during the
early part of the evening.[5]

Freudian psychology takes its viewpoint about the nature of
man from the orientation of this chakra. The basic theory of the
psychological nature of man in the original orthodox Freudian
system was derived from a study of sexual impulses. Sexuality
was thought of as underlying all motivation. All conflict and
discontent was initially thought to be associated with difficulties
which were basically of a sexual nature. Freud's perspective on
man seems to have been colored by the perspective of this
chakra.

The energies available at this level are, of course, so potent
that when one simply attempts to suppress them, they may
continue to influence motivation and personality. In the
tradition of yoga there are two methods of dealing with these
energies. One can continue to channel energies through this
chakra in an attempt to experience sex and sensuality in such
a way that it contributes to his self-exploration and growth.
Another possibility is to avoid focusing energy in this center
and to concentrate on channeling or "raising" it to higher
centers. This redirecting, which is called *sublimation* in psychoanalytic theory, allows the energy to be used for creative and
productive purposes, such as art, or the self-exploration involved
in meditation. This second path, that of sexual control or
brahmacharya is, therefore, not merely the outward suppression
and avoidance of sexual activity, but rather an inner rechanneling
of the energy that would be released sexually.

Sexual activity discharges a huge quantity of energy. Often we
can tolerate only so much of the tension that results from the
accumulation of energy in our systems. As energy builds up, we
tend to become restless and look for some route of discharge.
This may be in the form of emotional outbursts, "I've just got
to let it all out." Then there is a sense of relief. Things calm
down again. In other cases the release is accomplished through

sexual activity. If this has become the customary method of relieving tension, then suppression of sex for a while is likely to result in a state of tension and restlessness. There will be not only a physical tension and the sense of unease, but a psychological discomfort as well. But with the proper training, the same energy can be refocused at other centers. This becomes increasingly possible as the process of personal growth and evolution proceeds. Gradually the energy can be tolerated and pleasurably employed in a variety of ways. It's as though one's "circuits" mature and come to be able to handle a higher voltage.

According to the ancient yogic manuals, in Vedic times there was a particular initiation which was given by the yogis to a few advanced disciples who practiced sexual control. This method, called *urdhvaretas* or "leading upward," helped to lead the energy (which normally goes into the creation of offspring) to ascend to the brain and recirculate it in the body. It channeled consciousness from lower to higher centers. This method of "upward traveling" is still known to a few yogis today. They report that the joy which is found in discharging sexual energy, or releasing sexual tension, cannot be compared with that joy which results from conserving that energy and leading it to focus at the higher chakras.

But not all schools of yoga deal with sexual and sensual energies by non-expression and sublimation. There are certain practices in a "leftist" branch of tantra yoga where the use of what would ordinarily be sensual objects of experiences, e.g., the taking of meat, alcohol, or the practice of sexual intercourse, is a part of the process of self-exploration and spiritual development. What some may view as sources of dissipation are utilized as means of growth. This is a tricky undertaking and can easily degenerate into a sort of depleting indulgence. But, when correctly done, one's involvement with the external object is a means toward transcending his attachment to it.

The successful use of these practices might be best understood by recalling that the higher and more transpersonal levels of

consciousness can only be approached once the personal subconscious has been successfully explored and integrated. At the
deeper levels of the subconscious one encounters the tendency
within himself to become one with the objects of perception.
Here one encounters the massive attachments and the feeling of
total identification and absorption in another. Here where the
higher, more developed levels of mental function are not in
force, there is experienced a primitive, regressive merging. It is
on this level where psychic phenomena can occur, where one
manas becomes intermingled with the *manas* of another person.
Here, from the point of view of ancient yoga psychology, even
the basic psychic *prana* or *chitta* can come in contact with and
mix with that of another person.

The tantric practices of ritualized immersion in sensual
experience are methods of experimenting with these phenomena.
They are an approach to the experience of oneness and total
identification. They bring up from the depths of the personal
subconscious the tendency to fuse and merge with another.
They provide a framework within which one can play with and
explore the experience of becoming one with some other person
or thing by bringing into behavior and awareness these most
fundamental layers of mental life through rituals involving union
with external objects. They bring the student to discover the
inner dimensions of such experiences and to develop those levels
of consciousness in themselves from which union is more
transpersonal. Tantric techniques bring sensuality into awareness
so that it can become a means of transcending itself.

In the practice of tantra the student learns to redirect the urge
to transcend himself and merge with another from the physical
to the more subtle sheaths. At first he may regard an object or
person in sensual terms and seek fusion at the physical level. But
the ritualization of physical acts and the learning of observational
skills in the midst of sensual activities leads one to see beyond the
physical and sensory interaction and even beyond the fusion of
personalities. Tantra teaches one to see the latent all-inclusive

consciousness that exists within the other and to relate to and fuse
with that innermost level of the other's being. Thus the intercourse
between one and another becomes transformed. The male and
female come to experience themselves as the male and female
principle of the universe. In more advanced tantric practices
physical objects are no longer needed and the tendency toward
fusion is brought into consciousness at a more abstract level than
in external tantric ritual.*

Of course, such techniques can only be successful if their
practice is accompanied by at least some degree of non-attachment.
Observation is necessary if learning is to occur. To play with
these experiences means to not become caught up and lost in the
pleasure itself. There must be a certain restraint, a certain distance,
and in the case of sex, the sexual act an attitude of not being
rushed to attain the climax itself. Openness and control, a sense of
"foreplay" is necessary. In the words of one Western therapist
who has tried to use sensuality to evolve a growth-promoting
technique:

> If a person is living a sexual life and living out of his
> sexual feeling, then all of life is foreplay and one is
> ready to enter or be entered.

He says

> Pleasure is not only gratification, it is not only
> satisfaction.....it is that state of being which is itself
> gratifying....pleasure is really that state of feeling,
> acting which is truthful to one's becoming....Pleasure

---

* Traditionally in yoga three classes of tantric practices exist: 1) *kaula*—using
externals and making physical acts a means of worship; 2) *mishra*—a mixed form which
uses external worship but also focuses on raising the energy through the chakras to
develop one's creative potential; and 3) *samaya*—the most pure form of tantra where
the constituent principles from which the universe is manifest are merged with directly
through the use of ritual mantram and visualization.[6] Most Western conceptualizations
of tantra fall into the first or at best second category. The practice or understanding
of the more pure and evolved tantric practices are known only to a handful of
individuals.

then is not the search for itself by avoiding pain or the pursuit of hedonistic goals. It is more a *unitary* movement toward contact, self-expression, toward becoming who we are.

Here pleasure becomes redefined. It is really what we can call "joy."

Being who we are is pleasurable, self-revelation is pleasurable. It is the root of joy....*joy-pleasure is the feeling of our growth and aliveness.* We who think that we are gods because we have created a world are in our trap because we try to enjoy that which we have created, instead of really enjoying the creator in the act of creation.[7]

III. THE SOLAR PLEXUS CHAKRA:
DOMINATION AND SUBMISSION

Each of these chakras is experienced as being aligned along an axis. In the terms of the pranic sheath, this might be thought of as an "energy axis" that extends vertically through the center of the body from the base of the spine to the top of the skull. This axis runs centrally, not along the outer surface of the back. When one sits properly for meditation, the spinal column itself becomes aligned with this axis and the two are congruent. Under these conditions the experience of energy in the centers along the axis is easier to perceive.

The third center of consciousness is located at the level of the navel. This third center is associated with the element of fire. We often refer to this area of the body as the "solar plexus." It is a sort of internal sun produced by the oxidation or "burning" of food. In contrast to plants which can take their energy directly from the sun itself, animals must produce their own energy. They take that energy trapped in the plant matter and release it through the chemical processes of digestion. This creates an inner flame or fire which provides the energy for maintaining life. When this inner flame is properly regulated it allows the person to be healthy, to digest his food properly and to have a consistent energy level without being easily fatigued. If it is improperly regulated, it can lead to various disease states such as digestive problems like peptic ulcer. The flame may also, in other cases, be excessive but poorly centered so that one is red-faced, hot-tempered and irritable. Energy is ordinarily stored at this solar plexus center. When the solar plexus chakra is energized, one has the quality of being dynamic and assertive.

When the psychological issues related to this chakra have not been brought into consciousness and resolved, then the resulting conflict will lead to a preoccupation with control and the exertion of power over other people. The issue becomes one of domination versus submission. Such a person may be given to a tyrannical kind of assertiveness, spending all his time and effort in extending his personal power. Or he may be just the opposite: submissive and cowed. More often, however, he will alternate between the two, depending on the situation. Such people are often labeled "authoritarian personalities." They are unable to see other people as peers, but judge everyone as either superior or inferior. They cast others into the roles of either authority figures or underlings.

Other personality types may also reflect unresolved conflicts related to this center. Psychological studies of ulcer patients show that they are often the sort of people who force themselves to take on the responsibilities of a dominant, controlling position, although basically, underneath, they have a tendency to be passive, dependent and submissive.

One school of psychology which has focused on this aspect of functioning was founded by Alfred Adler who coined the term "inferiority complex." He dealt extensively with the way we compensate for inferiority feelings by creating a false sense of superiority. Adler tended to see his patients as being preoccupied with concerns about adequacy, competition, power and domination. He pointed out that even the sexual act can be experienced primarily in terms of conquest and domination rather than in terms of sexual pleasure. He felt that in childhood the feelings of inadequacy and inferiority experienced because of one's relative helplessness were very important and that much of human behavior could be explained in terms of an attempt to overcome this underlying feeling of inferiority and to gain a position of superiority. Out of this childhood experience, however, grew many of the positive aspects of control and autonomy that are necessary for mature functioning.

Although Freud did not approve of Adler's preoccupation with these issues, his own theory of psychology gradually developed in the direction of dealing with the more constructive aspects of ego-functioning. This grew into what is currently called "ego psychology." It is interesting to note the parallel between the psychoanalytic theory of development stages through which each person passes and the yogic hierarchy of chakras. Freud's anal and phallic stages seem closely related to the first two chakras.* Erik Erikson's extension of Freud's developmental model describes the next stage of development (corresponding to this third chakra) as centering on the issue of "industry vs. inferiority."[8]

* The issue of orality and trust which in the psychoanalytic model reflect the earliest stage in development are seen as being resolved at more advanced levels of development in the yogic system. See section on the fifth chakra.

The first three centers or chakras which have been described thus far are related to basic instinctual urges and needs for self maintenance.   They are concerned with self-protection, with propagation of the species and with functioning effectively in a competitive world.   There is a progressive movement from the most basic concerns to those which are more refined.   The first chakra is dominated by concern for self-preservation and the prevention of annihilation.   The second center is associated with sensual gratification, especially sexuality.   In a larger sense this relates to the maintenance of the species.   The third center is concerned with effective and assertive individual behavior which will permit one to provide for his personal needs: clothing, shelter, and the securing and digestion of food.*   As we move to the fourth chakra, however, we leave the field of domination by the instinctual and materially oriented aspects of life and move to a perspective that transcends the individual.

* As we shall see later Abraham Maslow has proposed a motivational hierarchy similar to that suggested here. In Maslow's theory, however, physiological safety and security needs are seen as more "primary" and once they are fulfilled the individual is motivated by more self-actualizing tendencies.

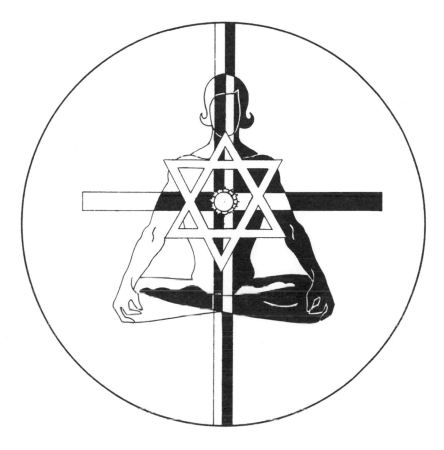

IV. THE HEART CHAKRA: FROM EMOTION TO EMPATHY

The heart chakra corresponds to a point between the breasts
and along the spine. It marks a sort of transition between those
chakras below it, which are concerned with the more biological
matters of self-maintenance and survival, and the chakras above it,
which are associated with a more evolved consciousness. The
higher chakras, as we shall see, relate to a kind of awareness that
is less tied down to the physical world, less bound up in attachments, and increasingly transpersonal in nature.

This chakra lies just above the diaphragm. The diaphragm is a dome-shaped muscular structure which separates the abdominal cavity from the chest cavity. Beneath the hollow of the dome lie the stomach, liver, duodenum, the major portion of the digestive apparatus, the solar plexus and, as we have seen, the third chakra. Lying on top of the dome formed by the diaphragm is the heart. It is surrounded by the two lungs and enmeshed in a network of nerves called the cardiac plexus. The center point of all this activity and energy is called the heart chakra, which is related to the element *air*.

This is the center of nurturance. The lungs are responsible for giving oxygen to the blood while the heart distributes this throughout the body, sending with it the nutrients that are necessary for growth and activity. It is at this level that the breasts are located. They are the only organs which are structured exclusively for the purpose of providing nourishment to another. Emotions and feelings for another person are often experienced as a welling up of energy in this region at the center of the chest. A feeling of going out toward, or relating strongly to, another person is traditionally expressed by the phrases "heartfelt," or "my heart went out to him." The heart is the symbol of emotion and feeling in the language of many cultures. Strong emotions are often accompanied by clearly identifiable physical sensations in the region of the heart and chest. For example, when ties to another are broken we often speak of "heartache" or "a broken heart." This sort of feeling and emotion marks a departure from the biological and survival concerns which are related to the lower three chakras. The diaphragm serves as a sort of boundary between the lower, more instinctual nature of man and the higher centers which become increasingly related to a more evolved consciousness.

In one American Indian tradition, the diaphragm is compared to the surface of the earth. Below this lies the subterranean level of instincts and man's animal nature. This is the realm of solid matter. Above this is the sky, the higher realms of man's more developed and evolved consciousness. Between heaven and earth lies the diaphragm. This body scheme is also echoed in the ancient symbols of Mexico, Egypt and the Middle East.[9]

The heart chakra is important because it represents the first dawning of consciousness above the horizon represented by the diaphragm. When the energy stored in the solar fire of the third chakra can be elevated to activate and bring to life the feelings and empathy which are the potential of the heart chakra, then the effect is, symbolically, likened to the rising sun. It radiates warmth. In biological evolution, the development of the capacity for feeling and compassion is a major step forward toward a higher consciousness.

Because this chakra is the center where our more basic impulses and our more evolved aspirations are integrated, the heart chakra is represented in many traditions by the six-pointed star. This symbol, which is found in ancient Indian writings as well as in the Hebrew tradition, is made up of two triangles, one pointing up, the other down. Their superimposition represents an integration of the higher and lower aspects of man's nature.

The heart chakra is of central importance in yoga theory because the heart is the meeting point between two separate polarities in the body's energy field. The first is that which exists between the chakras above and those below. The second is the polarity that exists between the right and left sides. As we have seen earlier, the right represents the active, the male, *yang* side of one's nature while the left corresponds to the passive, female, *yin* characteristics. A line drawn horizontally to represent this polarity between the right and left and one drawn vertically to represent the polarity between the higher and lower chakras forms a cross which has its point of intersection at the heart chakra. This cross is a symbol that appears almost universally, its form varying slightly from culture to culture. The heart chakra, then, represents a center of integration for these polarities. An outflow of energy or an interaction organized around this center potentially involves the whole of the person.

Breathing: Integration of Lower and Upper Chakras

A full use of the diaphragm is very important in creating the physiological conditions that promote the integration of the lower instinctual aspects of the system with the higher, more conscious ones. When the diaphragm moves rhythmically and naturally, there is a free interplay between the instinctual energies and the more evolved consciousness above, which can coordinate and control them. The natural process of breathing is to inhale by contracting the diaphragm muscle, flattening out its dome shape. This act pushes the abdomen out a bit while it lowers the floor of the chest, increasing the space inside the rib cage and expanding the lungs. With exhalation, the diaphragm relaxes and allows the tightening abdominal muscles to force it upwards once more into its rounded, dome position. This decreases the space in the chest and collapses the lungs, forcing air outward. When breathing is carried out in this natural, relaxed way, very little effort is required. With a minimum of exertion by the diaphragm and the abdominal muscles, a great deal of air can be moved in and out. This creates an effortless, rhythmic sort of flow that promotes relaxation and a feeling of calmness. The chest and shoulder muscles are not used at all and the rib cage remains relaxed.

The use of the shoulder and chest muscles to assist in respiration is normally and naturally employed only when there is a great deal of exertion; in those situations, for example, where there is a necessity of flight or fight. In these cases, the lungs are filled to their full capacity by using not only the action of the diaphragm and abdominal muscles, but the chest and shoulder muscles are used also to expand the rib cage to its fullest. A maximum of air is brought in to provide the largest possible supply of oxygen so that one might defend himself or escape in the most effective possible way. These are situations associated with self-preservation, or in some cases, with sexual or aggressive behavior.

Some people have been found to habitually breathe in a very

awkward and uncoordinated way. When at rest, they use primarily chest and shoulder muscles which are normally employed only in emergency situations to supplement the action of the diaphragm. Yet the diaphragm itself is held in a fixed position and does not contribute to the respiratory movement at all.

Since respiratory movements by the chest are biologically and instinctually tied in with the emergency responses of self-defense or escape, their use tends to stir up these feelings. One who is feeling calm and has no reason for fear or anxiety will find that if he deliberately imitates these movements, his emotional state shifts. He soon begins to experience a state much like stress and alarm, a sort of feeling of anxiety.

Alexander Lowen has studied the relationship between respiration and personality disorders in some detail. He finds that the schizoid, the person who is withdrawn, who has hidden much of his personality from himself and the world, typically breathes in this shallow way, using mostly the chest muscles. He holds the diaphragm, stomach area and lower part of the body in a tight, rigid position. In this way he tries to avoid the experience of feelings and impulses arising from the area of the first three chakras. Sexual and aggressive feelings are difficult for him to control or integrate. His solution to this problem is to try, by keeping the diaphragm stationary, to prevent arousing such feelings and in this way keep them out of awareness.[10]

Of course, the more primitive and biological impulses do not lose their potency or influence simply because they are kept out of awareness. In fact, providing for the needs they represent becomes even more difficult, causing increased tension and anxiety. In such a situation, they tend to operate outside awareness to push and pull one in directions he cannot fully understand. Reason and intellect are dragged along and do their best to justify the irrational behavior that results. Clarity of consciousness in the higher chakras is diminished and what would be a higher mental activity comes to be instead a servant of distorted and twisted instinctual urges, justifying or denying

them as best it can. Often, teaching diaphragmatic breathing to
such persons can help bring back into awareness the impulses
with which they are blindly wrestling. If they can overcome
their aversion to these aspects of themselves, these can then be
integrated and come under some reasonable control. The
movement of the diaphragm is of central importance in providing
a physiological basis for such integration.

Emotions: Effects of the Lower Chakras

Though emotions involve energy at the level of the heart
chakra, instinctual influences from the lower chakras are also
involved. The more feelings are dominated by fear, for example,
or by sexual urges, the more the experience brings into play the
lower chakras. According to yoga there are four basic well-springs
from which emotion arises. These are the four instincts or
primitive urges that serve as the foundation for all emotional
experience. As mentioned earlier, these are: the push toward
self-preservation or self-protection, which is related to the first
chakra; the sexual urge related to the second; and the need for
fuel or food which is in some respects related to the area of the
third chakra, where food is digested and energy stored. These
three instinctual urges serve as "automatic survival mechanisms"
insuring that we don't neglect to provide for our basic needs.
When the fuel in our system runs low, we get hungry. If we
fail to provide ourselves with food, we're not allowed to forget.
The fourth of these urges is that for sleep.* It's somewhat
different from the first three. If one goes without sleep for long
enough, he becomes disturbed and may develop behavior resem-
bling a psychotic reaction. As we saw earlier, this urge to sleep
represents the basic need for experiencing higher consciousness.

* Again note the similarity to Maslow's theory of motivation which suggests that
"the most basic, the most powerful, the most obvious of all man's needs are his needs
for food, liquid, shelter, sex, sleep and oxygen."[11]

When we sink into the deepest sleep, our awareness is allowed to escape the confines of its everyday, waking restrictions.

These four basic instincts or urges underlie all emotions. The quality of the emotion varies, depending on how the instinctual urge is handled and how one reacts to it. Initially the satisfaction of these urges does not depend on specific objects. The need for food is merely a general urge to eat something and keep the body going. But in the course of one's life he learns to want not just food, but, for example, elaborate dishes or delicate pastries. Eventually, that's the only thing that will satisfy his craving. A plate of simple food is boring. The instinctual urge becomes *attached* to a specific object. These attachments are what lead us to become emotional in one way or another. Attachment or "addiction" is the basis of emotional experience. This is called *kama* in the yogic texts and is the fountain of all other emotions.

If the struggle to satisfy one's addictions is frustrated, he may become angry. For example:

> I arrive at the bakery to find that the last strawberry pie has just been sold. I become frustrated and angry: "I *called* you and told you to hold that pie for me and you sold it? What's the matter with you people here?!" There follows a justified rage, a fit of "righteous indignation."

In the terms of yoga psychology anger comes from the frustration of a basic drive experienced in the form of an attachment to a specific object, goal or idea. When such an attachment is thwarted, frustration and anger inevitably result. Or, on the other hand, if I see someone else walking out the door with the last pie, the emotional experience becomes envy or jealousy.

> Or, suppose I reach the store in time to buy my strawberry pie. But going out the door I trip and the pie flips out of my hand, landing upside-down on the ground. My beautiful strawberry pie is all squashed and dirty—

and it was the last one! I become disappointed—
even slightly depressed.

Our more profound depressions are over those losses where
attachment was very strong.

Out of the permutations of what may happen to the object
or person to which one is attached, each of the emotions arise.
In each case there are two components to the emotion. There is
the inherent urge from within and there is the learned experience
of what specific object will satisfy that urge. All emotions can
be understood as coming from one of the four instincts operating
in combination with some particular object to which it has
become attached.

Emotions and the Heart Chakra

When little energy is being elevated and experienced through
the heart chakra, when there is little "feeling," one will appear
emotionless and cold. This does not mean that he is not motivated by the most primitive instinctual urges. But we say of
such a person that he "has no heart." He's ruthless and doesn't
care about anyone else. He just forges ahead, walking over
everyone in his way. In diagnostic terms, we refer to such a
person as "psychopathic" or "sociopathic." His energy is
channeled through the lower chakras in a manner that shows no
concern for, or awareness of, others.

When a person has some energy focused at the heart center as
well as at the third or solar plexus center, he may still be somewhat
aggressive and egotistical, but his behavior will be at least partially
tempered by some consideration for others, by some compassion
and understanding. There will be a certain amount of integration.
The influence of the heart chakra lends a feeling component to
one's experience.

Sometimes in psychotherapy we see a patient who is beginning
for the first time to experience some feeling for others. He's

managed to free up some of the energy involved with the lower chakras and experience it at the level of the heart center. There begins to be an element of true "relatedness" in his interactions with others. But because of the contamination of this feeling with the drives related to the lower chakras, he gets himself in all sorts of predicaments. He may suddenly become absurdly romantic, for instance, spending all his money on expensive bouquets for his new-found love or squandering his savings on extravagant gifts. The therapist, however, may find himself reluctant to discourage such behavior, sensing that there is an element of something new here. From the therapist's perspective, the experience can be seen as a movement in the direction of growth although it still involves much pathology.

When the consciousness experienced at the heart chakra is not contaminated by influence from the instinctual urges, its quality is different. It would no longer be called, strictly speaking, emotion, but more simply "feelings"; for example, "a feeling of compassion." The less attachments are involved, the more feeling is free from an emotional coloring.

Through concentration on this center during meditation, the experience associated with it is separated out in its purity. By focusing on and magnifying the consciousness here, the con taminants from other chakras can gradually be distinguished and come to fall away. It is then that one is able to experience less adulterated feelings which, in contrast to the turmoil of his previous emotions, are more joyful and peaceful. One is then experiencing the feeling that would usually accompany emotion without the coloration of attachment and addictions. He's then able to relate to others more fully, less hindered by instinct-dominated concerns for himself.

Unadulterated feeling and "pure compassion" or "selfless love" are not to be confused with the blissful state of oneness that will be experienced toward the culmination of the evolution of consciousness. For there is still here a sense of separateness from others. But, there is no longer the same craving to possess or use them for the enhancement of personal power or sensual pleasure or to merge with them in an infantile manner. For the person whose life has never before been free from narrow self-concerns, the experience can be one of great freedom and joy. Though the "other" is still sensed as separate, he is no longer the object of frenetic attempts to possess, conquer or defeat.

Compassion is possible only when there is a certain sense of fullness, when there is no longer so much outside oneself that is craved. This fullness implies some internal integration: internal schisms must have been healed to some significant extent. One's experience with people and objects is more from the point of view of relatedness and harmony rather than merely separation and conflict. Beginning to experience a true empathy through the heart chakra indicates that paranoid tendencies have been to some extent resolved. That is, there is no longer a drastic split between good and bad. There is less of a bad part of oneself which he must deny and project onto others. There remains some separateness between himself and those to whom he relates, but less of a schism between the parts of himself. This means that he is beginning to become whole, integrated, and full, and has less need to fuse with objects or people in the world to regain the projected parts of himself. There is no longer such a pressing need for attachment.

Rogerian therapy with its refusal to judge others and its emphasis on "unconditional positive regard" for another seems to promote empathy which is related to this chakra. The perspective of this chakra is also clearly elaborated in Erich Fromm's book, *The Art of Loving.* This is perhaps the most clear presentation of regarding the world from the point of view of the heart chakra in contemporary Western psychology. As Freud saw all motivation as primarily sexual, Fromm suggests that our various behaviors are based on the need for union.

> What Freud...ignores, is...the masculine-feminine polarity, and the desire to bridge this polarity by union....[12]

The sadistic person wants to escape from his aloneness and his sense of imprisonment by making another person part and parcel of himself.[13]

According to him, this desire for self-transcendence is best expressed through loving. In defining love Fromm enumerates those qualities which characterize the heart chakra. They include giving, care, responsibility (responsiveness), respect, and knowing the other.

The active character of love can be described by stating that love is primarily giving...

The person whose character has not developed beyond the stage of the receptive, exploitative, or hoarding orientation, experiences the act of giving.... but only in exchange for receiving; giving without receiving for him is being cheated.

But of the more mature person, Fromm says:

In thus giving of his life, he enriches the other person, he enhances the other's sense of aliveness....He does not give in order to receive; giving is in itself exquisite joy.[14]

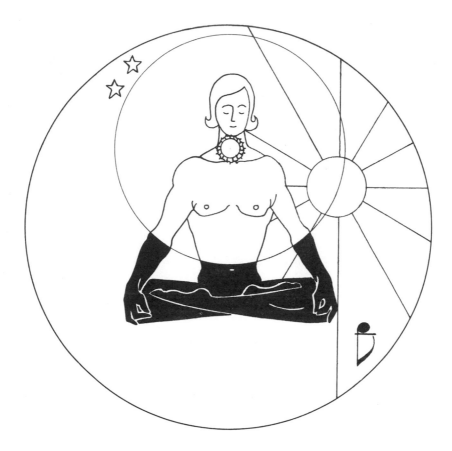

V. THE THROAT CHAKRA
NURTURANCE AND CREATIVITY

    The fifth chakra is located in the area of the throat. It is through here that nurturance in the form of food and air are taken into the body. The thyroid gland which regulates the metabolism of food and oxygen is also situated here. Physiologically, then, this chakra has to do with being nurtured. Psychologically, too, energy focused in this area is related to receptivity, to taking in what is given. This area is very much related to the feeling of being cared for and experience here varies according to whether one feels open or closed to being nurtured. Learning to accept, to receive, is very much related to the throat chakra. It has to do with having a certain sense of trust, a sort of natural, comfortable connection with the source of nurturance.

Receiving Nurturance

The heart center has to do with being able to give nurturance as a mother gives to her child. But the throat center is more related to the role of the child, to receiving. This doesn't necessarily imply an infantile way of relating as we are prone to believe. Rather we would see the child's way of relating as being an imitation of the mode of relating characteristic of this chakra. Both have to do with a feeling of being tied into a reliable source of nurturance, of feeling basically secure.

There is an interesting comparison here between yoga psychology and modern concepts of development. In modern psychology, the oral phase of development is the first. It's regarded as the most primitive mode of consciousness. It's thought to be predominant when the infant is born, as though, in terms of yoga psychology, there were another chakra below, and even prior to the anal one. Energy is said, at this earliest stage of development, to be concentrated around the mouth and involved with taking in nurturance. As we have noted earlier, with growth, the infant is thought to move through this oral stage to the next, which is called the anal stage, and which in the yoga system corresponds to the first chakra. In psychoanalytic theory there next comes a genital stage which is similar to the second chakra. Beyond that is the development of competence and effectiveness in the world which would be related in yogic theory to the third center of consciousness. The two theories show a striking correspondence except that what is considered the earliest and most primitive level of development in the psychoanalytic scheme and associated with orality and feeding is not parallel in the yogic conception of the evolution of consciousness. Instead, the issues related to receiving nurturance are thought to be resolved much further along in the developmental scheme. How can we understand or resolve such a major theoretical disparity?

In the psychoanalytic theory there is the tendency to move from the lower to the higher, from the pathological to the normal, seeing the more evolved state as built on the foundations of the more primitive—a sort of mimicry of earlier stages of development. In yogic theory, just the opposite is true. The most evolved states and the most subtle aspects of our being are seen as the center out of which more gross levels of our existence are manifest. The outer sheath is a projection of the inner. Similarly, the more primitive, less conscious levels of development are seen as a cloudy and more or less distorted reflection of more evolved states. The primitive oral stage of human development, for instance, is seen as a somewhat distorted *imitation* of the tendency toward trust and devotion that characterize the fifth chakra. In the infant, this attitude may be distorted by a lack of consciousness, an impulsiveness, a demandingness and an oscillation to states of distrust. In the mystic, as we have noted, such inconsistency and confusion is not likely to occur.

Both psychoanalysis and yoga psychology recognize that one level of development can "imitate" another, but the fundamental difference in the direction of imitation that is hypothesized has profound implications for our understanding of human nature. The psychoanalytic attitude is more pessimistic. It remains anchored to the primitive, the primordial and tends toward an emphasis in reduction to the infantile or pathological. The yogic approach, on the other hand, is more growth-oriented and leads the student toward a more evolved form of what he is currently experiencing.

Psychoanalytic theory grew largely out of studying people with severe emotional problems. Patients who are the most severely disturbed are often thought to have regressed to the most primitive levels of development. Severely paranoid and psychotic patients, for instance, may show a great deal of concern with being engulfed and annihilated. In psychoanalytic terms such a person is often thought of as having marked oral cravings which he projects onto those around him. In this way he comes to believe that others intend to get so close to him and take such control of his life that they will "swallow him up." This fear of being taken over or engulfed is understood by psychoanalysis as a projection of the patient's own extreme oral needs. Working with patients who remain preoccupied with unresolved infantile conflicts has often led to seeing all orality and longing for nurturance as a basically primitive and severely regressive phenomena.

However, this sort of psychological state is quite distinct from what is associated with the throat chakra in yoga psychology. The paranoid state involves fear of the ego being lost or swallowed up in a regression to a more primitive undifferentiated stage of development; while in yoga, the longing and seeking associated with the throat chakra relates to the ego searching for some "nurturance from above," for some contact with a higher potential, some way to outgrow itself. The former is associated with the intense oral craving which leads to both the desire to engulf and the fear of engulfment. The latter is the search for guidance from a consciousness beyond one's present limits. Although both are related to having consciousness centered at the throat chakra, one is a higher step in the evolution of consciousness while the other is contaminated by the influence of the most primitive levels of development.

The distinction here is the one discussed earlier in relation to the mystic and the psychotic. It involves differentiating between two kinds of merging or oneness. What is longed for by the mystic is a sort of psychological nurturance from a transpersonal consciousness, sought out in an attempt to escape his present limitations and to grow. The psychotic, on the other hand, in becoming one with whatever is appearing on the screen of the lower mind, is often pulled toward stronger, more massive attachments and regression.

We saw earlier that many psychotherapists tended to explain the mystical experience in terms of the psychotic or tried to understand it by likening it to the primitive oral urges of the infant. The mapping of the centers of consciousness provided by yogic theory may help in clarifying the distinction between these two states. It suggests that the striving to contact a transpersonal source of nurturance is associated with the move toward higher levels of awareness and the uncontaminated experience of the fifth center of consciousness, whereas the fear of attack, penetration and engulfment indicate that considerable energy is still bound up in the first chakra.

There are a number of techniques for resolving difficulties centered at the throat chakra. Alexander Lowen uses the initiation of the gag reflex to deal with muscular tensions in this area. It is interesting to note that in yoga training there is also an exercise which is called the "upper wash." This involves taking a large quantity of water in and repeatedly stimulating the gag reflex in order to throw it out. Although this serves in part to remove mucus from the esophagus and stomach, it has psychological effects as well. Some students experience great difficulty in performing the exercise because they are either unable to take the water in or unable to let it come out once it has been swallowed. Through repeated performance of the wash and the repetitive stimulation of the gag reflex, the student usually becomes able to comfortably take the water in and throw it out. This is often followed by an increased sense of well-being. In this way the physiological and psychological constriction related to fears of nurturance are partially worked through. As pointed out by Lowen, such exercises alone are not sufficient for creating a therapeutic effect. But in hatha yoga this exercise is part of a comprehensive program which leads, along with meditation and other practices, to a gradual transformation of the personality.

Creativity

The capacity to accept nurturance is a prominent theme in the psychology of religion. For example, the Madonna and Child occupies a central position in Christian art where there is an emphasis on raising consciousness to the heart and throat chakras. Moreover, the "prayer posture" *(mudra)* that is used in this and other traditions may also be related to working with these centers. When the hands are folded with palms together and held between the heart and throat, energy and awareness seem to be concentrated at these two chakras and a "devotional attitude" is created.

The yoga of devotion (bhakti yoga) and devotional practices in other religious traditions also emphasize ritual, worship, prayers and the frequent use of chanting and sacred music. This may be related to the fact that in a certain psychological sense one's words, his utterances, create the universe within which he exists. The throat chakra is the focus of vocalization and singing, of verbalization and creativity. Traditionally in yoga, artists and musicians are said to have their energy concentrated here. It is through sound vibrations, words and verbal symbols that we create our world.* By forming verbal concepts which structure our reality in a certain way, we determine which stimuli will be rejected, which accepted, and how they will be interpreted. Through the repetition of verbal ritual, one's reality can be restructured and recreated. New words and new thoughts create a new world, at least temporarily.†

The words that we say, the music that we sing, the artistic

---

* The element associated with the throat chakra is *akasha,* usually translated "ether." The ether is sort of the underlying medium in which other things exist, the field in which things happen. The throat chakra involves creation within this field. It is the symbolizations mediated through this chakra that fill this field with the reality that we construct for ourselves.

† Anthropologists have provided many examples of how linguistic concepts shape our concept of reality; see e.g., Benjamin Lee Whorf. [15]

activities we undertake, these express the more inventive and
creative aspects of our personality. So the throat chakra not only
involves nurturance: it involves creation. Though the two seem
on the surface to be two distinct functions, on closer examination
they turn out to be two sides of the same coin.

The Hopi Indians say of man's relation to this center:

> It tied together those openings in his nose and mouth
> through which he received the breath of life and the
> vibratory organs that enabled him to give back his
> breath in sound....New and diverse sounds were given
> forth by these vocal organs in the forms of speech and
> song, their secondary function for man on this earth.
> But as he came to understand its primary function, he
> used this center to speak and sing praises to the
> Creator.[16]

Historically, in both Eastern and Western culture, art and
music developed out of expressions of such devotion. Historians
of classical Western music trace its origins back to early Christian
music, such as the Ambrosian and Gregorian chants, which
survive today and are still sung in certain churches and monasteries.
Even as music evolved it remained primarily a spiritual endeavor
until after the time of Bach. The visual arts were also almost
exclusively devoted to the depiction of spiritual themes until
relatively recently in the history of Western art. Gradually,
these forms of creative expression became secularized and were
used to serve other diverse purposes. Nevertheless, art and music
still remain a principal means of keeping alive the process of inner
growth.

Art has often been used as a part of psychotherapy. It's often
found that by means of painting or through music the patient is
able to symbolize something important to him and to use this
symbol in reintegrating himself. Carl Jung focused considerable
attention on the way in which creative symbolization of the
unconscious helped in the process of growth. Jung's extensive

study of *mandala* and archetypal symbols in artistic expression and myth underscores the importance of the creative act in integrating the personality and expanding consciousness. Thus, it seems that in much of his work Jung was dealing with this, the creative aspect of the throat chakra, although he was not able to integrate it with the other, the devotional aspect of this center.

Art may be useful in the process of psychotherapy because it provides a symbolic expression of some aspect of the person that was previously unknown. But actually, on closer examination, all the symbolizations and formulations evolved during the course of the patient's free exploration of himself are no different. Work with dreams, for example, is basically the same thing: the dream symbols bring to consciousness something of importance that was outside the patient's awareness. The therapist takes hold of the dream symbol and helps the patient to use it in conceptualizing and understanding himself. All of these processes involve using a symbol creatively to bring into awareness something which was before unknown. When the patient is able, from the point of view of a higher perspective (the "observing ego"), to formulate and bring to the verbal level some part of himself, he has, in fact, performed an artistic or creative task. This is more or less the basis of art. The artist is one who allows the better part of himself to have its say. He gives his underlying consciousness a means of expressing itself that is relatively uncontaminated by his ego-oriented thoughts and concerns. He stands aside, in other words, and lets the inner voice "speak."* Therefore, the artistic achievement is not merely to create art but to transform one's personality. For it is by the symbol that has been outwardly created that one is

* The use of the word or sound vibration to create an outward form is the very basis of psychotherapy. For it is around this outward form that one is able to integrate himself at a new and higher level. This is only useful and valuable, of course, when the outward form takes shape during a more evolved consciousness, i.e., from the point of view of detachment (observing ego).

able to reintegrate and reach a new level of awareness. Hence, the act of creation and the act of being created are part and parcel of the same phenomenon. By contrast, when art becomes ego-entangled, creativity stagnates. It is then that an artist comes to "imitate himself"; his symbols no longer evolve and his personal growth ceases.* In the act of being creative, one nurtures himself by giving himself and accepting for himself guidance from the higher consciousness that lies within. It is in this sense that we say that the act of nurturing and being nurtured are one and the same. A traditional yogic blessing at meal time says: "The food is Brahman (universal consciousness), the food is offered to Brahman and it is Brahman who offers the food." Similarly, the English word "grace" is used both for the words that are said before eating and also that which is given in the way of nurturance and sustenance as a gift from a more evolved level of consciousness.

When consciousness is first focused at the throat chakra, one's role is still that of the receiver of "grace." The ability to receive grace is a step above the capacities of the heart chakra where one is limited to being compassionate, to sharing as a separate being with a limited other. Now, instead, one is able to accept from an inner, unlimited source. Eventually, through the experience of receiving this grace, one's consciousness moves towards the next center (the one above the throat chakra) and the realization that giver and receiver are one and the same begins to dawn. The artist, for example, realizes through his art his essential identity with that inner voice which inspired him. At this point, the notion that "higher consciousness is within," that it is an underlying potential that can be increasingly developed begins to make more sense.

* See Otto Rank, "Art and the Artist." [17]

VI. THIRD EYE: THE SEAT OF INTUITIVE KNOWLEDGE

The next chakra is the *ajna* chakra which is located between the eyes and slightly above at the space between the two eyebrows.* This is sometimes called "the third eye" because it has to do with a certain kind of seeing. Behind the area of the "third eye" is located the pineal gland. There is a traditional relationship between this and the sixth chakra. The pineal gland was said by the ancients to be sensitive to "a light within."

* There are no elements associated with the highest two chakras which lead one beyond even the most subtle forms of matter.

Centuries later, in his treatise on higher reason, Descartes included diagrams demonstrating rays of light entering the skull and affecting the pineal gland. He felt that somehow the most essential aspects of seeing were involved there. Though this was long discounted as a mere carryover from the pre-scientific era, recent research has begun to show that there may be some validity to this persistent belief. Although there is no direct connection of the pineal with the outside of the body, it has been shown in some animals to be sensitive to the level of light that exists in the environment. Its response varies according to seasonal and daily variations in light levels.[18]

Consciousness that is centered at the *ajna* chakra involves "introspection" or "the ability to see within." In ancient times a "seer" was one who had focused his consciousness here and was able to see intuitively. The term "clairvoyance," though it has acquired "psychic" connotations, actually comes from the French which means "seeing clearly," and also refers to the centering of consciousness at this chakra. But the "third eye" has the ability to "see" in a way that the physical eyes cannot. This is a deeper vision or *intuitive* means of gaining knowledge.

In modern terms, "intuition" has also assumed a vaguely pejorative connotation. It is often used synonymously with the term "hunch." It is regarded as either unreliable or imaginary. It's certainly not considered something that a sensible person would rely on. If one had an intuitive feeling that the stock market were about to collapse, he probably would not hurriedly sell all his stock. Even if he became a bit concerned, most likely he'd simply reassure himself, "It's only a matter of superstition—a fantasy." In those cases where an intuition does turn out to be accurate, the tendency is to attribute it to coincidence. In modern psychology there is no systematic and scientific study of the intuitive faculty and how it may relate to and grow out of other psychological functions.

In Eastern psychology, by contrast, intuition is a clearly defined phenomenon. It is, moreover, something which can be distinguished from superstition and hunches. A "hunch" may involve an element of intuition, but it is one that is contaminated and confused with material from the personal unconscious. One's complexes and problems intermingle themselves with what little access he might have to something beyond his usual limited consciousness. His premonitions are, then, more often than not mistaken and, at best, unreliable. But "getting hunches" is a natural tendency of the human mind. When the mind spontaneously goes to a state of calmness and relaxation, one is likely to receive such an impression. But when he becomes aware of that potential, he more often than not begins to intervene in the process and intellectualize. Then, even the hunch, contaminated as it is, evaporates.

By contrast, true intuition is a stable, reliable function of the higher levels of consciousness and awareness from which a wider range of information is accessible. There intellect and emotion flow together and become integrated, permitting a new kind of knowing, a kind of knowing which both depends on and promotes self-realization. Intuition unquestionably comes from the highest source of knowledge. It dawns bit by bit with the growth of consciousness. Techniques of meditation provide one with the means through which he can discover and develop within himself that level from which intuition operates.

Intuition has two aspects: there is a difference between creative intuition and higher or inward-directed intuition. Examples of creative intuition are Newton's discovery of gravity or Kekule's discovery of the ring structure of benzene discussed earlier. It brings the superconsciousness into productive contact with the outer world. The higher intuition, on the other hand, is not used for working with the more material, outer sheaths, but is used to grasp the innermost nature of our being. It is unalloyed and useful in helping one find his way deeper to even more advanced levels of consciousness.

In the advanced practice of meditation, a focusing of consciousness on the sixth center leads to gradually separating out the contaminants from the pure experience. Eventually, an accurate and reliable intuitive knowledge begins to dawn. We might say that the intuitive mode of consciousness that is associated with the right side of the brain is finally brought to its perfection. "Opening the third eye" means integrating the right and the left. It means bringing together the judgment and discrimination which characterize the left side with the openness and access to the intuitive world that characterizes the right. It means putting an end both to dry, sterile intellectualization as well as to superstition and "hunches." It means bringing together these two partial, inaccurate ways of knowledge into an integrated whole that is more profound and penetrating.

A well-known symbol, which has survived in the West, portrays the integration that occurs between these two poles when consciousness is properly focused on this chakra. This is the caduceus or medical symbol. Although it is commonly used in medicine, its origins and significance are not generally understood, even by physicians. It is apparently no accident* that this symbol is so strikingly similar to the traditional yogic way of depicting the relationship between consciousness, *prana* (energy) and the chakras. The central staff is analogous to the spinal cord, the coiled snakes as the left and right—*ida* and *pingala,* female and male, passive and active—aspects of human nature which we have discussed in Chapter Two. Like the *nadis* in yogic illustrations, the snakes of the caduceus intertwine, finally meeting at the sixth center where two wings are depicted.†

* The caduceus is a replica of the Staff of Mercury or Hermes and the "Hermetic Science" of the Middle Ages was closely related to the practice of medicine, as taught by such Masters as Paracelsus (whose studies and wanderings are said to have taken him to Russia, the Near East and eventually India). As we saw in Chapter Two, these medieval "alchemists," the forerunners of modern chemistry and medicine, were very much aware of the right-left polarity and its significance.

† Here again the symbolism parallels that of the yogic chakras, for each chakra in traditional symbology is shown with its own particular number of subtle nerve currents depicted as lotus petals. The *ajna* chakra is shown with two such petals at a point corresponding to that where the wings of the caduceus are found.

Perhaps the caduceus represents that ideal which should be attained by each person who seeks to heal others: his consciousness must be awakened to that deep intuition and understanding which characterizes this center, so that his efforts at healing come from the deep fountain of knowledge found here. This requires long and systematic training.

Even when preparation is not systematic, however, some fleeting contact with a more universal consciousness may be momentarily experienced. This may occur in people who have, through their life experience, reached a level of unusual maturity and personal evolution. Sudden flashes of an altered state of consciousness may be experienced and reported as overwhelming. Such experiences have been described by philosophers and poets through the ages, such as Spinoza, Walt Whitman, and William Blake.* Their recollection may serve as a constant source of inspiration for years, but without any systematic preparation or well-designed discipline, such persons are usually unable to find their way back at will to these moments of illumination. They must wait for them to happen spontaneously. Their experience remains an important influence on their life and a crucial center of integration around which they can be creative, but it cannot grow into a completely integrated consciousness. It never develops into a constant, underlying awareness, but remains only an occasional, transient experience. However, through the practice of yoga, under the guidance of an accomplished teacher, the student is trained to systematically attain the highest states of consciousness at will.

Opening this inner vision means opening modes of awareness for which we have potential, but which we are at present not able to imagine. It means escaping the confines of our culturally endorsed, everyday reality. It means escaping the limited concepts of a consciousness which is oriented around material,

* For detailed studies of such reports, see *Cosmic Consciousness* by Richard Maurice Bucke, M.D. 19

externally observable phenomena. It means moving beyond the limitations of time, space and causality.

One who knows how to meditate on the space between the two eyebrows or *ajna* chakra gains a new perspective on the principles of time, space and causality. The one-pointed inward focusing of awareness leads to a point from which the multiplicity of phenomena and events can be seen as one interrelated whole. The causal sequence of phenomena in the world is then transcended and "future" events can be apprehended. Though this may sound absurd to the hard-nosed, intellectualizing materialist, according to the exact and well-defined science of meditation, the network of past, present and future is a flow of many events on the bed of time. And this entire bed can be visualized, with proper training.

Ramakrishna tried to describe to his close disciples the transcendent experience resulting when the mind is fully centered on this chakra. One day he said:

> "I'll tell you everything today and will not keep anything secret." He described clearly the centers and the corresponding experiences up to the heart and throat, and then, pointing to the spot between the eyebrows, he said, "The supreme Self is directly known and the individual experiences *samadhi* when the mind comes here. There remains then but a thin transparent screen separating the supreme Self and the individual self. The *sadhaka* then experiences...," saying this, the moment he started to describe in detail the realization of the supreme Self, he was plunged in samadhi. When the samadhi came to an end, he tried again to describe it and was again in samadhi.[20]

After repeated attempts, Ramakrishna breaks into tears and tells his disciples that, although he has a desire to tell them everything "without concealing anything whatsoever," he is unable to speak:

> Whenever I try to describe what kinds of visions I experience when it goes beyond this place (showing the throat) and think what kinds of visions I am witnessing, the mind rushes immediately up, and speaking becomes impossible.[21]

Describing this state further, Ramakrishna says:

> If...anybody's mind reaches the spot between the eyebrows....He then has direct knowledge of the supreme Self....There is only a screen transparent like glass....The supreme Self is so near then that it seems as if one is merged in Him, identified with Him. But identification is yet to be.[22]

When consciousness moves to the next and final center, however:

> ...the distinction between the subject of consciousness and the object of consciousness is destroyed. It is a state wherein self-identity and the field of consciousness are blended in one indissoluble whole.[23]

VII. THE CROWN CHAKRA:
THE HIGHEST STATE OF CONSCIOUSNESS

The seventh or highest center is located at the vertex or top of
the head. It is called the "crown chakra." When consciousness is
most evolved it comes to be focused primarily here. The custom
of placing an ornate crown on the head of a monarch seems to be
rooted in the idea that the person with the most evolved
consciousness should be the one to lead the state. His understanding should be beyond that of his subjects. This is the concept of
the "philosopher king."

A reverence for this center of consciousness is also seen in the symbology of certain religions. In the Christian tradition it has been customary for certain monks to shave the crown of the head and leave a bare circle there. In the Jewish tradition a skull cap is worn which covers that same area. Religious art often highlights the area of the crown chakra with a burst of light or a halo.

The Hopi Indians say of man's relationship to this center:

> Here, when he was born, was the soft spot...the 'open door' through which he received his life and communicated with his Creator...At the time of...the last phase of his creation, the soft spot was hardened and the door was closed. It remained closed until his death, opening then for his life to depart as it had come.[24]

The yogic tradition gives a similar significance to the soft spot of the infant, noting that it gradually hardens as the child's intuitive qualities are diminished during the development of rationality and ego functions. The yogic viewpoint, however, emphasizes that this door may be reopened through the attainment of the highest state of *samadhi*. It is said that highly evolved yogis have access to this center. These accomplished yogis become aware of the course future events will take. They have been known to announce and prepare for the exact date and time when their consciousness quietly and calmly, in the company of their closest students, abandons the physical body. Of course, the mastery, control and highly evolved consciousness which this presupposes is rare.

At the level of this center, all the distinctions of ordinary consciousness break down. Awareness is expanded beyond the point that can be explained in verbal terms.

At this center there is a vast awareness that knows no limits. Even the differentiation between the experiencer and the experienced ceases. In the traditions of yoga this chakra is represented by a thousand-petaled lotus and the experience is one comparable only to the dazzling light of countless suns. Any descriptions of the experience involved here must of necessity be couched in such highly symbolic terms that they are difficult to deal with in the context of psychological theory.

Though in a sense this experience lies beyond modern psychology, since it departs from the limitations of the psyche, it is obviously of vital importance to the subject. It offers the vantage point from which the mind can be most clearly appreciated. It serves as a crucial point of orientation. Though it lies beyond the realm of mental functioning, it provides the key to a framework in which the functioning of the mind becomes intelligible, and all the aspects of experience can be integrated into a unified theory. Furthermore, the nature of this state is so fundamental to the nature of man's being that to be completely successful any psychological theory must at least be compatible with its existence.

THE CHAKRAS: YOGA AND PSYCHOTHERAPY

Proper meditation on each successive chakra results in a new level of integration.* Each of these levels of integration is a result of a synthesis that occurs between two polarities. The polarity synthesized at the level of the *ajna* chakra is that between *ida* and *pingala,* or the right and left aspects of the personality. Polarities involved at the throat chakra can be symbolized by the mother and child; that is to say, the nurtured and the nurturer. Polarities that are synthesized during meditation of the heart chakra have to do with the upper and lower halves on the body, and the positive and negative energies that they symbolize. This may be roughly conceptualized in terms of "heaven and earth," self-interest and the transpersonal, or *purusha* and *prakriti* (consciousness and matter). The polarity involved at the navel chakra has to do with activity and passivity in the sense of domination and submission. At the genital chakra the polarity is that which is between the male and the female. The polarities involved at the first chakra level are between the attacker and the attacked, the hunter and the prey, the devil and the divine or, simply, the "bad" and the "good."

Characteristics of each chakra after synthesis is accomplished are as follows: at the first chakra the synthesis of the good and the bad gives one the quality of solidity, of earthiness. One is not solid until he has overcome the basic tendency to split off and project onto others his own capacity for violence and aggression; until he has conquered the primitive fear that results from the

* One of the most famous books of Sanskrit literature is called *The Wave of Bliss,* which explains this science. It has two parts: one is the 'Wave of Bliss' and the other the 'Wave of Beauty.' There are more than thirty-five commentaries available on this book. The complete knowledge of this highly sophisticated science remains secret for the lack of its practical counterpart called *'prayoga shastra.'* We have heard that this manuscript is preserved in Baroda and Mysore, but we have not seen it. One respected swami reported that this is the most comprehensive and useful of the ancient works, dealing with human problems on all levels—psychological, pathological and psychosomatic. Our search still continues.

creation of such a "good-bad," black and white world.

The synthesis occurring at the genital chakra is between the concepts of masculinity and femininity. It brings into awareness those aspects of one's own personality which correspond to the opposite sex, but which he has exiled from his awareness in order to create a functional sexual role for himself. This brings an appreciation on a deeper level of the meaning of both maleness and femaleness so that one is able to effectively and genuinely assume his particular role.

The synthesis at the navel chakra has to do with the resolution of the issue of domination and submission. When this is resolved, it gives one the quality of being forceful and dynamic without being either cruelly aggressive or weakly passive. It also lends one the ability to be cooperative without being bothered about questions of authority and submission or driven by the need to be competitive. The traditional yogic symbol of this chakra is fire. Successful integration at this level allows one to act in the world dynamically and energetically.

Integration at the heart chakra brings one the quality of sensitivity, empathy and the ability to experience compassion and selfless love. Synthesis at the level of the throat chakra gives one the ability to be creative and to recreate himself; in other words, to grow and evolve.

Integration or synthesis at the *ajna* chakra occurs between *ida* and *pingala,* the polarities of right and left, and results in the activation of *sushumna* and the opening of the third eye. This gives one access to intuition and the ability to see clearly with the inner vision. The polarity resolved at the crown chakra is the final resolution of that distinction between self and other and results in what may be called "cosmic consciousness."

On close scrutiny the successful Western approaches to psychotherapy involve raising consciousness from one chakra to a higher one despite the fact that the growth process is generally not conceptualized in these terms. The paranoid person is led toward contact-sensuality, ego-oriented persons toward concern for others, etc. The processes in each case involve detaching oneself from the limited perspective which has led to unhappiness and suffering. Each of the practices in yoga exists to help the student free himself of the narrow perspectives of the lower chakras and to view the world from those which are higher. Devotional practices, austerities, service to others, and the study of philosophy, *pranayama* and meditation, all exist to decrease attachments to more primitive levels of functioning, allowing the unfoldment of a more comprehensive awareness.

A focus on the first three chakras, and to a lesser extent the fourth and fifth, has been associated with particular schools of psychology which view the world from the perspective of each of these chakras. When we study the higher chakras, however, we pass beyond the perspective of most of modern psychology and we leave the realm of experience which they ordinarily encompass. The movement from the third to the fourth chakra, the fourth to the fifth, and so on, may instead be related to the psychologies developed within various spiritual traditions. Within the yogic traditions there are various practices which help awaken the state of consciousness characteristic of particular higher centers. Bhakti yoga or the yoga of devotion, for example, helps to channel one's emotional tendencies toward pure love and service to one's ideal, thus bringing consciousness from the lower chakras to the heart center. It also emphasizes prayer, worship, chanting and other devotional practices which focus energy on the throat center. By contrast, jnana yoga, the yoga of self-study and study of the written wisdom, leads one to a focus of energy at the two highest centers of consciousness. Which approach the student takes depends on his temperament and abilities.

Another method for raising consciousness to higher centers involves the meditational practices of raja yoga. Here one focuses the attention on a certain selected chakra during meditation. Traditionally in yoga there are two separate approaches to the meditation on centers of consciousness or chakras. One is to begin at the lowest, or first chakra and concentrate on it until one has a thorough grasp of the energies and emotions that are involved there. After this process has led to a synthesis or resolution of the confusions existing on that level, he then moves his attention to the next highest chakra and begins to work there. This process, however, is very difficult and time consuming since one is attempting to find his way through the more primitive sides of himself without having cultivated any of the more advanced levels of consciousness which could be used by him as a tool. For this reason there is a danger in becoming involved in pathological versions of the lower chakras, being distracted from progress and led into more disturbed states.*

The other traditional, and perhaps more common, approach in yoga is to avoid completely any concentration and meditation on the lower chakras and focus on a selected higher center. In this case the guru prescribes a center of meditation for his pupil based both on this student's pathology and on his strengths.

The Application of Meditational Therapy

The human being is a nucleus and the universe is the expansion of this nucleus. To study the nature of the universe the human being can study his internal states and the subtler levels of his own being. The mind is the main instrument for consciousness lying between the physical body and pure consciousness. When this mind is distracted and dissipated, there is little will power. But when the mind is made one-pointed, it becomes dynamic and will power develops. The issue of attention is the key here, for

---

* This is similar to what occurs in psychotherapy when a patient explores in detail his areas of pathology. The therapist becomes quickly aware that many patients can lose their way here and permanently adopt those modes of functioning which arise during the regression to pathological stages. Moreover, any therapist who has attempted an in-depth, exploratory uncovering has discovered how time-consuming is the detailed study and working through of primitive levels of pathology.

will power is, in essence, a property of the one-pointed mind. The less will power one has, the more anguish and suffering will be experienced. Moreover, if the mind is weak and distracted, even the healthiest body can become diseased.

The purpose of meditational therapy, which is a highly sophisticated and specialized branch of yogic science, is to change the basic pattern of mental habits which form the fabric of our personalities. Before personality is transformed and character changed, the habits must be dealt with. Meditational therapy does this by the use of three principal means to rechannel the mind. Auditory or visual objects of concentration may be used or, thirdly, the mind may be redirected without any object, using negation or disidentification with the thoughts parading before it. In this latter method the mind is led toward the source of consciousness.†

There are several preliminary practices which prepare the student for meditational therapy. These include breathing-therapy and concentration exercises such as gazes *(trataka)*. Psychosomatic, physiological and psychopathological disorders which are not easily treated by the psychotherapist can be treated with the proper application of meditational therapy. In order to prescribe the appropriate meditational techniques for working with mental habits, the capacity of the patient should be examined and the patient led through a specific program of preparatory exercises to develop his awareness. This can only be done by those therapists who have themselves systematically practiced meditation for a long time (just as psychoanalytic techniques can only be applied by those who have themselves undergone psychoanalysis).

Meditational therapy which uses sound as the object of concentration is effective in helping with a variety of problems; the specific concentration technique is prescribed according to

---

† For further description of this method of meditation, see the works of Ramana Maharshi.

the disorder.   There are two types of sounds—the sound created
in the external world and another set of unalloyed sounds
coming from within as a result of the vibrations of various
energy channels overlapping from all over the body.   These
latter sounds are sometimes experienced in the deeper states of
meditation and may help to lead the mind through to the
higher dimensions of consciousness.   In the yoga manuals these
are called *anahad nada.*   Christian and Jewish mystics also
reported that these sounds lead to higher visions.   The Book of
Revelations of the New Testament describes sound functioning
in this manner.*

The Western world is slowly becoming aware that music has
powerful and potentially therapeutic effects on humans as well as
on animals and even plants.   The precise science of sound therapy
is not generally understood in the West, however, where this
science will have to be systematized and validated through
continuous experimentation.   *Nada* (sound) therapy is interdependent with the science of chakras.   Music therapy has come
out of the exact science of sounds and chakras which was used
centuries ago by the ancients of all great religions.   There are
only seven key notes in all the various forms of music throughout
the world.   They are related to the levels of consciousness associated with the seven chakras.   These seven key sounds may be
heard within when one opens the "ear of his mind."

Many diseases originate in the mind and are then expressed in
the body. Sound, along with the visualization of forms *(mandalas)*,
has been used to treat such psychosomatic diseases.   When the
mind is allowed to flow on these two objects, sound and
mandala, they seem to help in clearing the unconscious of
repressed material which, though subtle and unseen, often plays
a very powerful role in molding the personality.   Usually,
characterological problems are deep rooted, related to the strong

* The conflict of John was removed by the sound he heard and the visions he saw.
As a result, he attained a fearless state of mind, despite the fact that he was confined in
a lonely prison cell on the island of Patmos.

memories and impressions which, suppressed or repressed, operate from the unconscious. With the help of meditation on the appropriate *mandala,* chakra and sound, the entire personality can be transformed.

According to the science of chakras, specific sounds and forms for visualization are related to specific chakras. If this science of visual and auditory therapy is understood properly, it can be used effectively in most psychological and psychosomatic disorders, serving as a catalyst in the integration of mind and body. For example, a person who has recurring nightmares can be cured if he is taught to meditate properly on the solar plexus. Our experience bears this out. When the heart chakra is prescribed as a center of concentration along with certain sounds, it has been found that those who were emotionally unstable and immature were enabled to gradually develop emotional control. For those who are highly intellectual and emotionally insensitive, the space between the two eyebrows *(ajna* chakra) is used. Concentration here, along with sound and visualization, help in gaining balance between the intellect and emotions. Those with psychogenic impotence and premature ejaculation due to lack of command over emotions, can often be guided to develop more natural and comfortable control when the sacral plexus and the proper sound are prescribed as a focus of attention.*

With a few exceptions (for example, Jung, Maslow) study of the higher chakras in the West has been the domain of theologians or relegated to the partial and often inaccurate descriptions given by occultists. The unscientific approach and the aura of superstition that surrounds such descriptions have caused psychiatrists and psychologists to shy away from approaching these areas of consciousness. In many cases this distrust and suspicion is sufficient to lead professionals to dismiss entirely the relevance of this study to their field. We feel that it is

---

* The authors are still in the process of experimentation with the therapeutic use of the science of chakras. But this approach seems to be very effective, helpful and quite authentic.

because the study of expanded awareness has been neglected that psychodynamic theory has been unable to formulate a unified, comprehensive understanding of personality and development.

There have long been two major schools of Western psychological thought which have been at odds with one another in describing the basic nature of man and what motivates him. On the one hand there are those that insist that instincts, habits and basic physiological needs are the prime movers of human behavior. At the other extreme are the humanistic psychologists who see man primarily as a conscious, growth-oriented upward striving being. Abraham Maslow has provided a more comprehensive model which incorporates and integrates these two perspectives. He suggests that man has a hierarchy of motivational needs ranging from the most physiological needs for food, shelter, sleep and sex, through less physiological but still basic needs for safety and security, and more evolved needs of love, belongingness and esteem. Finally, in Maslow's schema if the basic needs are fulfilled, man can turn his attention to what Maslow calls growth needs, those which lead to the self-actualization of the individual. These include motivation to seek meaningfulness, self-sufficiency, simplicity, perfection, beauty, goodness and truth.[25]   Although his conceptualizations of these higher stages of growth remain embryonic, the similarity between Maslow's concept of a motivational hierarchy in man and the yogic schema of the chakras is striking. It may well be that the more detailed and elaborated yogic conception of the hierarchy of motivational perspectives, especially those most related to what Maslow calls "self-actualization," can contribute significantly to a more comprehensive and integrated theory of motivation in modern psychology.

CONCLUDING THOUGHTS

Essentially yoga is based on a philosophy of evolution. From the lowest form of animal life to the most highly developed human intelligence, there lies a scale within which most of our familiar concepts of biological and psychological growth and development fit. From the point of view of yoga, the process is a continuous one. The evolution of physical and mental potentialities as well as those of the higher consciousness are not considered to be separate, unrelated phenomena. They are part and parcel of the same process.

As we have seen, this process is most succinctly summarized in terms of observation, control and synthesis: growth is always based on the attainment of some degree of disentanglement from attachments, which allows one to observe something about himself and his world to which he was previously blind. This is the expansion of awareness. As awareness grows, one inevitably discovers within his new definition of himself a new ability to control. What he was previously blind to and controlled by is now within his power to regulate. Increased capacity for observation leads to increased capacity to control. We've seen how this principle applies in working with the body, in working with the mind, as well as in working on other levels.

As parts of oneself which were previously operating outside awareness are brought under conscious control, they gradually come to be more coordinated. When they are controlled from the point of view of a consistent, unitary consciousness, then they lose their tendency to work in opposition to each other. What previously gave rise to conflict is now brought together in a harmonious whole. The ability to control results in a new degree of synthesis. For example, when desires and impulses which were before repressed are brought into conscious awareness, they not only are subject to increased control, but they become synthesized into the total personality and there is no longer energy wasted in internal conflict. This process of increased observation leading to increased control and increased synthesis is what makes up each step in the long journey of evolution. With each repetition it carries one to a new level of awareness and a new way of being in the world which before was beyond his imagination.

This process of growth moves ultimately toward the higher states of consciousness which have been the subject of the most respected and, at the same time, most misunderstood writings in literature, philosophy and even religion. The higher levels of consciousness are the most difficult to understand because they are furthest from the ordinary, everyday awareness. But they are neither "other-worldly" nor beyond the reach of ordinary men. On the contrary, they are seen to be simply the outcome of an orderly process of growth in which each of us is, at least to some extent, involved.

Modern psychology has dealt with alternate states of consciousness only in a vague and undifferentiated kind of way. The tendency has been to lump together all those varieties of consciousness that differ from the ordinary waking consciousness. Hallucinations, feelings of emotional ecstasy, and states of enlightenment are often grouped together as "altered states of consciousness" and treated as though they are more or less the same since they are all different from the ordinary, ego-level awareness. Eastern psychology, on the other hand, has a long tradition of exploring and differentiating between these various states of altered consciousness. Yoga psychology is one of a number of systems which have grown out of the techniques of meditation and it offers a sophisticated and refined conceptualization of the various modes of consciousness that can be experienced. This is one of the great values of yoga psychology. It can provide a guide, an orientation, to areas of study that modern psychology is only now beginning to approach. In our first attempts to grapple with a scientific understanding of altered states of consciousness, the traditional understandings of yoga psychology offer at the very least a set of extremely useful hypotheses.

Beyond this, however, the implications of yoga psychology are deeper. For the Eastern meditative approach supplies a key to a more feasible approach to the study of alternate states of consciousness than what we have so far used. The technique of meditation can free us from the bind which has hampered our ability to extend our understanding of the psyche. It provides us with a new orientation toward the scientific study of consciousness. It permits us to see that higher states of consciousness, the inner world, can be studied in a genuinely scientific way.

Science is difficult to define. But perhaps the most essential feature of it is that it involves the study of something which is external to the observer. The techniques of meditation offer an approach which allows one to be "external to" internal states. This apparent paradox becomes clear in the context of our discussion of levels of consciousness. Once one accepts, at least as an operating hypothesis, that there are distinct and discernible levels of consciousness, he has firmly within his grasp a powerful tool, for it becomes quickly apparent that each of these levels offers a vantage point from which the one below can be observed. From each level one is "external to" the one beneath. He can observe it and study it. In this sense he has become a scientist whose field of study is the inner world. As long as this study is as meticulous, careful and conscientious as that carried out in a laboratory, it will continue to merit the title "science." The techniques of meditation, if properly applied, create for one an "internal laboratory."

The word *yoga* comes from the Sanskrit root *yuj,* which means "to yoke." This means that the lower levels of consciousness, the lower aspects of oneself, are yoked to the highest center of consciousness so that they become guided, directed and regulated by it. They become tools in the hands of the higher consciousness. When this is one's underlying orientation, then diverse schools of training and various disciplines can be each employed when appropriate to serve the purposes of the user.

Yoga offers to modern psychology the possibility of integration. Our techniques for the scientific and laboratory study of behavior, our analytic and dynamic approaches to therapy, are not lacking in sophistication and detail. Their diversity is not objectionable. It could be an asset rather than a liability. But our inability to integrate the various disciplines has been our shortcoming. The rich variety of techniques and theories we have at our disposal never seem to get pulled together, so our efforts become fragmented. It is the lack of a common point of orientation that has stymied growth and turned what could be complementarity into opposition. Western psychology and psychotherapy find themselves uncoordinated and scattered. It is at this point in the evolution of our thought that fresh input from a totally different culture, another system for defining man and the universe, might be most helpful.

When Western mathematics was encumbered by the awkward use of Roman numerals, the influx of the so-called "arabic" numerals, which originated in India, led to a breakthrough in the science of math. The system became simpler, more streamlined and more manageable. One could hardly imagine a science of calculus based on the use of Roman numerals. And without a highly efficient system of mathematics airplanes wouldn't fly and rockets wouldn't land on the moon. At this juncture in the development of psychology, the refreshing yet perennial insights of yoga psychology and philosophy may offer a simple but profound understanding which can reorient our thinking and free psychology from its narrowness, thus opening it to a new way of seeing human nature and the universe in which it is embedded.

APPENDIX

An example of the clinical application of yoga in psychotherapy:

One of the authors* had the opportunity to apply the principles of yoga therapy in an innovative in-patient treatment program for those convicted of sex offenses. Many of the patients involved in this program had repeatedly gotten into difficulty because of their impulsive, unthinking reactions. They had not known how to take control of themselves in a stressful situation. For example, if the bills piled up, if there was conflict in the family or if they felt strong sexual desires with no appropriate outlet, they acted impulsively without thinking of the consequences. This lack of impulse control seemed a sort of common denominator among the various types of personalities present. With this in mind, a group of twelve patients who chose to participate in a "self-mastery" class were brought together for an hour-and-a-half once each week. The group consisted primarily of patients convicted of rape and child molesting.

A program of yoga therapy was developed to instill the attitude in these patients that control over oneself in situations of internal or external stress is both possible and satisfying. Comprehensive training in several aspects of self-mastery were taught, following the traditional structure of yogic discipline. The class began with several sessions on how to control the

* Swami Ajaya

body. This provided the most basic and concrete experience in self-control. Yoga postures and breathing exercises were taught to calm the nervous system, relax the body and mind and to teach concentration. Later, meditation techniques became the focus and, finally, interpersonal situations occupied the last part of the therapy. The first and second phases occupied about two months. The third and last phase of the program extended over six months and emphasized core principles from yoga psychology such as the development of non-attachment and the disengagement from a restrictive and disabling concept of *I-ness*.

FIRST PHASE: WORK WITH THE BODY

The therapeutic program began with an emphasis on hatha yoga postures and relaxation techniques. A bare, cinderblock, concrete-floored basement was converted into a yoga class. Patients brought blankets and laid them on the floor, stretched out and relaxed, gradually becoming more comfortable in this formerly stark environment.

At first, the postures struck some as humorous. A few patients would look at one another, commenting on how silly they were being, smirking as though they knew this was a lot of nonsense, or laughing at the strange positions their friends were assuming. At times, there would be a feeling of embarrassment. What would their friends think about these weird exercises?

Some patients who had not done much physical work for a number of years were rather embarrassed by their lack of coordination and inability, at first, to do even the simple postures. However, after a few weeks, a great deal of improvement in body control was evident. Patients, who at first had trembled and strained to hold a position became able to remain still long enough to focus their attention for increasing periods of time. Gradually, after several weeks of practice, they noticed that they were feeling better physically and began to take the project more seriously, some of them getting up an hour earlier each day to practice. One patient reported that an officer, looking into the window of his room and seeing him doing the postures, ordered him to stop "that strange behavior," assuming it was a part of his "craziness." This patient decided to get up and practice in the middle of the night in order to avoid such difficulties.

During these initial meetings the participants were somewhat tense and uncertain. Techniques were taught for the systematic relaxation of muscle tension throughout the body. During this phase of the training, breathing exercises, such as diaphragmatic breathing and the complete breath were also introduced. As the patients learned that they could gain control over physical and mental tension, their restlessness, discomfort and concern with others' reactions diminished markedly. As the sessions continued, they began to be less concerned about what others were doing and thinking and began to bring their energy more within themselves to concentrate on their own feelings and experiences.

SECOND PHASE: MEDITATION

Gradually, the patients began to ask for more training in the mental aspects of yoga. Following these requests, the classes shifted gradually toward instruction in meditation. Patients were taught to calm the mind and observe the thoughts flowing through it, instead of reacting to them. They learned simple methods of watching the breath or concentrating on sounds around them as a way of bringing the mind away from the distractions and worries with which it was usually preoccupied. Surprisingly, the patients took to this practice quite readily. Within two meetings, some reported that they were practicing as much as an hour each day, sitting quietly in their rooms with their eyes closed.

Several patients described beneficial effects within a few weeks of practice; for example, experiencing a sense of mastery in difficult emotional situations. One extremely impulsive patient, who had recently kicked in his window following a disappointment, observed that at the time of his outburst he had been tense and worried, feeling upset and angry because his parents hadn't written to him. Now, he said, his practices enabled him to avoid becoming caught up in and overwhelmed by such thoughts and frustrations. Another patient had been quite obsessive, constantly preoccupied with ruminations about his trial, how he had been mistreated and taken advantage of, and why he should have never been put in the hospital at all. This had been his constant, tiresome theme in every conversation or discussion. Gradually, however, he began to give up these preoccupations, describing how he replaced such worrysome, recurring thoughts with concentration on his breathing and the sounds around him. Another slightly retarded man, who had been in prison over twenty years, remarked that he finally learned that when he became tense and emotional, all he had to do was to breathe deeply and relax, and he could quickly overcome these feelings. The patients also began to notice that these techniques were carrying over to, and affecting, their interpersonal relations. One patient commented, "I used to get uptight when somebody put me down, but now I just watch my breath and it doesn't bother me."

Five of the twelve patients in the self-mastery class had also participated in more traditional therapy groups with the same leader. In the group therapy situation, prior to the self-mastery training, these patients seemed to be isolated by preoccupation with their own individual problems. Repeatedly, conversations started by one patient would be interrupted and diverted to a completely different track by another. One patient might be talking about the poor meals in the dining room when the second would suddenly cut in and ask if he could visit his family. Then a third would begin talking about a dream he had the night before. There was little or no continuity between comments. As the patients began to learn self-observation skills in the self-mastery class, however, they began to be less limited to their own individual concerns, becoming more interested in what other members of the group were experiencing.

Previously, they had projected their strong, negative feelings toward authority figures onto the therapist. It was characteristic for most of these patients to externalize blame and to be preoccupied with the way they had been mistreated. Their hatred and distrust of those in authority led them to attack the therapist verbally, rejecting any input from him. But, those patients who became involved in the self-mastery class began to show a dramatic change in their attitude. Rather than focusing on the therapist and rejecting his observations, they began to observe their own feelings and behavior. As a result, they seemed less caught up in and overwhelmed by the intensity of the moment. The notion of objectively observing themselves in the midst of activity had been unknown to them before. In their work with postures and meditation, they became acquainted with a means of standing outside the situation and observing it. Learning to observe their bodies during the practice of yoga postures and the flow of thoughts in their minds during meditation, served as a preparation and model for objectively observing their actions and reactions during everyday living. They seemed, almost spontaneously, to apply this newly developing skill to their emotional life and to interpersonal situations.

These skills were eventually of benefit even to those members of the therapy groups who had not undergone self-mastery training. When these patients became intensely emotional, losing perspective and objectivity, the patients trained in self-observation would no longer join them in a gripe session against the therapist, the institution or the world in general, as they had previously done. Instead, the trained patients led the others to look at their behavior more objectively. Moreover, self-observation was leading them to an increasing acceptance of responsibility for what they were experiencing.

Before the yoga and meditation training, such patients invariably responded to stress with accusations, hostility, cries of
injustice and, at times, violence. If an officer was hostile or
seemed to treat one of them unfairly, he would become negativistic and seek to retaliate in some way. Such a patient would
often be preoccupied with resentment and the wish "to get even"
for days on end. If a fellow patient mistreated him, he might
respond impulsively, perhaps becoming involved in a fist fight.
He would respond automatically without thinking about the long
range consequences of what he was doing, reacting more on the
basis of primitive "survival mechanisms" than from the perspective
of a more evolved and objective consciousness.

THIRD PHASE: MEDITATION IN ACTION

As the patients in the self-mastery group became interested
in how their self-observations could apply to these interpersonal
situations, attention was turned away from the study of meditation to focus on interactions with others. This was the third
phase of the training program, beginning to look at interactions
from the point of view of yoga psychology, developing a
philosophy of how to deal with stressful or emotionally arousing
situations. This aspect of the training program received the
greatest attention and occupied them most of the time. The
basic principles of hatha yoga and meditation had been taught
in two months of weekly sessions. However, understanding the
way in which meditational principles applied to everyday living
situations, involved the group for the next six months.

In retrospect, three core principles were emphasized in applying
yoga to everyday living:

Non-attachment: the ability to maintain objectivity
rather than becoming emotionally engulfed by situations.

Karma and Responsibility: the concept that our actions lead to reactions; that we are each responsible for whatever comes our way.

Identity: differentiating between identities based on role identifications and our true or core identity (Self).

Non-attachment

One of the main principles of yoga therapy is learning how to become non-attached in the sense of not being caught up and overwhelmed by the emotions, desires or reactions of the moment. This leads to the ability to gain control of situations rather than be controlled by them. In the self-mastery group, we discussed the application of this principle to the everyday situations faced by the patients. The therapist acquainted the group with the yogic concept that emotions and anxieties are derived from attachments to goals, objects or people and the frustrations of desires and expectations based on these attachments. We used examples of uncontrolled emotionality from the patients' everyday experiences to see how instability arose out of attachments. Each time a patient became anxious or emotional, we focused on his lack of objectivity. The therapist encouraged the participant to become aware of the underlying attachment or expectation that brought the emotion about. Instead of dealing with the emotion itself, as is characteristic of most psychotherapeutic approaches, the patient was encouraged to examine the attachment or expectation in some detail. Where did it arise? Was it really necessary that it be fulfilled? Was it realistic? Could he have control over or change these expectations and attachments? In many cases, participants quickly understood the way in which attachments were the cause of their distress, although, of course, their intellectual understanding did not lead them immediately to give up dependencies which had been built over many years.

Initially, some patients accused the therapist of being unrealistic when he suggested that their intense frustrations and
anxieties over not being released from the hospital could be
minimized by being less attached to what they imagined they
would have "out there." When first encouraged to experience,
enjoy and learn from the immediate moment and present
situation, they looked at the leader as if he were crazy, as though
he belonged in the hospital as a patient. "You've never been
locked up, so you don't understand what it's like," was their
attitude. However, gradually they began to see how the principle
of non-attachment could be applied to such aspects of their
lives. They began to see the effects of lessening attachments in
small "temporary" situations, later extending their work to
more established relationships with girlfriends and families.

One day a participant in the program came to the therapy
group just after taking part of an exam for a high school diploma.
He had become very anxious during the exam when he ran into
some rather difficult problems. He had begun to be afraid of
failing and this fear and anxiety had led to errors in problems
he would have ordinarily solved easily. He observed that a
similar panic often plagued him when things were not going well.
As we discussed his exaggerated concern over passing the examination, it became clear that he was afraid of what his parents
would say if he failed. The discussion began to focus on how
attached he was to fulfilling his parents' expectations. He came
to the conclusion that this preoccupation with living up to such
expectations had been there throughout most of his school years
and was both unrealistic and irrational. He decided then and
there that there was no need to be so attached to others'
evaluation of him. The next week he took the remaining portions
of the exam, reporting that for the first time ever, he was able
to take a test without feeling anxious about the results. "I just
did the best I could and performed much better than I usually
do when I'm worried about the outcome," he said. In subsequent
sessions, this patient began to generalize what was learned, stating

that, in the past, he had repeatedly sought to discover what others' expectations were and became anxious and in conflict about fulfilling these.   As he began relinquishing his attachments to what others expected of him, he became more comfortable with himself and more confident.   Working with this technique over several months, he gradually overcame his panic and fear of his girlfriend or parents abandoning him.

Of course, other therapeutic approaches could also have led to an uncovering of this patient's underlying fears of disappointing his parents and his investment in their expectations. Yoga therapy differed by focusing more quickly and directly on attachments as the common underlying root of such problems. In the example presented, there was a definite tact to be used: we moved directly to the underlying attachment from which the anxiety arose. The personalities and the drama were not, *in themselves*, of interest

Karma and Responsibility

The principle that we create our environment rather than having it imposed upon us is basic to yoga psychology. We are responsible for the situation in which we find ourselves. If our present situation was brought about by our past actions, thoughts and desires, this implies that we can also transform this environment through our present and future actions. Characteristically, these patients blamed others for their predicament. Most were preoccupied with seeking justice and "getting even" for the way they had been and were currently being mistreated. Therefore, understanding how we are responsible for our circumstances was important in helping these patients change their lifestyles.

After the therapist introduced the principle of non-attachment and the group worked with this concept for some time, we focused more directly on the issue of responsibility.

Patients were encouraged to look at the way in which they initiated positive or negative responses in others toward themselves.

It was repeatedly pointed out during several classes how the individual himself helped to initiate the response he was receiving from others and for which he was actually blaming the other person.

As the day-to-day interactions were discussed, patients learned to see how their actions created reactions in others. It was suggested that they could create any scene they wish. Conversely, we looked at how patients were allowing themselves to react to the situation created by others, introducing the notion that, through observation and non-attachment, they could avoid being pulled into an automatic reaction to the provocations of others.

The patients often claimed that they were provoked by the staff; for example, a new officer coming on the ward may not be familiar with the routine. In contrast to the usual ward officer, he may prove rigid, turning the lights off at an early hour and harshly ordering all of the patients to their rooms. Typically, patients would react to this by becoming sullen toward the officer. As a result, disciplinary action was often taken. If the response was too hostile, the patient might even be removed to a more restrictive ward.

In discussing such situations as they occurred, the leader first tried to develop an observing attitude in the group, encouraging participants to look at the situation from an objective vantage point instead of becoming caught up in their usual "us against them" attitude. The therapist asked whether their responses to provoking situations were actually responses they chose to make. Did the officer's action lead to an automatic emotional reaction on the part of the patient? Was the patient merely becoming caught up in the role in which an authority figure had placed him? If an officer was authoritarian and "bossy," would the patient predictably respond by playing the reciprocal role of the sullen and negativistic child who feels mistreated and who wants to get even?

In each situation that was discussed, the group explored to what extent the patient felt locked into a prescribed role, and to what extent he felt free to avoid playing out this scene in the expected way. During these situations some patients began to realize that they had been reacting automatically to authority figures for years. As a result, they would experiment at times with altering their response; at other times they lost perspective and again became involved in the melodrama.

After examining the way in which the officer may have initiated the scene, the group turned to look at how the patient might play the role of director in arranging and redirecting such confrontations between oppressor and oppressed. In some cases, patients saw that by acting in a negativistic manner, they actually encouraged punitive behavior on the part of the authorities. They were, at times, leading the officers to react with their own automatic, emotionally driven, authoritarian behavior. As the group members analyzed their interactions further, it became difficult to tell whether the chain of reactions actually began with the provocations of the guards or with those of the patients, since their roles seemed to mesh together in an unending cycle.

Once the group began to clearly observe these interactions, the therapist introduced the notion that the patients could modify the script, producing a completely different set of reactions on the part of authority figures. The therapist asked, "What would happen if you treated the guards more kindly than you were treated?" It was suggested that instead of reacting to officers as authority figures, they relate to them as human beings who might, themselves, have emotional problems and conflicts that lead them to behave in an irrational and immature way. The patients were asked to experiment with being friendly towards the officers instead of responding by their "immature and defensive" behavior and to note the effect of disrupting the typical interaction pattern. They were to avoid bringing on a confrontation or a struggle between "us and them." It was also suggested that the patients refuse to lose their role as an observer in the midst of the interaction.

When similar suggestions had been made in therapy groups,

before the introduction of the self-mastery class, they had been quickly put down. The patients had immediately become defensive. Their typical reaction had been, "Well, you don't know what it is like. You've never been a patient here. You can talk that way about treating others more friendly because you've never experienced how we get treated." But, when this step-by-step procedure of introducing observation, then self-control, was used (through postures, meditation and, later, social interactions), the patients were now ready to accept such suggestions and work with them. They began experimenting with becoming more friendly to the officers, often going up to an officer to strike up a conversation. The officers, of course, were quite surprised, having difficulty in understanding such a change in behavior.

One patient described a conversation in which an officer was emphasizing the importance of punishment when someone does something wrong. In the past, this patient's typical reaction would have been defensive, asserting the "patient's point of view." In this case, however, he realized immediately that his usual reaction would bring about the usual confrontation and stand-off between himself and the officer. So, instead of confronting the officer with the opposite point of view, he decided to look at things from the other's perspective, reasoning along with him. As a result, he found that the conversation, instead of ending up in a confrontation, led to a feeling of mutual understanding. As patients took the officer's point of view, the officer also became less defensive and more willing to see things from the patient's perspective.

A number of such interactions began to convince some of the patients in the self-mastery class that they could change the atmosphere of the institution by refusing to become caught up in the typical role-interactions and by offering, instead, genuine concern for others, both staff and patients. Of course, there were a number of staff and patients who remained only slightly affected, and the patients periodically became caught up in grievances. But, over the course of several months the predominant feeling in the institution began to change. A more positive caring feeling was often noticeable in place of the paranoia which had predominated earlier. Patients in the self-mastery group, along with others in the institution, developed and led a "big brothers organization" in which the brighter and more stable patients visited each evening with those who were more disoriented or retarded. An evening self-help group was started in which the patients provided additional group therapy for themselves without staff members present. Patients often met together in twos or threes for the purpose of uncovering and working on emotional problems. As one patient put it, "We're creating our own institution."

Identity

One traditional technique in yoga is to focus on the sense of *I-ness* by asking the question, "Who am I?" When a patient in the group was asked to answer this question, he at first responded somewhat superficially, based on physical appearance and possessions. He said, "I am thirty-two years old, I'm male," and so on but then he came to the way he saw his personality and said, "I'm somebody who is sneaky. I like to see what I can get away with. I'm also very bossy. I like to have control over other people." The group members began to work with these self definitions that he had of himself, asking, "Is this who you really are at your deepest core? Or is this just a facade, a more superficial aspect of yourself?" In this way the patients were encouraged to become aware of the concepts they imposed on themselves and to see how these concepts created a personality and a way of reacting.

After the limitations of such self-concepts were pointed out, the participants were led to question the validity of these concepts. It was suggested that they were valid at only a relatively superficial

level of self-description and that they could *choose* to define
themselves at a more basic level, beneath personality.* The
patient described above was encouraged to continue asking,
"Who am I?" to see if he could get to a deeper level of answering
this question. As this confrontation continued, he began to get
a sense that the way in which he was defining himself was really
not necessary. It occurred to him that there were many possibilities for self-definition. The therapist continued asking,
"Who are you?" to each response he would give, attempting to
bring him to a more core self-definition than one based on the
roles he had been consistently playing. As this process continued,
he seemed to become confused about his identity, unable to
really define who he was. He realized that the self-definitions
given earlier were somewhat superficial but there seemed to be
no alternatives. He felt at a loss without these "negative"
identities.

This patient's confusion was regarded by the therapist as a
very positive sign in that he was no longer willing to stick by
his older definitions and was beginning to come to grips with
the search for a deeper self-definition. Over the next several
months, this man began experimenting with new identities. It
was a time of uncertainty as he tried new ways of relating in
place of manipulating others. He became a leader in the "big
brothers" organization and invested a considerable part of his
time in helping others. He began reading extensively about
Zen and other Eastern philosophies. He concluded that he had
been *using* people all of his life, but now felt that living in that
manner was hollow. Two major disappointments followed within
the next few months: he was refused a parole and his girlfriend
broke off their relationship. He responded with an attempt to
return to his previous cynicism regarding relationships with
others. However, subsequent attempts to resume his stance

---

* For a more complete description of techniques in this area, see Vargiu, James G.,
"Subpersonalities," *Synthesis*, Vol. I-1, 1974, pp. WB-9-47.

in this old identity have not been fully successful and he is still struggling to integrate his disparate self-concepts.

Other patients also benefited from this working on self-definition. One patient reacted intensely to a "Who am I?" session. He became very excited in the midst of this discussion and suddenly burst out, "I know who we really are—we're everything." This seemed to be more than a superficial statement; he felt he had gained some feeling of sharing and some escape from the isolation of egoism and he talked about this "realization" for some weeks afterward.

Other Principles of Yoga Psychology

A number of other principles were also worked with in the self-mastery group. Some of these will be mentioned briefly:

Equanimity: This involves learning to see every situation that we are in as a means of growing. Every experience has enormous potential value in helping us to learn and develop. This principle carries the notion one step further that we create our environment. Here it is suggested that the reason we create or place ourselves into a particular situation is because it is the best possible learning experience for us at that time. This is so, even though it may seem painful. There are no good and bad experiences—all have equal potential for helping us to grow.

This psychology contrasts sharply with the patients' typical approach to the situation in which they find themselves. They typically view their incarceration only in terms of deprivation and are frequently preoccupied with figuratively shaking the bars and shouting, "Let me out of here so I can resume my life!" They do not look around to see that even their restricted environment offers excellent opportunities for growth and the development of self-mastery.

It was suggested that instead of reacting to their incarceration,

they learn to treat equally all situations in which they find themselves and try to find how they can grow from the circumstance.
The extent to which the patients were able to adopt and use this
new method of facing their predicaments is brought home in the
following example:

> During several group sessions a patient had been
> complaining vigorously about his boss in an insti-
> tutional job.   This boss was described by several
> patients as extremely abusive, demanding and irrational.
> However, when the patient in question complained of
> his fate to be working under such a tyrant, instead of
> sympathizing with him the group suggested that this
> might be the most useful learning opportunity he
> could have. What better means, they asked, is there to
> learn self-mastery and self-control than through working
> under such a person?   They felt it was excellent
> preparation and an opportunity for self-testing to
> determine if he would be able to handle stress when
> he was released from the institution.

Levels of Consciousness: The therapist introduced the yogic
concept that there are different centers of consciousness (chakras)
each of which involve completely different perspectives for
seeing the world.   It was suggested that one can see the world
primarily in terms of either basic security, sensuality, power,
compassion, trust and creativity, understanding and intuition. A
comprehensive system was presented for understanding how
these perspectives developed.   Patients were encouraged to be
aware of which perspectives they and others used in experiencing
the world by asking them to take specific experiences and
determine whether they responded in terms of one or the other
of these orientations.

This schema provided the patients with a comprehensive
framework for taking an observing attitude toward themselves.

It was quite easy for patients to see how, in each case, their behavior arose out of one of these orientations. Some patients were quite surprised to see how applicable this hierarchy was to them.

When the possibilities of seeing the world were divided into these categories, patients could then see how behavior, which seemed to be expressing one need, was often actually expressing another lower need on the hierarchy. For example, one patient discussed his difficulty in "getting" his girlfriend to grow toward more independence. He seemed to feel that he was quite altruistic and compassionate in trying to help her but the group suggested that he was really reacting from power needs. They pointed out that to "get her" to do anything, he was actually trying to control her rather than allow her to be independent.

Once this hierarchy of perspectives was understood we discussed ways of re-orienting oneself in order to be less caught up in the lowest needs in the hierarchy since it was actions based on the security, sensuality and power needs that had caused these patients to be incarcerated. The idea of gradually replacing habitual ways of thinking and reacting with new ones was introduced. We looked at the possibility of learning to replace seeing the world from one of these lower orders of need perspectives with seeing the world from a higher order need perspective.

Replacement of Habits: Yoga training offers a number of specific techniques for accelerating one's progress from lower order to higher order needs. One method we focused on in the self-mastery class was the replacement of unwanted habits which included habits of thought as well as action. Patients were asked to avoid dwelling on the undesirable habits; instead it was suggested that they become occupied with positive patterns, thoughts and actions which would, of themselves, replace their habitual ways of being. They were asked to develop routines of meditation, thought patterns and behaviors which would, in

304 Yoga and Psychotherapy

themselves, overrun and replace undesirable habits which had been developed earlier.

CONCLUSION

The descriptions here are, perhaps, suggestive of the range of effective interventions available to the yoga therapist, but this is by no means a comprehensive list. These are aspects of yoga psychology which were particularly useful with this patient population.

Certainly not all of the concepts taught in this self-mastery class were understood or adopted by the majority of patients. As of this writing, some of the patients have been parolled with, as yet, little follow-up information; others have improved considerably in their self-mastery skills while they remain confined. A few have shown little apparent change. Perhaps the biggest change has been the subtle influence on the atmosphere of the institution. A few patients with bitter, paranoid outlooks have learned to replace this with a stance of compassion and understanding and they in turn are affecting others in a similar way. A slight but definite shift toward a more constructive and growth-oriented atmosphere can be sensed.

After several months the formal group meetings were discontinued. However, a few of these patients continued to pursue the study of yoga psychology in much greater depth. They met together on their own, reading and discussing traditional texts on yoga and meditation. These few made a deep commitment to this new approach to living and remain markedly different in their attitudes and behavior.

One of the patients whose uncontrolled emotional violence was described earlier, came up to the therapist one day and said, "Who would have ever thought I would become so involved in studying Eastern psychology? When you first began teaching about non-attachment a year ago, I thought you were crazy. We were worlds apart. Now I spend a lot of my time studying these ideas and applying them to my life, and, do you know, they really work."

Variations of many of these techniques are, of course, also used in modern psychotherapy. From bioenergetics to behavior modification, from psychoanalysis to rational emotive therapy and "the power of positive thinking," are found echoes of the methods described here. However, as we have seen throughout this book, yoga therapy seems to be unique in its comprehensiveness and inclusiveness. It is not a hodge-podge of separately developed techniques of growth but an integrated system that works with the full range of habits and emotions, rational and irrational aspects of our being.

Yoga therapy integrates a behavioral and introspective approach to growth. In contrast to much of modern psychology, it views roles and personality as superficial and easily changed when one is not caught up at that level of being. It provides a perspective from which one can become disengaged from involvement in the unhappy personalities he has created for himself and in the negative roles he has adopted. It does not encourage the patient to indulge in elaborating the superstructure of his personality; instead, it moves quickly to a training program for changing habits, thought patterns and self-concepts.

Our book has concentrated on outlining the vast and significant theoretical implications of yoga psychology. We feel it has the potential for stimulating fundamental and needed revisions in the concepts of modern psychology. This appendix is offered to demonstrate that from our clinical experience thus far, the timeless insights of yoga psychology seem to provide simple and effective therapeutic techniques. It would appear that the theoretical profundity of yoga psychology is matched by a practical utility.

REFERENCES

CHAPTER 1

1. Alexander Lowen, *Language of the Body*. New York: MacMillan, 1971.

2. Alexander Lowen, *Betrayal of the Body*. New York: MacMillan, 1967, pp. 43-47.

3. Sam Keen, "My New Carnality," *Psychology Today*, October 1970, pp. 59-61.

4. Richard J. Davidson and Gary E. Schwartz, "The Psychobiology of Relaxation and Related States: A Multi-process Theory," in D. Mostofsky, ed., *Behavior Control and Modification of Physiological Activity*. New York: Prentice Hall, in press.

5. See also Chapter 3.

6. Swami Kuvalayananda, *Pranayama*. Bombay: Popular Prakashan, 1972. See also references herein to articles in the journal, *Yoga Mimamsa*, giving details of experimental work in this area.

7. Neal Miller, "Learning Visceral and Glandular Responses," *Science* 163 (1969): 434-445.

8. Norbert Wiener, quoted in Marvin Karlins and Lewis M. Andrews, *Biofeedback*. Philadelphia: J. B. Lippincott Co., 1972, p. 26.

9. Miller, *op. cit.*, pp. 436-438.

10. T. Budzynski, J. Stoyva and C. Adler, "Feedback-induced Muscle Relaxation: Application to Tension Headache," *Journal of Behavior Therapy and Experimental Psychiatry* 1 (1970): 205-211.

11. Elmer Green, *Psychosomatic Self-Regulation of Migraine and Tension Headaches.* Topeka:Menninger Foundation, 1973.

12. Gary Schwartz, David Shapiro, Bernard Tursky, "Learned Control of Cardiovascular Integration in Man Through Operant Conditioning" in *Biofeedback and Self-Control, 1971.* Chicago: Aldine-Atherton, 1972, p. 245.

13. Herbert Benson, "Decreased Systolic Blood Pressure through Operant Conditioning Techniques in Patients with Essential Hypertension," in *Biofeedback and Self-Control, 1971.* pp. 528-531.

14. C. H. Patel, "Yoga and Biofeedback in the Management of Hypertension," *The Lancet,* November 10, 1973, pp. 1053-1055.

15. C. H. Patel, "Twelve-month Follow-up of Yoga and Biofeedback in the Management of Hypertension," *The Lancet,* January 1975, pp. 62-67.

16. Theodore Weiss and Bernard T. Engle, "Operant Conditioning of Heart Rate in Patients with Premature Ventricular Contractions," in *Biofeedback and Self-Control, 1971,* pp. 509-527.

17. Gorman and Kamiya, "Voluntary Control of Stomach pH" quoted in Eric Peper, "Frontiers of Clinical Biofeedback," *Seminars in Psychiatry,* 1973.

18. D. J. French, et al., "Self-Induced Scrotal Hypothermia in Man, a Preliminary Report," quoted in Peper, *op. cit.*

19. Elmer and Alyce Green and E. Dale Walters, *A Demonstration of Voluntary Control of Bleeding and Pain.* Topeka: Menninger Foundation, 1972.

20. Marion A. Wenger, Basuke Bagchi and B. K. Anand, "Experiments in India on Voluntary Control of the Heart and Pulse," *Circulation* 24 (1961): 1319-1325.

21. J. Hoenig, "Medical Research on Yoga." *Confinia Psychiatrica* 2 (1968): 88-89.

22. Marion A. Wenger, et al., *op. cit.*

23. A. S. Dalal and T. X. Barber, "Yoga, Yogic Feats and Hypnosis in the Light of Empirical Research," *American Journal of Clinical Hypnosis* 2 (1969): 156.

24. Elmer Green, "Biofeedback for Mind-Body Self Regulation: Healing and Creativity," in *Biofeedback and Self-Control: An Aldine Annual, 1972.* Chicago: Aldine, 1973, pp. 152-166.

25. L. K. Kothari, A. Bordia and O. P. Gupta, "The Yogic Claim of Voluntary

Control over the Heart Beat," *American Heart Journal* 86 (1973): 282-284.

26. Eric Peper, "Frontiers of Clinical Biofeedback," *Seminar in Psychiatry,* 1973.

CHAPTER 2

1. Hazrat Inayat Khan, *The Sufi Message of Hazrat Inayat Khan*, Vol. 7. London: Barrie and Rockliff, 1962.

2. Wilson Van Duren, *The Presence of Other Worlds: The Findings of Emanuel Swedenborg.* New York: Harper and Row, 1974, pp. 19-20.

3. W. Edward Mann, *Orgone, Reich and Eros: Wilhelm Reich's Theory of Life Energy.* New York: Simon and Shuster, 1973, p. 87.

4. Magda Proskauer, "Breathing Therapy," in *Ways of Growth,* edited by Herbert Otto and John Mann. New York: Viking Press, 1969, p. 27.

5. Khan, *op. cit.*, p. 104.

6. Proskauer, *op. cit.*, p. 27.

7. C. H. Patel, "Yoga and Biofeedback in the Management of Hypertension," *The Lancet*, November 1973, pp. 1053-1055.

8. Alfred L. Scopp, "Anxiety Reduction Through Breathing and Muscle Relaxation Training: Cognitive and Affective Components," Ph.D. dissertation, Duke University, 1973.

9. Robert Ornstein, *The Psychology of Consciousness.* New York: Viking Press, 1972, pp. 49-73.

10. G. William Domhoff, "But Why Did They Sit on the King's Right in the First Place?" *Psychoanalytic Review* 56 (1969-70): 590-591.

11. Ornstein, *op. cit.*, p. 64.

12. *Ibid.*

13. Gay Luce, *Body Time.* New York: Bantam Books, 1973, p. 10.

14. Vijayendra Pratap, "Diurnal Patterns of Nostril Breathing," *Chakra* (Winter 1970): 14-15.

15. Rama Prasad, *Nature's Finer Forces: The Science of Breath and the Philosophy of the Tattvas.* Mokelumne Hill, California: Health Research, 1969, pp. 201-203.

16. *Ibid.*, pp. 200-201.

17. *Ibid.*, pp. 212-217.

18. *Ibid.*, p. 204.

19. John W. White, "The Consciousness Revolution," *Saturday Review* (February 22, 1975), p. 18.

20. Mann, *op. cit.*, p. 86.

21. Shafica Karagulla, *Breakthrough to Creativity*. Santa Monica, California: Devorss, 1967, p. 124.

22. Mann, *op. cit.*, p. 88.

23. Leonard J. Ravitz, "Electromagnetic Field Monitoring of Changing State-function, Including Hypnotic States," in Harold S. Burr, *The Fields of Life*. New York: Ballantine Books, 1972, pp. 175-176.

24. Burr, *op. cit.*, pp. 28-29.

25. Paul A. Robinson, *The Freudian Left*. New York: Harper and Row, 1969, p. 60.

26. Gopi Krishna, *Kundalini: The Evolutionary Energy in Man*. Berkeley: Shambala, 1971, p. 67.

27. William A. Tiller, "Some Energy Field Observations of Man and Nature," in Stanley Krippner and Daniel Rubin, *The Kirlian Aura*. Garden City, New York: Anchor Books, 1974, p. 123.

28. Frank Waters, *Book of the Hopi*. New York: Ballantine Books, 1963, pp. 10-11.

29. Karagulla, *op. cit.*, pp. 124-127.

30. Karagulla, *op. cit.*, p. 127.

31. Tiller, *op. cit.*, p. 123.

CHAPTER 3

1. J. Sinha, *Indian Psychology: Vol. I and II*. Calcutta: Sinha, 1958-1961.

2. There have been numerous commentaries on Patanjali's aphorisms which have explained them and elaborated on their meaning. The most helpful and authoritative of those available in English are the following:

Swami Hariharananda Aranya, *Yoga Philosophy of Patanjali*, trans. P. N. Mukerji. Calcutta: University of Calcutta, 1963.

James Haughton Woods, *The Yoga System of Patanjali*. Delhi: Motilal Banarsidass, 1914.

Swami Vivekananda, *Raja Yoga*. New York: Ramakrishna-Vivekananda Center, 1955.

I. K. Taimni, *The Science of Yoga*. Wheaton, Illinois: Theosophical Publishing House, 1961.

3. *Ibid.*

4. Swami Rama, *Lectures on Yoga*. Honesdale, Pennsylvania: Himalayan International Institute of Yoga Science and Philosophy, 5th edition, 1976.

5. B. G. Tilak, *Gita-Rahasya*. Poorna, India: J. Tilak Bros., 1971, p. 182.

6. Solomon P., ed., *Sensory Deprivation: a Symposium held at Harvard Medical School*. Cambridge, Massachusetts, Harvard University Press, 1961, pp. 231-232.

7. Robert White, "Ego and Reality in Psychoanalytic Theory," in *Psychological Issues*, V. 3, No. 3. New York: International Universities Press, 1963, p. 49.

8. Aurobindo, *The Synthesis of Yoga*. Pondicherry: Sri Aurobindo Ashram, 1971, p. 625.

9. *Ibid.*

10. B. G. Tilak, *op. cit.*, pp. 186-187.

11. Sigmund Freud, *Future of an Illusion*. Garden City, New York: Doubleday Anchor Books, 1953, p. 4.

12. Franklin Merrell-Wolff, *Philosophy of Consciousness without an Object*. New York: Julian Press, Inc., 1973.

13. Roberto Assagioli, *Psychosynthesis*. New York: Viking Press, 1971.

CHAPTER 4

1. Robert E. Ornstein, *The Psychology of Consciousness*. New York: Viking Press, 1972, pp. 16-22.

2. William James, *Varieties of Religious Experience*. New York: The New American Library, 1958, p. 298.

3. Georg Groddeck, "Uber den Symbolisierungezwang," *Imago* 8: 72, 1922, quoted by Franz Alexander (see 5 below).

4. Roberto Assagioli, *Psychosynthesis.* New York: Viking Press, 1971, p. 35.

5. Franz Alexander, "Buddhistic Training as an Artificial Catatonia," *The Psychoanalytic Review* 18 (1931): 143.

6. *Ibid.*, p. 141.

7. Carl Jung, *Collected Works of C. G. Jung*, Vol. 9, Part 1: *The Archetypes and the Collective Unconscious*, trans. R. F. C. Hull. Princeton: Princeton University Press, 1969, p. 3.

8. *Ibid.*, pp. 3-4.

9. Carl Jung, *Man and His Symbols.* Garden City, New York: Doubleday and Company, 1964, p. 52.

10. Edward Edinger, *Ego and Archetype.* Baltimore: Penguin Books, 1972, p. 110.

11. Jung, *Man and His Symbols*, p. 67.

12. Carl Jung, *Collected Works of C. G. Jung,* Vol. 9, Part 2: *Aion: Researches into the Phenomenology of the Self.* Princeton: Princeton University Press, 1969, p. 69.

13. Edinger, *op. cit.,* p. 113.

14. *Ibid.,* pp. 115-116.

15. Jung, *Collected Works,* Vol. 9, Part 1, p. 283.

16. Jung, *Man and His Symbols*, p. 64.

17. Jung, *Collected Works,* Vol. 9, Part 2, p. 24.

18. Jung, *Collected Works,* Vol. 9, Part 1, p. 287.

19. *Ibid.*, pp. 287-288.

20. Sam Keen, "A Conversation with Stanley Keleman," *Psychology Today,* September 1973, p. 5.

21. *Ibid.*

22. Jung, *Collected Works,* Vol. 9, Part 1, p. 288.

23. Carl Jung, *The Undiscovered Self.* New York: New American Library, 1958, p. 119.

24. Jung, *Man and His Symbols,* p. 67.

25. *Ibid.*, p. 69.

26. Jung, *Collected Works, Vol. 9, Part 1,* pp. 43-44.

27. Jung, *Collected Works, Vol. 9, Part 2,* pp. 62-63.

28. Franklin Merrell-Wolff, *The Philosophy of Consciousness without an Object.* New York: Julian Press, 1973, p. 40.

29. Jung, *Man and His Symbols,* pp. 50-51.

30. *Ibid.*, pp. 51-52.

31. *Ibid.*, p. 64.

CHAPTER 5

1. Elmer Green, et al., *Autogenic Feedback Training.* Topeka, Kansas: The Menninger Foundation, 1973, p. 7.

2. *Ibid.*, p. 8.

3. *Ibid.*, pp. 6-7.

4. E. Green, A. Green, and D. Walters, *A Demonstration of Voluntary Control of Bleeding and Pain.* Topeka, Kansas: The Menninger Foundation, 1972, pp. 2-3.

5. E. Green, A. Green, and D. Walters, *Biofeedback for Mind-Body Self Regulation: Healing and Creativity.* Topeka, Kansas: The Menninger Foundation, 1971, p. 21.

6. E. Peper, *Frontiers of Clinical Biofeedback.* Yellow Springs, Ohio: Antioch College, 1973, p. 25.

7. Green, et al., *Autogenic Feedback Training,* p. 17.

8. E. Green, D. Walters, and A. Green, *Brainwave Training, Imagery, Creativity and Integrative Experiences.* Topeka, Kansas: The Menninger Foundation, 1973, p. 12.

9. Assagioli, *Psychosynthesis.* New York, Viking Press, 1971, preface.

10. Robert Keith Wallace and Herbert Benson, "The Physiology of Meditation," *Scientific American,* February 1972, pp. 84-90.

11. Daniel Goleman, "Meditation and Stress Reactivity," Ph.D. dissertation, Harvard University, 1973.

12. *Ibid.*

13. William Linden, "Practicing of Meditation by School Children and their Levels of Field Dependence-Independence, Text Anxiety and Reading Achievement," *Journal of Consulting and Clinical Psychology* 41 (1973): 139-143.

14. W. T. Winquist, "The Effect of the Regular Practice of Transcendental Meditation on Students Involved in the Regular Use of Hallucinogenic and 'Hard' Drugs." Report for Dr. G. T. Slatin, U.C.L.A., 1969.

15. Gary E. Schwartz, "Pros and Cons of Meditation: Current Findings on Physiology and Anxiety, Self-Control, Drug-Abuse and Creativity," (paper presented at the American Psychological Association Convention, Montreal, August 1973, p. 5).

16. W. Seeman, S. Nidich, and T. Banta, "Influence of Transcendental Meditation on a Measure of Self-Actualization," *Journal of Counseling Psychology* 19 (1972): 184-187.

17. R. A. C. Stewart, "States of Human Realizations: Some Physiological and Psychological Correlates," *Psychologia* 17, No. 3 (1974): 126-134.

18. Terry V. Lesh, "Zen Meditation and the Development of Empathy in Counselors," *Journal of Humanistic Psychology* 10 (1970): 39-74.

19. A Kasamatsu and T. Hirai, "An Electroencephalographic Study on the Zen Meditation (Zazen)," in *Altered States of Consciousness,* ed. Charles T. Tart. Garden City, New York: Doubleday, 1972, pp. 501-514.

20. B. K. Anand, G. S. Chhina, and Baldev Singh, "Some Aspects of Electroencephalographic Studies in Yogis," in *Altered States of Consciousness,* ed. Charles T. Tart. Garden City, New York: Doubleday, 1972, pp. 515-518.

21. Kasamatsu and Hirai, *op. cit.*

22. Green, et al., *Bio-Feedback for Mind-Body Self Regulation: Healing and Creativity,* p. 22.

23. W. C. Dement and Merrill Mitler, "An Introduction to Sleep," in *Basic Sleep Mechanisms,* ed. Olga Petre-Quadens and John D. Schlag. New York: Academic Press, 1974.

24. Ralph J. Berger, "The Sleep and Dream Cycle," in *Sleep, Physiology and Pathology,* ed. Anthony Kales. Philadelphia: J. B. Lippencott Co., 1969, pp. 23-28.

25. E. Hartmann, "Sleep Requirements: Long Sleepers, Short Sleepers, Variable Sleepers and Insomniacs," *Psychosomatics* 14 (1973): 95-103.

26. *Ibid.*

27. Swami Prabhavananda and Frederick Manchester, trans. *The Upanishads.* New York: New American Library, 1957, pp. 50-51.

28. Green, et al., *Bio-Feedback for Mind-Body Self Regulation: Healing and Creativity*, p. 23.

29. Swami Akhilananda, *Hindu Psychology.* Boston: Branden Press, 1946, p. 2.

30. *Ibid.*

CHAPTER 6

1. Swami Hariharananda Aranya, *Yoga Philosophy of Patanjali.* Calcutta: University of Calcutta, 1963, pp. 129-142.

2. T. G. Manikar, *Samkhya Karika of Isvarakrsna with Gaudapadabhasya.* Poona, India: Oriental Book Agency, 1972.

3. J. Krishnamurti, *Freedom From the Known.* New York: Harper and Row, 1969, p. 77.

4. *Ibid.*

5. Fritz Perls, *The Gestalt Approach and Eye Witness to Therapy.* Ben Lomond, California: Science and Behavior Books, 1973, p. 131.

6. Stella Resnick, "Gestalt Therapy, The Hot Set of Personal Responsibility," *Psychology Today*, November 1974, pp. 110-117.

7. Chogyam Trungpa, *Cutting Through Spiritual Materialism.* Berkeley: Shambala, 1973, p. 128.

8. *Ibid.*

9. Paramahansa Yogananda, *Autobiography of a Yogi.* Los Angeles: Self Realization Fellowship, 1969, pp. 149-150.

10. John Custance, "Wisdom, Madness and Folly," in *Inner World of Mental Illness*, ed. Bert Kaplan. New York: Harper and Row, 1964, pp. 47-53.

11. Franz Alexander, "Buddhistic Training as an Artificial Catatonia," *Psychoanalytic Review* 18 (1931): 130-145.

12. Swami Saradananda, *Sri Ramakrishna The Great Master.* Madras: Sri Ramakrishna Math, 1952, p. 497.

13. Bert Kaplan, ed., *Inner World of Mental Illness.* New York: Harper and Row, 1964, pp. 55-61.

14. R. D. Laing, *The Politics of Experience.* New York: Pantheon Books, 1967, pp. 96-97.

15. K. Dabrowski, *Personality Shaping Through Positive Disintegration.* Boston: Little, Brown & Co., 1967, p. 92.

16. *Ibid.*

17. Roberto Assagioli, *Psychosynthesis.* New York: Viking Press, 1971, p. 53.

18. Franklin Merrell-Wolff, *Pathways Through to Space.* New York: Julian Press, 1973, p. 113.

19. Bhagavad Gita, Chapter 2.

20. Geraldine Coster, *Yoga and Western Psychology.* Delhi: Motilal Banarsidass, 1934, p. 81.

21. Merrell-Wolff, *op. cit.,* p. 285.

22. Richard M. Bucke, *Cosmic Consciousness.* New York: E. P. Dutton, 1969, p. 123.

23. Merrell-Wolff, *op. cit.,* p. 286.

24. *Ibid.,* p. 288.

25. *Ibid.,* p. 288.

26. *Ibid.,* p. 286.

CHAPTER 7

1. Gopinceth Kaviraj, *Aspects of Indian Thought.* Burdwan, India: The University of Burdwan, 1966, pp. 229-237.

2. Sir John Woodruff, *The Serpent Power.* Madras: Ganesh & Co., 1918, p. 137.

3. Frank Waters, *Book of the Hopi.* New York: Ballantine Books, 1969, p. 11.

4. Chogyam Trungpa, *Meditation in Action.* Berkeley: Shambala, 1970, p. 23.

5. Ken Keyes, Jr., *Handbook to Higher Consciousness*. Berkeley: Living Love Center, 1973, p. 62.

6. Pandit S. Subrahmanya Sasri and T. R. Srinivasa Ayyanger (Transliteration, translation and commentary), *Saundarya Lahari (The Ocean of Beauty) of Sri Samkara-Bhagavatpada*. Madras: Theosophical Publishing House, 1972.

7. Stanley Keleman, *Sexuality, Self and Survival*. San Francisco: Lode Star Press, 1971, pp. 40, 110, 111.

8. Erik H. Erikson, *Childhood and Society*. New York: W. W. Norton, 1963, pp. 258-261.

9. Erich Neumann, *The Origins and History of Consciousness*. Princeton: Princeton University Press, 1954, pp. 24-25.

10. Alexander Lowen, *The Betrayal of the Body*. New York: Collier Books, 1967, pp. 151-152.

11. Frank G. Goble, *The Third Force*. New York: Pocket Books, 1970, p. 38.

12. Erich Fromm, *The Art of Loving*. New York: Harper and Brothers, 1956, p. 36.

13. *Ibid.*, p. 20.

14. *Ibid.*, pp. 24-25.

15. Benjamin Lee Whorf, *Language, Thought and Reality*. Cambridge, Mass.: MIT Press, 1956.

16. Waters, *op. cit.*, p. 12.

17. Otto Rank, *The Myth of the Birth of the Hero*. New York: Vintage Books, 1959, pp. 99-245.

18. Gay Gaer Luce, *Biological Rhythms in Human and Animal Physiology*. New York: Dover, 1971, pp. 123-132.

19. Richard Maurice Bucke, M.D., *Cosmic Consciousness*. New York: E. P. Dutton and Co., Inc., 1969.

20. Swami Saradananda, *Sri Ramakrishna The Great Master*. Madras: The Jupiter Press, Private LTD, p. 364.

21. *Ibid.*

22. *Ibid.*

23. Franklin Merrell-Wolff, *The Philosophy of Consciousness without an Object*. New York: The Julian Press, Inc., 1973, p. 24.

24. Waters, *op. cit.*, p. 11.

25. Abraham H. Maslow, *Motivation and Personality*. New York: Harper and Row, 1970.

INDEX

A

Abhinivesa (fear of death), 193
Acupuncture, 54, 60
Addiction. *See* Attachment
Adler, Alfred, 241
Aesthetics, 91
Aggression, 221, 227, 246, 247, 250, 273
Ahankara, 70, 71, 73, 84-90, 107, 154
Air, 228, 244, 254
Ajna chakra, 263-269, 273-274, 279
Akasha, 259
Alchemists, 39
Alcohol, 187, 235
American Indian, 244-245
Amphetamines, 56
Anahad Nada, 278
Anal chakra, 226-231, 273-274
Anand, 212
Anger, 34, 78, 79, 205, 249, 290
Animals,
    body structure of, 117
    and chakras, 220, 226-230, 240, 264, 278
    and learning, 66-68, 93
    and perception, 105
Anxiety,
    and attachment, 152-154, 185-187, 201, 293-294
    cause of, 176, 227, 247
    reduction, 37, 155-157

and the unconscious, 123
Archetypes, 116-118, 120, 124, 147
    in art, 261
    and the "self," 125, 127
    use of in therapy, 136-137
Art, 117, 135, 145, 224, 225, 234, 259, 260, 261, 262, 271
Asanas (postures), 6-9, 10-12, 52, 288
Asmita (limited self concept), 176
Assagioli, Roberto, 113, 148, 200
Assertiveness, 221, 240
Astanga Yoga, 2, 75, 76-77
Asthma, 15, 17
Atman, 72
Attachment, 78, 249
    and anxiety, 152-154, 176, 250
    and growth, 179-188, 192, 211-213, 236, 275, 292-295
    and "I-ness," 201
Aurobindo, 91, 92
Autogenic training, 9
Automatic mechanisms, 67
Aversion, 176, 179, 180, 182, 183, 186, 192
Avidya (ignorance), 175, 176

B

Behavior, 65, 69, 76, 85, 114, 116, 122, 179, 183, 184, 250, 291, 297, 303
Behavior modification, 305

Creativity, 259-262, 274,
302
Cross, 245
Crown chakra, 220, 270-272,
274
Culture, 231

D

Dabrowski, K., 199
Death, 176, 192-194, 271
Defense mechanisms, 87
Defensive patterns, 67
Depression, 176, 250
Descartes, 264
Detachment, 192
Dharana (concentration), 76
Dukkha (pain), 176
Dhyana, 76
Diaphragm, 243-245, 246-248
Diarrhea, 229
Digestion, 30, 219, 221, 222,
223, 240, 242
Disappointment, 190-192, 250, 290
Disease, 15-16, 41, 59, 223, 225,
240, 277
Disintegration, positive, 199-200
Domination, 239-242, 274
Dreams, 116-119, 127, 134-137,
161, 168, 171, 174, 192, 199,
261, 290
Drugs, 15-16, 56, 156, 182
Dvesa (aversion), 176, 179, 180

E

Earth, 228, 230, 273
Ecstasy, 121, 131, 212, 281
Eczema, 15
Ego,
in chakras, 257, 274
and Freud, 241
and Jung, 115-120, 122-127,
135
limitations of, 165-188
as part of mind, 71, 95-96,
147-148
transcending, 130-131, 146,
154, 166, 176, 178, 199-207,
301

Western and yogic views on, 66,
86-90, 210-211
observing, 112, 136-137, 261
Electro-dynamic fields, 47-49
Elements, 228, 230, 232, 240, 244,
259, 263
Emotions, 5, 6, 16, 34, 79, 170, 175,
182, 183, 194, 201, 217, 222,
229, 243-253, 265, 279-280,
281, 290, 291, 293, 297, 299,
305
buddhi, 91, 92
children, 85
distractions, 68
experiences, 109
imbalance, 178
outbursts, 57, 234
repressed material, 111
Empathy, 157, 243-253, 274
Endocrine glands, 222
Energy. *See also Prana*, 27, 45-61,
76, 218, 219, 222, 234, 239,
240, 245, 255
Envy, 249
Equanimity, 301-302
Erikson, Erik, 88, 241
Eskimo, 59
Ether, 228, 259
Evolution, 93, 185, 186, 187, 191,
198, 199, 201, 205, 208, 210,
211, 257, 275, 280, 281
Extrasensory Perception, 131, 133

F

Fairy tales, 116
Family counseling, 28
Fantasies, 82, 83, 129, 152, 189,
191, 194, 201, 225, 264
Fasting, 14
Fear, 34, 68, 78, 99, 176, 180,
182, 183, 186, 187, 189, 191,
192, 198, 201, 205, 226-231,
247, 248, 257, 273, 296
Feeling, 251, 290, 291
Field theory, 47-49
Fire, 221, 223, 225, 228, 240, 245,
274
Fixation, 179
Fludd, Robert, 33

THE HIMALAYAN INTERNATIONAL INSTITUTE

The Himalayan Institute was founded by Sri Swami Rama as a non-profit organization whose charter outlines the following goals: to teach meditational techniques for the personal growth of modern people and their society; to make known the harmonious view of world religions and philosophies; and to undertake scientific research for the benefit of humanity. This challenging task is met by people of all walks of life and all faiths who attend and participate in the courses and seminars. These continuous programs are designed for people of all ages in order that they may discover how to live more creatively. In the words of the founder, "By being aware of one's own potentials and abilities, one can become a perfect citizen, help the nation and serve humanity."

Located in Honesdale, Pennsylvania, the National Headquarters serves as the coordination center for all of the Institute activities across the country. Five buildings, on four hundred and twenty acres, house the various programs as well as research and publication facilities of the Institute.

The Institute staff includes physicians, scientists, psychologists, philosophers and university professors from various fields of learning. These professional men and women share a common involvement both as students themselves and as pioneers in realizing the aim of the Institute.

GRADUATE STUDIES The Institute offers coursework in Eastern Studies with three areas of specialization: Eastern Studies, Comparative Psychology and Holistic Therapies. The University of Scranton, by an agreement of affiliation, will award a Master of Science degree upon successful completion of the coursework.

The University of Scranton is accredited by the Middle States Association of Colleges and Secondary Schools.

RESIDENTIAL COURSE FOR MEN AND WOMEN Residential programs for both men and women are available for systematic training in all phases of yoga.

SEMINARS AND WORKSHOPS   Classes are available throughout the year which provide intensive training and experience in such topics as Superconscious Meditation, hatha yoga, philosophy, psychology and various aspects of holistic health. *The Himalayan News* announces the current programs.

THERAPY PROGRAM   The Institute offers a two-week Combined Therapy Program emphasizing a natural, holistic approach to physical and psychological problems. A comprehensive medical and nutritional evaluation is provided by staff physicians, and the program includes daily consultations, individualized work with diet, biofeedback training, joints and glands exercises, relaxation techniques, training in various methods of breathing, and meditation.

INTERNATIONAL CONGRESS   The Institute sponsors a yearly international congress devoted to the scientific and spiritual progress of modern man. Through lectures, workshops, seminars and practical demonstrations, the Institute thus provides a forum for professionals and laymen to share their knowledge and research.

ELEANOR N. DANA RESEARCH LABORATORY   The psychophysiological laboratory of the Institute specializes in research on breathing, meditation and holistic therapies. Utilizing the full range of equipment for the measurement of respiration, stress, and relaxed states, the staff investigates Eastern teachings through studies based on Western experimental techniques.

HIMALAYAN INSTITUTE PUBLICATIONS

Living with the Himalayan Masters	Swami Rama
Freedom from the Bondage of Karma	Swami Rama
Book of Wisdom	Swami Rama

Lectures on Yoga   Swami Rama
Life Here and Hereafter   Swami Rama
A Practical Guide to Holistic Health   Swami Rama
Marriage, Parenthood & Enlightenment   Swami Rama
Emotion to Enlightenment   Swami Rama, Swami Ajaya
Yoga and Psychotherapy   Swami Rama, Rudolph
                                    Ballentine, M.D., Swami Ajaya
Science of Breath   Swami Rama, Rudolph
                                    Ballentine, M.D., Alan Hymes, M.D.
Superconscious Meditation   Pandit U. Arya, D. Litt.
Philosophy of Hatha Yoga   Pandit U. Arya, D. Litt.
Meditation and the Art of Dying   Pandit U. Arya, D. Litt.
God   Pandit U. Arya, D. Litt.
Yoga Psychology   Swami Ajaya
Foundations, Eastern & Western Psychology   Swami Ajaya (ed)
Psychology East and West   Swami Ajaya (ed)
Meditational Therapy   Swami Ajaya (ed)
Diet and Nutrition   Rudolph Ballentine, M.D.
Joints and Glands Exercises   Rudolph Ballentine, M.D. (ed)
Freedom from Stress   Phil Nuernberger, Ph.D.
Science Studies Yoga   James Funderburk, Ph.D.
Homeopathic Remedies   Drs. Anderson, Buegel, Chernin
Hatha Yoga Manual I   Samskrti and Veda
Hatha Yoga Manual II   Samskrti and Judith Franks
Swami Rama of the Himalayas   L. K. Misra, Ph.D. (ed)
Philosophy of Death and Dying   M. V. Kamath
Practical Vedanta of Swami Rama Tirtha   Brandt Dayton (ed)
The Swami and Sam   Brandt Dayton
Sanskrit Without Tears   S. N. Agnihotri, Ph.D.
Psychology of the Beatitudes   Arpita
Theory and Practice of Meditation   Himalayan Institute
Inner Paths   Himalayan Institute
Meditation in Christianity   Himalayan Institute
Faces of Meditation   Himalayan Institute
Therapeutic Value of Yoga   Himalayan Institute
Chants from Eternity   Himalayan Institute

Spiritual Diary   Himalayan Institute
The Yoga Way Cookbook   Himalayan Institute
Himalayan Mountain Cookery   Himalayan Institute